CONFESSING JESUS CHRIST

CONFESSING JESUS CHRIST

Preaching in a Postmodern World

David J. Lose

William B. Eerdmans Publishing Company
Grand Rapids, Michigan / Cambridge, U.K.

Wm. B. Eerdmans Publishing Co.
255 Jefferson Ave. S.E., Grand Rapids, Michigan 49503 /
P.O. Box 163, Cambridge CB3 9PU U.K.

Printed in the United States of America

07 06 05 04 03   7 6 5 4 3 2 1

Library of Congress Cataloging-in-Publication Data

Lose, David J.
Confessing Jesus Christ: preaching in a postmodern world / David J. Lose.
p.   cm.
Includes bibliographical references (p.   ).
ISBN 0-8028-4983-0 (pbk.: alk. paper)
1. Preaching. 2. Postmodernism — Religious aspects — Christianity. I. Title.
BV4211.3.L67   2003
251 — dc21

2002192547

www.eerdmans.com

Contents

Acknowledgments

At the outset of his influential work, *The Tacit Dimension*, Michael Polanyi describes the curious phenomenon that "we can know more than we can tell." In many ways, this project has been an effort to tell what I have known, or at least believed, about preaching for some time. The process of bringing to conscious expression what I intuitively believed about preaching, while not always corroborating all that I thought I knew, has greatly clarified my understanding of, and deepened my appreciation for, the practice of preaching to which I am committed. This, in turn, confirmed one of the significant themes of this work: that in order to appropriate one's beliefs fully one must articulate them.

The process of completing this dissertation has also confirmed another of the major themes of this work: that one comes to such understanding and articulation through critical conversation. I have been greatly blessed in a number of my conversation partners at the Lutheran Theological Seminary at Philadelphia, Wartburg Theological Seminary, Princeton Theological Seminary, Luther Seminary, and the Academy of Homiletics, and I give thanks for all of them. Central to this effort has been James F. Kay, the chair of my dissertation committee. I have benefited tremendously from his depth as a theologian, his expertise as an adviser and editor, and his fidelity to the gospel. Janet L. Weathers and Donald H. Juel, the two other members of my committee, improved this manuscript significantly through their considerable theological, biblical, and rhetorical acumen, and I am richer for my association with them.

I also want to acknowledge my debt to the parishioners and pastoral staff of the three congregations I have served, St. John's Evangelical Lutheran Church in Summit, NJ; Holy Trinity Lutheran Church in Audubon, NJ; and Prince of Peace Lutheran Church, in Princeton Junction, NJ. They have listened to me preach both appreciatively and critically and have patiently taught me what it means to confess Jesus Christ. Particular thanks go to the Rev. R. Gregg Kaufman, with whom I shared pastoral duties at Prince of Peace while completing this project, and whose friendship and encouragement were always a blessing.

The circumstances of the year in which this dissertation was written demanded that Karin and I rely on the support of our extended family to a tremendous extent. I am therefore thankful to them not only for their love and example that has shaped the entirety of my life, but also for the significant help they provided during the year past. In particular, we are indebted to my father and mother, the Rev. John F. and Susan G. Lose, and Karin's mother and sister, Thelma K. McNulty and Nancy L. Miller.

Since the completion of this project as a dissertation, I have been aided tremendously by the editorial staff of Eerdmans Publishing Company, especially Roger Van Harn and Jennifer Hoffman.

Finally, I would be able to accomplish little, if anything, of worth were it not for the love and encouragement of my family and the joy they bring me. This work is therefore offered with thanksgiving to God for my children, Jack and Katie, and it is dedicated to my beloved wife and partner, Karin. No one believed more, hoped more, or endured more. Thank God for you.

Reaping the Whirlwind

In many quarters of our common world there exists an increasingly shared conviction that the modern world is dying, if not already dead. Born some three centuries ago in the aftermath of bloody religious conflict, the modern era was founded upon an optimism that by the enlightened application of reason humanity might eradicate disease and suffering, establish a basis for just and moral behavior, foster personal and social liberation, and subdue nature for the good of all people. At the dawn of the twenty-first century — awash in the blood of ideological and nationalistic conflict, beset by pandemic viruses, and standing at the brink of ecological disaster — such confidence has been all but sentenced to the gallows, and the name of its executioner is "postmodernity."

The effects of the "postmodern turn" appear perhaps most dramatically in the scholarly world. Raging like a whirlwind of relative values and subjective truths through the ivory towers of the academy, postmodernity has in one fell swoop severed the connection between language and its referent, divested history of its purely academic character, banished the pretense of objectivity from the sciences, betrayed the lie of social progress, and killed the authors of literary texts. It has, in short, irrevocably altered our intellectual landscape.

But traces of the de(con)structive force of the postmodern gale are felt in our churches and communities as well. Churchgoers report a greater sense of "homelessness" in this "post-denominational" age, and church leaders admit less confidence in their roles and responsibilities

I

as the church's influence in society wanes.[1] The larger culture continues to adjust to changing perceptions about the "traditional" roles of men and women and the increasingly pluralistic nature of our communal life.[2] In the wake of the cold war, national boundaries and identities continue to shift, while global security remains elusive. In light of all this, several theologians have aptly described the plight of our church and society as "de-centered" and "disestablished."[3]

Not surprisingly, the discipline of homiletics has not been exempted from its own set of disruptions, some of which reflect the trends just noted. With the annihilation of the historical-critical synthesis in biblical studies, for instance, so also perished the two-step hermeneutical waltz danced by so many twentieth-century preachers. Similarly, as the New Hermeneutic collapsed under the weight of its modernist presuppositions about the referential properties of language, so also the new homiletic is buckling under the assault of postmodern critics who question its assumptions about the "universality" of human experience.[4] In a time when, as Yeats penned, "things fall apart" and "the center cannot hold," truth, like beauty, seems increasingly to be in the eye of the beholder, and proclamation of a message that claims both ultimate and universal significance seems a dicey venture at best. Little wonder, then, that postmodernism appears to more than a few acute observers as a threat to the very nature of Christianity.[5]

---

1. See Anthony B. Robinson, "Beyond Civic Faith," *The Christian Century* 115 (1998): 933-36; Martin B. Copenhaver, "Formed and Reformed," *The Christian Century* 115 (1998): 933, 937-40; and Loren B. Mead, *The Once and Future Church* (Washington, D.C.: Alban Institute, 1993), pp. 8-42.

2. Walter Brueggemann, *Cadences of Home: Preaching Among Exiles* (Louisville: Westminster/John Knox Press, 1997), pp. 24-37.

3. Brueggemann, *Cadences of Home*, pp. 38-42; Douglas John Hall, *Confessing the Faith: Christian Theology in a North American Context* (Minneapolis: Fortress Press, 1996), pp. 201-39.

4. See Lucy Rose, *Sharing the Word: Preaching in the Roundtable Church* (Louisville: Westminster/John Knox, 1997). For a defense of the new homiletic, see Robert Stephen Reid, "Postmodernism and the Function of the New Homiletic in Post-Christendom Congregations," *Homiletic* 20, no. 2 (Winter 1995): 1-13.

5. Paul Scott Wilson, for instance, describes postmodernity as "a form of religion" that "excludes the possibility of God except as a human construct" ("Postmodernism, Theology, and Preaching," *Papers of the Annual Meeting of the Academy of Homiletics*, December 1-3, 1994, p. 150).

But while I agree that the situation is clearly urgent, I am less sure that it is either dire or novel. In fact, I am increasingly convinced that within the postmodern whirlwind there lies, waiting to be reaped, an unprecedented opportunity to clarify the nature and import of our theology and preaching.[6] Postmodernity, I believe, not only offers some distinct challenges to Christians, but also may lend us a fresh perspective on the very nature of faith and in this way call us to greater fidelity. For this reason, this project seeks to respond to the challenges, and realize the opportunities, of the current age by fashioning the means by which to proclaim God's Word in a postmodern world.

In short, *I propose that preaching that seeks to be both faithful to the Christian tradition and responsive to our pluralistic, postmodern context is best understood as the public practice of confessing faith in Jesus Christ.* Preaching, to put it another way, is a particular *type* of confession, made in response to the reading of the biblical text and the particular context and circumstances of the hearers, and set within a pattern of corporate worship.[7] By describing such preaching as "confessional," I seek to reclaim a Christian practice that rests not on empirical proof but on a living confession of faith, leads not to certainty but to conviction, and lives not in the domain of knowledge and proof but rather in the realm of faithful assertion.

This proposal unfolds into three significant parts, each of which consumes two chapters. The first deals primarily with describing the postmodern challenge and outlining the means by which to speak of truth and reality with integrity. In Chapter One I contend that postmodernity is best understood as a reaction to the Enlightenment

6. In this regard, I concur with the sentiments of the great French preacher of the nineteenth century, Jean Baptiste Henri Lacordaire, who is said to have remarked that "sowing and planting are best done when the sky is overcast and the weather is stormy." Paraphrased and referenced by Karlfried Froehlich in *The Bible as Word of God in a Postmodern Age*, with Terence E. Fretheim (Minneapolis: Fortress Press, 1998), pp. 7, 64 n. 6.

7. Not all confessions of faith, of course, are preaching. Personal assertions of faith and public recitations of the Creeds, for instance, while undoubtedly sharing some attributes with preaching, remain distinct expressions of faith. Further, preaching is not *only* confession, but may also contain elements of catechesis and exhortation. Nevertheless, I believe that preaching that stands with integrity within the Christian tradition while seeking to be faithfully responsive to the postmodern condition has at its core a public, particular, and intentional confession of faith in Jesus Christ.

quest for rational certainty that animated the modern era. By challenging the possibility that we can ground our claims to knowledge in indisputable foundations, and by calling into question our ability to speak accurately of reality, postmodernists seek to overturn the modernist penchant for order, which they claim is only achieved at the expense of dismissing or destroying that which does not conform to the norms it imposes. Whatever its gains, however, postmodernity also exacts certain costs: namely, our ability to speak meaningfully of what we believe to be true. For this reason, in Chapter Two I propose that we can transcend the modern-postmodern debate only by refusing to accept its terms. I therefore outline a postfoundational position that proposes a critically fideistic epistemology that relies upon cross-contextual, critical conversation. The chapter outlines the need for such conversation, overcomes postmodern concerns about the limited ability of language to refer beyond itself, and proposes a model of "dialogical realism" that grants us a measure of confidence in the referentiality of our speech.

The second significant part of this project moves from general philosophical and theological inquiry into the challenges and opportunities of the postmodern context to a more specific concern for Christian proclamation by reclaiming the Christian practice of confession as the most apt term for describing speech about truth in our era. In Chapter Three I therefore define and describe "confession" by examining its New Testament use, surveying several recent theological works that have reclaimed it as an important theological category, and viewing it from the perspective of linguistic theory. From the results of this study, I suggest that "confession" has functioned in the church to describe (1) a summary of the "essential" faith and (2) the articulation of that faith in response both to the proclaimed word and the present needs and circumstances of the community and world. In Chapter Four I move forward to fashion a confessional homiletic by surveying two recent attempts to respond to the postmodern challenge. The first is the postliberal homiletic of Charles Campbell which stresses the ascriptive power of the biblical narratives, and the second is the postmodern homiletic of Lucy Atkinson Rose which reconceives preaching as conversation. Each of these proposals develops one of the two elements of "confession" I discern, but only at the expense of the other. I maintain that only by retaining *both* senses of "confession" can

4

we preach in our context both faithfully and adequately, and I therefore recommend placing the distinct contributions of Campbell and Rose in creative and critical conversation with each other.

In the third and final part of this work, I focus on the specific tasks that confront preachers by suggesting that they will profit by allowing the entire process of preparing sermons — from their engagement with the text to their concerns for sermonic form and language — to be shaped by the Christian practice of confessing faith in Jesus Christ. Therefore, in Chapter Five I explore the nature of the Scriptures as a collection of confessions and describe the demands such a view makes upon our exegetical practice and our understanding of the role of the preacher. In Chapter Six I then consider the conversation we hope to promote in the congregation through our preaching by giving attention to the way we conceive and execute our sermons. In particular, I seek to formulate a "confessional" or "kenotic rhetoric" patterned after God's self-disclosure in the cross and resurrection of Jesus Christ, and to explore the implications of that rhetoric for sermonic form and language.

Throughout this book, I draw material from a variety of philosophical, theological, and homiletical sources in order to fashion a useful way to think about preaching in the postmodern context. Ultimately, I conclude that, far from threatening the life of the church, postmodernism presses us to release deceptive foundational securities and live, once more, by faith alone; we therefore would do well in our preaching to reclaim the ancient Christian practice of confessing faith in Jesus Christ. Interestingly, in so doing we not only respond to the postmodern challenge but also overcome the major limitation of postmodernity and reclaim the means by which to speak of "truth" and "reality" with integrity.

I conclude this work by offering two sermons to illustrate what I have proposed.

Before proceeding to the main argument, two final notes are in order. First, while the project unfolds fairly neatly from (1) an analysis of the problem (Chapters One and Two) to (2) the construction of a recommendation (Chapters Three and Four) and (3) the application of its implications (Chapters Five and Six), such an order belies the actual origin of the argument, which comes only at the end. For far from believing that postmodernism holds the power to determine the church's present and future theology, I think that the cross and resurrection of Jesus

Christ exposes the lie — more devastatingly than postmodernism ever could — of any and all foundations upon which we would guarantee our faith. As Rudolf Bultmann noted half a century ago, Jesus Christ created — and still creates! — a crisis *(krisis)* for those he encounters by destroying every place of refuge to which we would flee other than the naked proclamation of the gospel.[8] Thus, the deconstructive force of postmodern criticism only renders us the timely service of reminding us, albeit at times painfully, of our essential nature and calling.

Second, the reader should note that this whole project is itself a confession of faith. That is, it rests upon several axiomatic assumptions about the nature of reality and of God's revelation that, while able to be described and defended, simply cannot be proved. This, I believe, is not only fitting but also, as we shall see, unavoidable in our postmodern context. I hope, therefore, that both the conception and execution of this project will, if not *prove* its major argument, at least offer a consistent and compelling witness to its usefulness to the Christian community in this day and age.

8. "God's revelation destroys every picture which man's desire makes of it, so that the real test of a man's desire for salvation is to believe even when God encounters him in a totally different way from that which he expected." Rudolf Bultmann, *The Gospel of John,* trans. G. R. Beasley-Murray, R. W. N. Hoare, and J. K. Riches (Philadelphia: Westminster Press, 1971), p. 228.

CHAPTER I

The End of the World as We Know It?

What's in a Name?

In this chapter I seek to accomplish two goals. First, I will describe postmodernity chiefly as a reaction to modernist assumptions about (1) the basis for knowledge and (2) language's ability to represent reality, and I will describe the implications of these challenges. Second, I will then both underscore postmodernity's contribution as a salutary corrective to modernity and also clarify the challenge that the era presents to those who wish to speak beyond the confines of their immediate community and experience; to those, that is, who wish to speak with any degree of meaningfulness of "truth."

In order to accomplish these goals, we must first admit that, at this bridge of two millennia, postmodernism appears to be simultaneously overwhelmingly present and frustratingly elusive. On the one hand, whether we are always aware of it or not, we probably listen to postmodern music, see postmodern films, overhear conversations about postmodern literature, fashion, or even architecture, and consume postmodern goods produced, marketed, and delivered by postmodern means. On the other hand, despite the preponderance of the "postmodern" — or perhaps because of it — few of us have a clear sense of what the term actually means.[1]

Part of the problem undoubtedly rests in its very name, as ungainly

---

1. Steven Best and Douglas Kellner offer a helpful overview of the variety of cultural forms that postmodernity takes in *The Postmodern Turn* (New York: Guilford Press, 1997).

7

as it is misleading. To the extent that we use the term "modern" to mean "contemporary," it is difficult to imagine how anything could be "post-" modern. Further, both self-described advocates of the postmodern and their critics regularly employ the term in a variety of ways, particularly in respect to different disciplines. (Despite some similarities, that is, there are also significant differences between postmodern literature, architecture, economics, and philosophy.) Finally, some are already heralding the end of the postmodern age and the advent of some future epoch yet to be named.

For all of these reasons and more, "postmodernism" remains a notoriously difficult term to pin down, and therefore I necessarily begin my investigation of it by first considering both the denotations and connotations of its name.[2] To put it most simply, in what way do we understand the postmodern era actually to be "post-" modernity? Answers to this question usually tend in one of two distinct directions.

For some, "post-" implies a complete "leaving behind" of what it modifies. Postmodernity therefore represents an absolute rejection of the modern period, stressing the discontinuity between the ages and roundly denouncing the goals of modernity.[3] Others, however, use the milder form of "post-" to imply "following after," and for this reason view the advent of the postmodern in less disjunctive terms, stressing the inherent relationship between the two epochs and sometimes describing postmodernity as the final stage, or inevitable evolution, of modernity.[4] Before reaching our own conclusions about "postmodernity," it may therefore prove useful to sketch briefly the dominant features of its antecedent age.

According to most historians, the modern era was inaugurated in the years following the Peace of Westphalia (1648) that brought an end to the Thirty Years War and marked the dawn of the period known as

---

2. The earliest known reference to the term is in Arnold Toynbee's *An Historian's Approach to Religion* (Oxford: Oxford University Press, 1956), p. 146; as cited in Fretheim and Froehlich, *The Bible as the Word of God in a Postmodern Age* (Minneapolis: Fortress Press, 1998), p. 64 n. 5.

3. E.g., Ihab Hassan, *The Postmodern Turn: Essays in Postmodern Theory and Culture* (Columbus: Ohio State University Press, 1987), p. 5.

4. E.g., Jean François Lyotard, *The Postmodern Condition*, trans. Geoff Bennington and Brian Massumi, Theory and History of Literature, vol. 10 (Minneapolis: University of Minnesota Press, 1984), p. 79.

the Enlightenment. Worn out by the religious wars that had ravaged Europe, increasingly skeptical of the sectarian dogmas and disputes driving those conflicts, and more aware of the fissures in the edifice of the post-Reformation church, the intellectuals of that generation assumed the humanistic mantle of their Renaissance forebears and sought the means by which to order society by rational, rather than religious, means.

It is difficult to underestimate the nature of the change that occurred as the early modernists sought to erect a society guided, not by superstitious belief, but by a universally valid rationality. While retaining the overarching belief in God that shaped the Christian world of medieval Europe, they nevertheless suspected that grounding one's understanding of the workings of the *creation* on theological speculation about the nature of the *Creator* (or, in earlier Greek thought, *Being*) was entirely inadequate, and therefore freely called into question the metaphysical convictions of the previous ages. The result, as Diogenes Allen points out, is an important philosophical shift in emphasis from ontology (questions of Being) to epistemology (questions of knowing).[5]

Having rejected the traditional theological and philosophical foundations they had inherited, however, the architects of the modern period found themselves intellectually and existentially moorless and were therefore driven by a sense of impending crisis to commence a relentless quest for an enlightened *certainty*.[6] This quest took shape in two distinct forms. In the *rationalism* of René Descartes, certainty came from subjecting every experience to radical doubt until one is left only with the undeniable reality of one's own existence. With his famous "*Cogito, ergo sum,*" Descartes argued that simply because our perceptions can — and often are — mistaken, certainty exists only in the mind. He therefore lodged his confidence in the rational consciousness of our own existence, from which the indisputable "first truths" of philosophy might be deduced through rigorous and logical introspection and then applied to make sense of our perceptions of the external world. In contrast, the *empiricism* of John Locke asserted that all of our rational ideas originally stem from our sensory experience. Therefore,

---

5. Diogenes Allen, *Philosophy for Understanding Theology* (Atlanta: John Knox, 1985), p. 171.

6. Allen, *Philosophy for Understanding Theology*, p. 171.

9

only a method of empirical observation and verification could establish a reliable foundation for all knowledge.

While apparently starting at opposite ends of the philosophical spectrum, both rationalists and empiricists held fast to the conviction that some indubitable "first truths" or "universal foundations" could (indeed, must!) be discovered upon which to ground all knowledge. That is, whether by introspection or observation, both variations of the quest for certainty sought to pierce through the superstition they charged had governed earlier ages and find some indubitable epistemological touchstone.

While they therefore debated the precise direction to follow, both camps concurred regarding not only the final destination, but also the path: enlightened human reason. Indicating the central significance human rationality would occupy in the emerging modern world, Immanuel Kant summarized the ethos of the age at the outset of his 1784 essay, "What Is Enlightenment?":

> Enlightenment is Man's leaving his self-caused immaturity. Immaturity is the incapacity to use one's intelligence without the guidance of another. Such immaturity is self-caused if it is not caused by lack of intelligence, but by lack of determination and courage to use one's intelligence without being guided by another. *Sapere Aude!* Have the courage to use your own intelligence! is therefore the motto of the enlightenment.[7]

Indelibly stamped by the confidence that human reason alone provided sure ground for certainty, modernity would come to be animated by a resolute and optimistic desire to discover, study, describe, and ultimately harness the universal laws of the created order.[8] It is the unmis-

---

7. Karl J. Friedrich, ed. and trans., *The Philosophy of Kant* (New York: Modern Library, 1949), p. 132.

8. Diogenes Allen suggests four dominant characteristics, or "pillars," of modernity that arise from such resolve: (1) the existence of a self-contained universe, (2) the possibility of establishing a rational basis for morality and society, (3) the belief in inevitable progress, and (4) the assumption that knowledge is inherently good. See *Christian Belief in a Postmodern World: The Full Wealth of Conviction* (Louisville: Westminster/John Knox Press, 1989), pp. 2-5. See also Darrell Jodock's helpful survey of the characteristics of modernity in his *The Church's Bible: Its Contemporary Authority* (Minneapolis: Fortress Press, 1989), pp. 15-19.

takable waning of both the resolve and optimism behind the modernist project that most clearly typifies postmodernity.

But even in identifying this significant discontinuity between the ages, we inadvertently touch upon the degree to which modernity defines the postmodern reaction to it. Other instances of continuity-in-discontinuity abound. Both periods are born out of the crisis of certainty, but understand and respond to that crisis differently.[9] Again, both eras possess a keen awareness of the fragility of the human condition, but understand the predicament of humanity in markedly different terms. Similarly, both ages despair of the solutions of a previous age and therefore confront the specter of a foundationless world, even as each adopts distinct means by which to address such tension.[10] Finally, both the modern and postmodern epochs inaugurate a period of radical experimentation in the face of a de-centered world, yet whereas the former eschewed religious foundationalism in favor of rationally or empirically based certainty (or at least the possibility of certainty), the latter has not only given up such a quest but, at least on a global level, has actually embraced uncertainty itself.[11]

To understand postmodernity aright, therefore, I believe we cannot afford to overlook the way in which it stems from the very originating impulses of modernity, even as we recognize its intentional repudiation of many of the outcomes of those impulses.[12] It is in this context that I find useful David Harvey's suggestion that a line from Baudelaire's seminal 1863 essay, "The Painter of Modern Life," well captures the spirit of the modern age. "Modernity," Baudelaire wrote, "is the tran-

9. Allan Megill characterizes the earlier crisis (to which Descartes and, later, Kant responds) as theological — the death of God and loss of the authority of the Bible — and the later crisis as historical — the demise of a belief in the linear, progressive nature of history. Interestingly, however, both crises inevitably involve, as we will see, questions of "truth," "meaning," and humanity's "place" in the universe. See Megill, *Prophets of Extremity: Nietzsche, Heidegger, Foucault, Derrida* (Berkeley: University of California Press, 1985), pp. xii-xiv.

10. See John McGowan, *Postmodernism and Its Critics* (Ithaca, N.Y.: Cornell University Press, 1991), p. 24.

11. We will have more to say about postmodernity's preference for the "local" below.

12. See Steven Best and Douglas Kellner, *Postmodern Theory: Critical Investigations* (New York: Guilford Press, 1991), pp. 29-30; and Jean François Lyotard, *The Postmodern Explained*, ed. Julian Pefanis and Morgan Thomas (Minneapolis: University of Minnesota Press, 1993), pp. 75-80.

sient, the fleeting, the contingent; it is one half of art, the other being the eternal and the immutable."[13] We may perhaps best characterize postmodernity as a frenzied celebration of the first half of Baudelaire's assessment and a marked despair over the second.[14]

At the heart of both the celebration and the despair is a vigorous rejection of the modernist quest for certainty and a spirited assault on modernist assumptions about (1) the basis of our knowledge and (2) the ability of language to refer beyond its own semiotic system and therefore the existence of a reality independent of our linguistic constructions. In order to perceive the scope of the postmodern challenge, I will briefly probe each of these elements in turn before comparing the relative "costs and benefits" of the two ages.

The Emperor Has No Clothes

Hans Christian Andersen's well-known children's story, "The Emperor's New Clothes," concludes with this scene:

> And so the emperor marched in the procession under the beautiful canopy and everybody on the street and in the windows cried out: "The Emperor's new clothes are peerless! What a beautiful train! How wonderfully they fit!"
>
> No one would let it be known that he saw nothing, for that would have meant that he was unfit for his office, or else that he was very stupid. . . .
>
> "But he has nothing on!" said a little child.
>
> "Just listen to the innocent!" said the child's father. But one person whispered to another what the child had said. . . .
>
> "But he really hasn't anything on!" at last shouted all the people. The Emperor had a creepy feeling, for it seemed to him that they

13. Cited by David Harvey, *The Condition of Postmodernity* (Cambridge, Mass.: Blackwell, 1996 [1990]), p. 10.

14. Lyotard asserts that postmodern thought and art are "undoubtedly a part of the modern," arguing that *whatever* challenges the reigning assumptions of the day is postmodern. Modernism is simply the reification of what was once avant-garde. "Postmodernism thus understood is not modernism at its end but in the nascent state, and this state is constant" (*The Postmodern Condition*, p. 79).

were right. But then he thought to himself, "I must carry the thing out and go through with the procession."

So he bore himself still more proudly, and the chamberlains walked along behind him carrying the train which was not there at all.[15]

In many respects, postmodern critics present themselves in a role akin to Andersen's young child. While they may not possess the guilelessness of the youngster, they nevertheless delight in pointing out the degree to which many of our most cherished beliefs about "the good, the true, and the beautiful" are simply convenient assumptions that we have agreed not to question. They name these assumptions philosophical foundations and have declared on them a war without surrender.

Formally defined, philosophical foundations are premises "whose truth is acceptable independently of any inference and whose status is accordingly indubitable"[16] and thereby serve as "non-inferential principles whose certainty and stability ground other epistemic claims."[17] Less formally, they are the unquestioned assertions of what is undeniably and self-evidently true, assertions that serve to undergird our sense that the world is, ultimately, a coherent, unified, and meaningful place.

Foundations play at least two important roles. First, they offer a sense of social cohesion by setting the parameters of shared convictions within which a society may flourish. Second, foundations offer a standard by which to assess competing claims to truth. Without such a standard, the process of validating, or legitimating, one claim to truth over another would be impossible, as each standard would depend upon another and one would enter into an infinite regression of validation. In both roles, then, foundations create a center to the world — socially and intellectually — and thereby serve to ground our sense of values, truth, and even ourselves.

Not surprisingly, the foundations of a given society are esteemed quite highly by those who live within the order they procure.[18] Because

---

15. *Hans Andersen's Fairy Tales,* trans. Valdemar Paulsen (Chicago: Rand McNally, 1916), pp. 115-16.

16. Bruce Aune, *Knowledge, Mind and Nature* (New York: Random House, 1967), p. 41.

17. John Thiel, *Nonfoundationalism* (Minneapolis: Fortress Press, 1994), p. 1.

18. Ironically, of course, foundations are rarely thought of as "philosophical foun-

they are generally viewed as self-evidently and eternally true by those who hold them, foundations are regularly conferred an almost semi-divine status by the group they define and, as Jean François Lyotard points out, are therefore often capitalized — as in God, Truth, Freedom, Capitalism, the American Way, Socialism, the Proletariat, and so forth.[19]

Postmodernists resist foundationalism out of the deep suspicion that the order and unity foundations provide entail the significant price of excluding whatever does not fit into, or agree with, the parameters allowed by the foundation. Following up particularly on the structuralist observation that things (e.g., words, ideas, signifiers) only have meaning in relation to other things (primarily in binary relationships), postmodernists are wary of the way in which certain elements of a larger "web of signification" are privileged over the rest. Hence, one does not simply differentiate between white and black, male and female, rich and poor, Western and Eastern, and so on, but regularly privileges one term or category over the other and therefore *discriminates* between the two in both senses of the word. Such privileging is normally justified on the basis of some tacitly held conviction about the good, the true, and the beautiful; it is justified, that is, on the basis of a foundation.

The difficulty comes, however, in proving or demonstrating the validity or legitimacy of a justifying foundation. Simply because foundations *cannot* be foundations if they depend on some prior justification, they are simultaneously self-evident to the holder and unprovable (if not improbable) to the skeptic. Inevitably, therefore, social groups happily (albeit often unconsciously) assume and assert their philosophical, religious, and cultural foundations as true to the point that, when confronted by the differing constructions of other groups, they just as happily (and often more consciously) judge, oppose, or condemn those differing foundations as inferior by their own unproven assumptions. Hence, one of the central and unifying tenets of postmodernity is that the process of legitimation (always) implies the (usually) tacit exercise of power.[20] Postmodernity resists the process of foundational legitima-

---

dations" by the vast majority of persons in any given society; rather, they are simply the self-evident, the obvious, and the given.

19. See Lyotard, *The Postmodern Explained*, p. 41.

20. See, in particular, Michel Foucault, *Power/Knowledge: Selected Interviews and Other Writings, 1972-1977*, ed. Colin Gordon (New York: Pantheon Books, 1977).

tion, then, because such a process masks one particular group's use of power to define the standards (legal, ethical, cultural, religious, philosophical) by which they judge — and sometimes violently quash — other groups.

What postmodernists seek, therefore, is continually to do away with the pretense of foundationalism, relentlessly forcing the reigning "Emperors" to admit that they are wearing no clothes. In this respect, postmodernity has been appropriately called a movement of resistance, contesting at every step the process of foundational legitimation and the unified totality that such a process seeks.[21] For this reason, Lyotard closes his prominent article, "What Is Postmodernism?" with a call to arms:

> The nineteenth and twentieth centuries have given us as much terror as we can take. We have paid a high enough price for the nostalgia of the whole and the one. . . . Under the general demand for . . . appeasement, we hear the mutterings of the desire for a return of terror, for the realization of the fantasy to seize reality. The answer is: Let us wage a war on totality; let us be witnesses to the unpresentable; let us activate the differences and save the honor of the name.[22]

Central to the postmodern critique, therefore, is that which stands beyond the pale of the foundationally defined structure or order. In this sense, postmodernists regularly do the unthinkable by, if you will, tenaciously questioning the "unquestionability" of whatever foundations they stumble across. Consequently, Lyotard, speaking of postmodern aesthetics, writes,

> The postmodern would be that which, in the modern, puts forward the unpresentable in presentation itself; that which denies itself the solace of good forms, the consensus of a taste which would make it possible to share collectively the nostalgia for the unattainable; that which searches for new presentations, not in order to enjoy them but in order to impart a stronger sense of the unpresentable.[23]

21. See A. K. M. Adam, *What Is Postmodern Biblical Criticism?* (Minneapolis: Fortress Press, 1995), p. 1.

22. Lyotard, *Postmodern Condition*, pp. 81-82.

23. Lyotard, *Postmodern Condition*, p. 81.

While postmodernists describe this presence of the unpresentable "Other" in different terms — the differend,[24] the play of *différence*,[25] the marginal[26] — each has in mind that which disrupts the reigning order simply by existing in its "otherness" and thereby calling into question the univocal totality of the foundational regime.[27] Such a strategy seeks to betray the extent to which foundations serve, not simply to create order, but also to restrict change, flux, instability, play, and the anxiety that often attends them. As Jacques Derrida writes in his seminal article, "Structure, Sign, and Play in the Discourse of the Human Sciences,"

> The function of this center was not only to orient, to balance, and organize the structure — one cannot in fact conceive of an unorganized structure — but above all to make sure that the organizing principle of the structure [i.e. the foundation] would limit what we might call the *play* of the structure. By orienting and organizing the coherence of the system, the center of a structure permits the play of its elements inside the total form. And even today the notion of a structure lacking any center represents the unthinkable itself.
>
> ... The concept of a centered structure is in fact the concept of a play based on a fundamental ground, a play constituted on the basis of a fundamental immobility and a reassuring certitude, which itself is beyond the reach of play. And on the basis of this certitude anxiety can be mastered, for anxiety is invariably the result of a certain mode of being implicated in the game, of being caught by the game, of being as it were at stake in the game from the outset.[28]

24. See Jean François Lyotard, *The Differend: Phrases in Dispute,* trans. George Van Den Abbeele (Minneapolis: University of Minnesota Press, 1988).

25. See Jacques Derrida, *Margins of Philosophy,* trans. Alan Bass (Chicago: University of Chicago Press, 1982); *Writing and Difference,* trans. and with an introduction and additional note by Alan Bass (Chicago: University of Chicago Press, 1978).

26. See Terry A. Veling, *Living in the Margins: Intentional Communities and the Art of Interpretation* (New York: Crossroad, 1996).

27. See also Emmanuel Levinas, *Totality and Infinity: An Essay on Exteriority,* trans. Alphonso Lengis (Pittsburgh: Duquesne University Press, 1961); and Wendy Farley, *Eros for the Other: Retaining Truth in a Pluralistic World* (University Park: Pennsylvania State University Press, 1996).

28. Derrida, *Writing and Difference,* pp. 278-79. (Unless otherwise noted, all uses of italics are original to the cited text.)

In place of a foundationally ordered, centered structure, post-modernists offer a picture of a heteronomous dissensus of competing claims and voices, where no one idea or voice is privileged over the rest. Instead of an ordered, centered structure, one discovers an undulating and ever-developing sense of reality that shifts in response to our changing perceptions and convictions. This is not to suggest that we can or should equate postmodernism with unrestrained anarchy. Rather, the objection postmodernists level against foundations is not that they *lend* a center or organizing principle to a structure or group, but rather that they *impose* and *enforce* that center in a way that limits the play of difference by excluding that which does not fit and by fixing meaning, value, or truth once and for all. It is the static, not the coherent, element of foundationalism that postmodernists oppose.[29]

Thus, rather than seek a universally valid rationality by which to legitimate competing truth-claims, postmodernists tend to call instead for pragmatic, ever-local determinations of the good, the true, and the beautiful, thereby shifting the process of legitimation to local, rather than global, grounds, but certainly not destroying it. As John McGowan points out, postmodernism "sets itself against the traditional theoretical aspiration to uncover essential and necessary truths that are not contingent upon the temporal and the human."[30] According to postmodernists, because whatever foundations we may adopt are all too human and inextricably temporal, they — and the larger structures they order — will ever be in flux. Therefore they steadfastly maintain that no single measure or standard should be permitted to gain permanent ascendancy over the rest. The ultimate goal of postmodern critics, we may conclude, is not simply that the emperors of this world admit they are wearing no clothes, but rather that this world might see an end to emperors altogether.

Innocence Lost

In his 1962 book *The Birth and Death of Meaning,* Ernest Becker suggests that postmodernity's antifoundational onslaught stems from human-

---

29. See Derrida, *Writing and Difference,* pp. 278-89.
30. McGowan, *Postmodernism and Its Critics,* p. 23.

ity's surprising ability to pierce through the "fictitious nature" of its own world. As he writes,

> The world of human aspiration is fundamentally fictitious. If we do not understand this we understand nothing about man. It is a purely symbolic creation, by an ego-controlled animal, that permits action in a psychological world; a behavioral world removed from the tyranny of the present moment, of immediate stimuli which enslave all lower organisms. Man's freedom is a fabricated freedom from boundness to the here and now. But the price he pays for this loftiness is not only a confinement of his perceptions to the world view he has learned. It is *the utter fragility of his delicately constituted fiction.* . . .
> It is one of the most remarkable achievements of thought, of self-scrutiny, that the most anxiety-prone animal of all would come to see through himself and discover the fictional nature of his action world.[31]

Becker's assessment of the human condition reflects the phenomena that Peter Berger and Thomas Luckmann later described as "the social construction of reality" and proffers a view that can be characterized as "constructionist," "semantical," "semiotic," or "aestheticist."[32] All these designations manifest the conviction that our various characterizations of the "world" are not neutral descriptions of "reality" but rather imaginative sociosymbolic constructs that produce, rather than reflect, the world(s) we inhabit. As a product of our own linguistic construction and psychological projection, what we call "reality" is both fragile and contingent. Hence, whatever the merits of the "achievement" Becker hails, it also bespeaks a loss of innocence no less profound than that described in Genesis; this for at least four reasons.

First, a postmodern perspective — where language cannot refer be-

31. Ernest Becker, *The Birth and Death of Meaning* (New York: Free Press, 1962), p. 109.

32. Peter L. Berger and Thomas Luckmann, *The Social Construction of Reality: A Treatise in the Sociology of Knowledge* (New York: Doubleday, 1966); on "constructivist," see Hassan, *The Postmodern Turn*, p. 172; on "semantical," see Arthur C. Danto, "Philosophy as/and/of Literature," in *Post-Analytic Philosophy*, ed. John Rajchman and Cornel West (New York: Columbia University Press, 1985), pp. 63-83; on "semiotic" see Fredric Jameson, "The Linguistic Model," in *Language and Politics*, ed. Michael J. Shapiro (New York: New York University Press, 1984), pp. 168-92; on "aestheticist," see Megill, *Prophets of Extremity*, pp. 2-4.

yond itself and "reality" is therefore a sociosymbolic construction — dissolves the teleological import of human history and thereby raises the specter of "meaninglessness," the possibility that human existence is ultimately void of intrinsic value.[33] While modernists launched their quest for certainty in optimistic defiance of that possibility, given the tragic failures of the modernist project, postmodernists can no longer stave off such a conclusion.[34]

Second, postmodernity holds humanity culpable for the world it produces. Simply because its constructions of "reality" are contingent — and therefore could have been otherwise — humanity is now responsible for the order and character of the world it creates and accepts.[35] Thus, the symbol-using human displaces the God of Genesis as the one burdened with creating order from the "formless and void" chaos of the universe. In this way, postmodernity's harsh critique of modernist foundationalism and the aestheticist view it tenders brings to fruition Friedrich Nietzsche's dark prediction of a century ago that "God remains dead. And we have killed him."[36] In God's place stands a humanity that is simultaneously potent and fragile but always, and inescapably, culpable.

Third, postmodernity offers a distinctly ironic view of language, in that while language can create entire worlds it is unable to penetrate the confines of its semiotic system and refer beyond itself. Language is therefore no longer simply the "house of Being," but also its cage, a prison that is as necessary to our existence as it is unyielding in its impotence to depict the "real."

Finally, if "reality" is but the product of our desire to tame primor-

---

33. See Megill, *Prophets of Extremity*, p. xiii; and Richard Rorty, "Solidarity or Objectivity?," in *Post-Analytic Philosophy*, ed. John Rajchman and Cornel West (New York: Columbia University Press, 1985), p. 3.

34. As Darrell Jodock writes, "Postmodern culture lives more anxiously in the shadow of the mushroom-shaped cloud and belching smokestacks of Auschwitz" (*The Church's Bible*, p. 8).

35. "Henceforth . . . it is the world that becomes culpable (for the first time in the Western world) in relation to the work; it is now arraigned by the work, obliged to order itself by language, compelled by it to a task of recognition, of reparation . . ." (attributed to Michel Foucault in Megill, *Prophets of Extremity*, p. 181). See also *Michel Foucault: Politics, Philosophy, Culture*, ed. Lawrence Kritzman (New York: Routledge, 1988), p. 156.

36. Friedrich Nietzsche, *The Gay Science*, trans. W. Kaufmann (New York: Random House, 1975), p. 181.

dial chaos by social or symbolic means, then "truth" itself becomes little more than a rarefied name for the popular opinion currently in favor.[37] Hence, the postmodern critique ushers in a world where the
possibility for reasoned judgments about ultimate right and wrong or
universal truth and falsehood withers, if not perishes altogether.

In place of modernist confidence to name and tame reality, we are
left instead with the troubling possibility that reality is *artificial,* nothing more than a linguistic construction of our own devising that can
guarantee neither "meaning" nor "truth" and leaves us implicated for
the shortcomings of our work. This has enormous implications not
only for how we "see" our world, but also for how we speak of it. For if
reality, like beauty, is increasingly "in the eye of the beholder," then
our hope to find common ground upon which we can speak meaningfully to anyone beyond the confines of our immediate cultural-
linguistic community diminishes severely. To appreciate the challenge
postmodernity offers to those who still desire to speak of truth, therefore, we must investigate the postmodern rejection of modernist conceptions of, and confidence in, objective knowledge. For in this central
repudiation of one of the cherished ideals of modernity we perceive
most perspicuously the abandonment of the idea of any truth independent of specific communities of knowers and a consequent shift in
attention from epistemology to hermeneutics that has characterized
the age.

In the modern era, the question of "truth" was construed largely as
one of "knowledge" and, as a consequence, epistemology — the study of
how we know — dominated the modern project. One might characterize the intellectual breach initiated by the Enlightenment, in fact, as
primarily a shift from understanding knowledge as logical and consistent belief to positing it as verifiable fact.

Premodern knowledge was comprised of two components, which we
may describe as coherence and fidelity. In the Aristotelian thought that
permeated the medieval academy, one demonstrated (and acquired)
knowledge through the syllogism, establishing one's claims through the
coherency and consistency of logical proof built upon undisputed first

---

37. Hence Lyotard's preference for a "politics of opinion" over one of "reason." See
Jean François Lyotard and Jean-Loup Thébaud, *Just Gaming,* trans. Wlad Godzich (Minneapolis: University of Minnesota Press, 1985), p. 82.

principles.[38] At the same time, premodern views of knowledge depended largely upon a sense of received tradition. The experience of past generations received in oral or written form constituted the body of mediated (as opposed to immediate) knowledge from which one might draw and to which one was required to be faithful.[39] Thus, one validated extended arguments through appeal to a collection of interrelated points logically established (coherence) and by citing the relevant tradition, be it Aristotle, Augustine, or the Bible (fidelity). Throughout, one sought to demonstrate the consistency of one's premise with some ecclesial or secular version of Vincent of Lérins's canon that "what is held everywhere, always, and by all is what is to be believed."

In both the rationality of Descartes and the empiricism of Locke, such a view of logical consistency is rejected in favor of the ideal of critical verifiability. Knowledge — to be accepted as knowledge — is not simply displayed, but proved. Hence, by submitting truth-claims to either the rigorous doubt of rational introspection or the strict examination of empirical observation, one gains knowledge through a critical process of observation, experimentation, and verification. The stress on coherency is not, of course, left entirely behind by the modernists, but alone it is insufficient. Knowledge is not only coherent belief, it is verifiable fact; it is no longer simply mediated by others, but immediate to our rational and sensory perception; not so much an account of the past, as one of the present; and therefore not the province of tradition, but instead of expertise. Knowledge, in short, is that which can be proven here and now through the exercise of critical human reason.

The reassessment of knowledge — and therefore of truth — as that which can be verified through reason promotes a similar movement from the metaphysical and theological speculation that dominated the scholastic academy to an emphasis on mathematics and the emerging natural and (later) social sciences that would become the hallmark of the modern university. In his critique of modernity, Michel Foucault identifies three central assumptions about knowledge that characterized the period. While each contributed to the great technological strides of the era, each has also come under intense scrutiny during the

38. Allen, *Philosophy for Understanding Theology*, p. 171.
39. See Edward Farley, *Ecclesial Reflection* (Philadelphia: Fortress Press, 1982), pp. 108-13.

postmodern turn. These beliefs are that (1) an objective body of knowledge exists that can be discovered, (2) such knowledge is not only attainable but also value-free, and (3) the pursuit of knowledge benefits all people.[40]

Foucault and other postmodernists typically assault such a view of knowledge on two fronts. The first consists of following up Nietzsche's perspectivalist approach to philosophy. As Nietzsche observed, once the foundations that guarantee meaning and/or truth have been denied or done away with ("God is dead"), all that is left are perspectives. Rational knowledge, from this point of view, is not simply *partial* (the modernist view), but also *particular,* reflecting the specific locale — understood in terms of geography, ethnicity, gender, race, economic status, etc. — of the "knower," reflecting his or her presuppositions, and protecting his or her interests. Where you stand, quite simply, affects what you see (even what you are willing to look at), and there is no "God's-eye view" free of such bias. What modernists offered as knowledge, postmodernists therefore charge, turns out instead to be only particular perspectives, influenced throughout by one's context, no more or less verifiable than any other claim, and ultimately enmeshed in the "power structures" of the time.[41]

While such arguments had been countenanced to some degree in the humanities during the modern period, Foucault and others extend them even to the "hard" sciences. Here they find a natural ally in Thomas Kuhn, whose pioneering work in *The Structure of Scientific Revolutions* similarly argued that even scientific theory amounts to sets of coherent and consistent rhetorical *claims* about the nature of reality that not only cannot be validated beyond the systems of thought they create but also change (sometimes dramatically) over time.[42] From this

40. See Stanley J. Grenz, *A Primer on Postmodernism* (Grand Rapids: Eerdmans, 1996), p. 131; see also Allen, *Christian Belief,* p. 5.

41. This theme runs throughout Foucault's works. See, in particular, *Power/Knowledge: Selected Interviews and Other Writings* and *Michel Foucault: Politics, Philosophy, Culture.*

42. "Science does not deal in all possible laboratory manipulations. Instead, it selects those relevant to the juxtaposition of a paradigm with the immediate experience that the paradigm has partially determined. As a result, scientists with different paradigms engage in different concrete laboratory manipulations." Thomas Kuhn, *The Structure of Scientific Revolutions,* 2nd ed. (Chicago: University of Chicago Press, 1970 [1962]), p. 126; for Kuhn's summary of his position, see pp. 1-9, 160-73.

point of view, universal, value-free, objective knowing is denied and all of our context-dependent knowledge turns out to be far more fragile than previously imagined.

Not only is knowledge not universal, however, it is also not neutral; in fact, according to Foucault, knowledge is always inextricably bound up with power. It is this link between power and knowledge (really an inversion of Francis Bacon's dictum that "knowledge is power") that forms the second front of the postmodern assault.

Who determines, Foucault asks in a series of provocative works, what counts for knowledge? The inevitable answer, he concludes, is those who hold the reigns of power. By studying the transformation of concepts as diverse as insanity, punishment, sexuality, the medical clinic, and humanity's sense of itself, Foucault consistently points out the degree to which not only our assumptions about what we *know* change over time (and are therefore only perspectives) but also that those assumptions are regulated by the governing authorities of any given epistemological structure.[43] Knowledge is thus neither neutral nor unbiased, as beneath perspectival claims to rational knowledge lie assertions driven by self-interest and enforced by force or the threat of its use.[44]

The postmodern emphasis on knowledge as governed by perspective and power accounts for the shift from epistemology (the science of knowing) to hermeneutics (the study of interpretation). Apart from foundations to guarantee the validity of knowledge, all that is left, as Nietzsche observed a hundred years ago, are interpretations.[45] Implicit

43. Foucault does not see this as entirely negative, but rather as an apt reflection of how thoroughly and inextricably enmeshed are power and knowledge. As he writes, "What makes power hold good, what makes it accepted, is simply the fact that it doesn't only weigh on us as a source that says no, but that it traverses and produces things, it induces pleasure, forms knowledge, produces discourse. It needs to be considered as a productive network which runs throughout the whole social body, much more than as a negative instance whose function is repression" (from *Power/Knowledge*, in *The Foucault Reader*, p. 61).

44. See Stanley Fish, *Doing What Comes Naturally: Change, Rhetoric, and the Practice of Theory in Literary and Legal Studies* (Durham, N.C.: Duke University Press, 1989), pp. 503-24.

45. See his *Beyond Good and Evil: Prelude to a Philosophy of the Future*, trans. Walter Kaufmann, in *Nietzsche's Basic Writings*, ed. Walter Kaufmann (New York: Modern Library, 1968).

in such a shift is a commensurate transmutation from viewing "truth" as the source of our observations to seeing it as the product of our interpretations. Hence, postmodernists commonly speak of all "reality" in terms of multilayered literary texts and therefore apply the methods of literary interpretation to philosophical, social, and natural studies. Knowledge and truth are therefore always bound up with issues of power and perspective, and hermeneutics — the art of interpretation — reigns supreme. For in a "sociosymbolic" view of the world, as Jacques Derrida asserts, "There is nothing outside of the text."[46]

At What Price Freedom?

I have so far attempted to sketch the contours of the postmodern turn as boldly as possible so as to state its challenges most sharply. But should we accept the postmodern verdict that Western philosophy and theology have perished and the modern world they supported has come to an end? After all, by its manifold technological advances, modernity presents a compelling case for itself.[47] Further, do most of our parishioners — do we ourselves! — believe that reality is artificial, indeed, *un*real? And what are the consequences of such belief? Finally, what kind of a world do postmodernists seek to create in place of the modernist one with which we are so familiar? These and other questions urge that we not "go gently" into the postmodern night without first evaluating more rigorously the strength and implications of its

46. Or, "there is no outside-text" *(il n'y a pas dehors-texte);* Jacques Derrida, *Of Grammatology,* trans. Gayatri Chakravorty Spivak (Baltimore: Johns Hopkins University Press, 1977), p. 158. See Megill, *Prophets of Extremity,* pp. 2-9, 261-67.

47. In defending his controversial program of stripping the New Testament of its premodern, mythic elements to reveal its modern, existential essence and import (demythologization) Rudolf Bultmann wrote, "We cannot use electric lights and radios and, in the event of illness, avail ourselves of medical and clinical means and at the same time believe in the spirit and wonder world of the New Testament." "New Testament and Mythology: The Problem of Demythologizing the New Testament Proclamation [1941]," in *New Testament and Mythology and Other Basic Writings,* ed. and trans. Schubert M. Ogden (Philadelphia: Fortress Press, 1984), p. 4. Similarly, those of us who board airplanes, visit our doctors for an annual physical, and save for retirement — not to mention use light bulbs — may wonder about the relevancy of debates raging in ivory towers over the status of philosophical foundations.

claims. Because the understanding of postmodernity I have advanced is inextricably bound to the modernity it seeks to overturn, I will offer this evaluation by comparison, attempting an abbreviated version of what accountants call a "cost-benefit analysis" by weighing the contributions and limitations of each period in turn.

Modernity

It will be difficult to assess modernity's accomplishments if we fail to perceive that it was an age born out of a hunger for freedom.[48] Emerging from the ruin of the Thirty Years War, the early modernists sought to free themselves from a blind obedience to religious tradition.[49] This is not to say, however, that they sought to banish faith. On the contrary, as Diogenes Allen has pointed out, Christian faith in the goodness and rationality of God granted the early modernists a confidence in the orderliness and intelligibility of the universe and spurred their efforts to realize the Genesis command to "exercise dominion" over all creation.[50] It was therefore not Christian faith, but rather sectarian dogma, that the early pioneers of the modern era sought to overcome by subjecting every claim, sacred or secular, to the acid test of rational inquiry.

At one level, this search for universally rational criteria by which to assess all claims to knowledge and truth led modernists to affirm their premodern intellectual inheritance positing a rational and coherent "reality" where competing descriptions can and must be resolved. At another level, however, this flight from religious authority prompted the early modernists to disavow premodern methods of investigation.[51] No longer would it suffice to determine the nature of

48. Recall Kant's description of the "Enlightenment" as humanity's releasing itself from its "self-caused immaturity."

49. Metaphors of blindness and sight, darkness and light, will come to dominate not only modernity — the era begun by the Enlightenment — but also color our own perceptions, as we regularly refer to those centuries before the advent of modernity as the "Dark Ages."

50. Diogenes Allen, *Christian Belief in a Postmodern World*, pp. 23-34.

51. See Jeffrey Stout, *The Flight from Authority: Religion, Morality, and the Quest for Autonomy* (Notre Dame: University of Notre Dame Press, 1981).

the universe via speculation on its rational nature. Rather, in the wake of the sectarian conflict that devastated Europe, evidence meeting universally valid criteria was now the requirement.[52] While the modernists therefore shared the same passion for reason as did their premodern forebears, they shifted their admiration and attention from the rationality of the universe to that of humanity, thereby commencing what Calvin Schrag has described as a slide from interest in *logos* to a demand for logic.[53] This move led eventually to a privileging of science as the paradigmatic example of human reason, which in turn has led to the momentous technological advances that have marked not only Western history but also left virtually no corner of our globe untouched.[54]

Postmodernity

Perhaps ironically, the source of modernity's greatest virtues is identical to what postmodern critics charge is the source of its greatest vices: its relentless search for certitude. As we observed above, postmodernist critics assert that certainty demands a homogeneity of experience that simply does not exist. Rather than contend with the uncertainty heterogeneity implies, modernists imposed their own order. As a consequence of their demand for universal orderliness, proponents of modernist rationality not only subdued nature but all too often subjugated those who differed from their imposed norm.[55] Latent beneath the achievements of modernity, postmodernists therefore charge, exists a reservoir of fear of chaos and meaninglessness

52. J. Wentzel van Huyssteen, *The Shaping of Rationality: Toward Interdisciplinarity in Theology and Science* (Grand Rapids: Eerdmans, 1999), p. 189. See also his *Essays in Postfoundationalist Theology* (Grand Rapids: Eerdmans, 1997), pp. 120-28.

53. Calvin O. Schrag, *Resources for Rationality: A Response to the Postmodern Challenge* (Bloomington: Indiana University Press, 1992), p. 18.

54. For accounts of how this privileging of rationality and science impacted theology and preaching see, respectively, Diogenes Allen, *Christian Belief in a Postmodern World*, pp. 6-9; and Ronald J. Allen in Ronald J. Allen, Barbara Shires Blaisdell, and Scott Black Johnston, *Theology for Preaching: Authority, Truth, and Knowledge of God in a Postmodern Ethos* (Nashville: Abingdon Press, 1997), p. 90.

55. As Levinas writes, the history of Western philosophy has most often been a history of reducing "the 'other' to the 'same'" (*Totality and Infinity*, p. 43).

that has ushered in as much terror and coercion as it has technological advance.[56]

More acutely aware of the ecological and social cost of modernity's "advancements" and rocking in the wake of the most violent century of our history, we may therefore welcome postmodernity's resolute rejection of the modernist penchant to totalization in its relentless quest for a sure place to stand. Having written the epitaph for modernity, postmodernity reverses modernist tendencies at almost every juncture. In place of an imposed homogeneity, postmodernity cultivates rampant heterogeneity; as opposed to seeking consensus, it celebrates dissensus; instead of order, it glorifies unlimited play; and so on. For this reason, and as we have seen, in the postmodern world nothing is sacred. Every claim to truth is subjected to an ever-suspicious critique, and every boundary between "right and wrong" and the "seemly and unpresentable" is willfully transgressed, all in the steadfast pursuit of resisting the "terror" of modernist totalization.

But at what cost? Ultimately, perhaps the most damaged item in the postmodern fray is not so much a unified sense of the truth (was there ever really one?), but the very possibility of even speaking about, let alone asserting, a truthful description of our physical and moral world. To some postmodernists, the very notion of "truth" is entirely suspect.[57] At its best, the claim to "truth" represents the collective values of particular communities, while at its worst it disguises a tacit claim of a superior value by which to justify — and enforce — one's own predilections.

Amid the relativistic free play of postmodern transgression, therefore, the one thing one cannot speak about is the truth. Thus, and ironically, the postmodern flight from totality renders only another, even if inverse, form of totality. As Donna Haraway observes, both modernist foundationalism and postmodernist constructionism are "mirror-twins" in that they each purport to describe ultimate reality, though in opposite ways. For whereas modernity sought to lay bare the eternal essence of the universe, postmodernity declares that there is no essence; and whereas modernity promised to reveal the truth, postmodernity denies its existence. Each option makes its prescriptions

56. See Allan Megill, *Prophets of Extremity*, pp. xii-xiv.
57. See, for instance, Richard Rorty, *The Consequences of Pragmatism* (Minneapolis: University of Minnesota Press, 1982), p. xii.

from some universal dictum: one can/cannot describe reality. Hence, as Haraway writes, modern foundationalism and postmodern antifoundationalism "are both 'god-tricks' promising vision from everywhere and nowhere equally and fully."[58]

The shadow side of postmodern antifoundationalism and its constructivist view of reality is that in attempting to free discourse from the restraints of an imposed order it inadvertently renders us mute by robbing us of the power of conviction. That is, apart from at least some *sense* that there exists a universal standard of the good, the true, and the beautiful (apart, that is, from some conviction of foundational truth), can one claim any sense of universal rights to defend or extend? While postmodernists aver that local criteria are sufficient (indeed, are all that exist), far too many situations demand judgments of greater force and cultural dexterity. As John McGowan writes, postmodernism inevitably

> finds itself between a rock and a hard place. . . . Unable either to ground or to construct an ethics within the terms of its critiques of foundationalism and of dominating, humanistic reason, postmodern politics is often reduced to the ironic, anarchistic effort to transform the existing order by means of play, *jouissance,* or other textual strategies.[59]

Consequently, there exists the danger of what we might call postmodern "malaise," a condition where Derrida's "deferral of meaning" devolves into a "deferral of responsibility." A major proponent of "the postmodern turn" in his book of the same name, Ihab Hassan suggests that retreats to textualism can be made by persons "only in comfort, when life makes on them no real demand."[60] Similarly, Donna Haraway urges that "social constructivism cannot be allowed to decay into the radiant emanations of cynicism."[61] More ominously, Allan Megill warns against the dangers of denying all reality that we ourselves have not created: "if one adopts, in a cavalier and single-minded fashion, the

---

58. Donna J. Haraway, *Simians, Cyborgs, and Women: The Reinvention of Nature* (New York: Routledge, 1991), p. 191.

59. John McGowan, *Postmodernism and Its Critics,* p. 28.

60. Ihab Hassan, *The Postmodern Turn,* p. 195.

61. Haraway, *Simians, Cyborgs, and Women,* p. 184.

view that everything is discourse or text or fiction, the *realia* are trivialized. Real people who really died in the gas chambers at Auschwitz or Treblinka become so much discourse."[62]

From the point of view of our brief cost-benefit analysis, modernity and postmodernity each exacts a significant toll, resulting in a "zero-sum difference." We may assess part of the responsibility of this cost and its unsatisfactory result, I think, to the inherent fearfulness of each position. In the case of modernity, this has become more readily apparent in recent years, as several commentators have underscored that the era was born not simply from a benign quest for freedom and knowledge but also, and perhaps to a greater degree, from a fear of chaos.[63] But if modernity was driven by what Richard Bernstein aptly names its "Cartesian Anxiety" to secure certainty "at any price," postmodernity appears no less fearful. Driven by its dread of totalizing modernist truth-claims and metanarratives, postmodernists seek to alleviate their anxieties by encouraging an endless plurivocity of local narratives and perspectives. Ironically, the resulting cacophony nearly silences all claims to truth, making it extremely difficult to offer constructive critique or proclaim a universally liberating word. Ultimately, one is left in the unhappy position of having to choose, as Dennis Olson puts it, between either the "Tower" of modern foundationalism or the "Babble" of postmodern relativism.[64]

Where, then, are we to turn? Is there a way to reject modernist totalization without succumbing to postmodern nihilism? Does a passage exist through the foundationalist-antifoundationalist impasse? Can we negotiate the means by which to reclaim authentic speech about truth and reality that does not negate the validity of counter-assertions? Can we, that is, find the means by which to transcend our fears, or at least refuse to be dominated by them? It is to these questions that I turn in the next chapter.

62. Megill, *Prophets of Extremity*, p. 345.

63. See Richard J. Bernstein, *Beyond Objectivism and Relativism* (Philadelphia: University of Pennsylvania Press, 1983), pp. 16-20; Susan R. Bordo, *The Flight to Objectivity: Essays on Cartesianism and Culture* (Albany: State University of New York Press, 1987), esp. pp. 13-31; Stephen Toulmin, *Cosmopolis: The Hidden Agenda of Modernity* (Chicago: University of Chicago Press, 1990), esp. pp. 45-87.

64. Dennis Olson, "Biblical Theology as Provisional Monologization: A Dialogue with Childs, Brueggemann, and Bakhtin," *Biblical Interpretation* 6 (1998): 171.

CHAPTER 2

Critical Conversation

Reframing the Issues

The first chapter concluded by registering a distinctly mixed assessment toward the postmodern turn. On the one hand, postmodernism presents itself as a much needed corrective to the modernist penchant of totalization. Through its relentless exposure of the weaknesses of modernist foundationalism, postmodernism nurtures diversity, cultivates dissensus, and privileges free play over imposed order so as to keep modernist schemes of totalization at bay. On the other hand, postmodernism's antifoundational rejection of speech about truth and its conception of the artificial nature of reality fail to provide the means by which to engage in meaningful cross-cultural critique and risks trivializing the pain and suffering of those it purports to protect. Trapped by an inverse "Cartesian anxiety" (fear *of* Descartes, not Descartes's fear), postmodernism inadvertently sets the stage for a return to the terror it seeks to resist.[1]

We find ourselves, then, at an impasse. The way back is forbidden, as much by Auschwitz as by any intellectual critique; yet the way forward is unclear, even unsafe. At the same time, remaining where we are presents its own hazards. As Allan Megill has suggested, while the "crisis" occasioned by the postmodern turn burst through modernist hegemony, one sustains a posture of crisis only at great risk.[2]

---

1. See Ihab Hassan, *The Postmodern Turn: Essays in Postmodern Theory and Culture* (Columbus: Ohio State University Press, 1987), p. 200.

2. In particular, Megill suggests that crisis often leads in one of two equally peril-

Megill not only points to the problematic nature of "crisis," he also invites us to call the notion into question altogether. Crisis, he writes, "is essentially *reactive* in nature. In postulating various breaks, leads, mutations, and divine deaths, it is reacting against an implied assumption of continuity over time."[3] Crisis, that is, is only a crisis if you accept the hegemonic claim of the reigning world order to represent the "One True Way" in the first place. Megill's observation illuminates once again the extent to which postmodernity is tied to modernity. It also suggests that a large part of our problem stems from accepting a false dichotomy — really a whole host of false dichotomies — between the modern and the postmodern and thereby being driven by the fear latent in both positions.

Nancey Murphy lends some helpful perspective on this issue by pointing out that modern philosophy is defined not so much by a fixed canon of seminal positions as by sets of ongoing debates. She mentions three such debates as central, including the two concerns I have identified as (1) the way to establish epistemological foundations and (2) the relationship between language and reality.[4] She then defines as "postmodern" those scholars who have transcended these debates.[5] I am less confident than she, however, that postmodernists have "transcended" the debates, but instead suspect that they have been inadvertently pulled into quarrels already defined by modernist assumptions. From this point of view, modernist disputes about the correct means by which to construct foundations (rationalism vs. empiricism) are countered by protests that building foundations is an impossible task, and modernist discussions of how language refers to reality (logical positivism vs. expressivism) have been silenced by postmodernist assertions that language does not refer and that reality is therefore a fic-

---

ous directions: either it leads to a degraded view of the present that warrants extreme actions (e.g., religious apocalypticism) or (2) it leads to metaphysical generalities that obscure the immediate situations of concrete need and crisis at hand (e.g., Heidegger's inability to see through the "National Socialist Movement"). See Allan Megill, *Prophets of Extremity: Nietzsche, Heidegger, Foucault, Derrida* (Berkeley: University of California Press, 1985), pp. 347-48.

3. Megill, *Prophets of Extremity*, p. 297.

4. Nancey Murphy, *Anglo-American Postmodernity: Philosophical Perspectives on Science, Religion, and Ethics* (Boulder, Colo.: Westview Press, 1997), pp. 9-18.

5. Murphy, *Anglo-American Postmodernity*, pp. 18-35.

tive construction. While the debates have obviously increased in scale, the central and defining issues remain unchanged.

For this reason, I propose that the only way to "resolve" these philosophical deadlocks is to sidestep them altogether and reframe the questions at hand by paying attention, not first to the metaphysical issues involved, but instead to our actual practices. This is not a novel goal; others are engaged in similar work, and I am profiting by their guidance and expertise.[6] I must also admit that this is not a goal lacking in ambition, as a full execution of such a project would demand far more space than a single chapter or even a single book affords. My intent, however, is far more modest. I hope only to sift through recent attempts to move beyond the modernist-postmodernist standoff so as to sketch the broad contours of what I describe as a "postfoundational" response to the current challenges.[7] The response is *post*foundational in the sense that it seeks to leave the traditional debates over foundationalism and representationalism largely behind, approaching questions of truth and reality only indirectly, via a "critical conversation of convictions." Further, I also want to keep in mind the pragmatic goal, not of determining absolutely the existence (or lack thereof) of "truth" and "reality," but rather to ascertain whether we have good reason for saying something about these things with a measure of confidence.

I take up this project in the next three sections of this chapter. The first, on "critical fideism," is given over to the issue of foundationalism, suggesting that even in the absence of demonstrably ultimate foundations we can nevertheless approach knowledge claims on pragmatic grounds through critical conversation. Because "conversation" entails language, in the second section on "adequate translation," I give specific attention to the question of the ability of language to refer beyond itself. In the third section, on "dialogical realism," I then discuss the

---

6. Richard J. Bernstein, for instance, writes at the outset of *Beyond Objectivism and Relativism* (Philadelphia: University of Pennsylvania Press, 1983) that "there is a growing sense that something is wrong with the ways in which the relevant issues and options are posed — a sense that something is happening that is changing the categorical structure and patterns within which we think and act — a sense that we have an urgent need to move beyond objectivism and relativism" (p. 2). See also pp. 48-49.

7. I borrow the term "postfoundational" from J. Wentzel van Huyssteen, *Essays in Postfoundationalist Theology* (Grand Rapids: Eerdmans, 1997).

possibilities and limitations of speaking of the real and the true. All this provides the backdrop for exploring the utility of "confession" to articulate our convictions and facilitate critical conversations, an exploration that will continue into Chapter Three.

Critical Fideism

It will be helpful in each of these three sections to explore the modernist-postmodernist impasses as different sets of answers to similar questions. In the case of foundations, for instance, the questions at hand are firmly epistemological: What can we know? How do we know? What is the foundation for our knowing? Modernity answers these questions by positing that there are foundations and therefore we can know; or, inversely, because we can — indeed, must! — know, there are obviously foundations. While such reasoning is inherently circular, postmodernity's response — while formally very distinct — is in this sense not terribly different. There are no foundations and so we cannot know; or, inversely, we cannot know because there are no foundations. Hence, Donna Haraway's description of the modern and postmodern as "inverse twins" rings true once again.[8]

The two are linked by more than just their (perhaps unavoidable) recourse to circular reasoning; they are also joined by the level of apprehension motivating their distinct pursuits. With modernism, as we have seen, it is the fear of the chaos, the anarchy, the meaningless that a world without foundations poses.[9] With postmodernists, it is the fear of oppression, hegemony, the reduction of all "others" to the "same"; in short, the fear of totalization.[10]

But rather than accept the terms of the debate thus posed, I suggest that we refuse to surrender to the fear each position bespeaks and live in the tension of unanswered questions long enough to observe that, regardless of our ability to prove *whether we know* or demonstrate

8. Donna J. Haraway, *Simians, Cyborgs, and Women: The Reinvention of Nature* (New York: Routledge, 1991), p. 191.

9. See Bernstein, *Beyond Objectivism and Relativism*, pp. 16-19; Megill, *Prophets of Extremity*, pp. xii-xiv.

10. Jean François Lyotard, *The Postmodern Condition*, trans. Geoff Bennington and Brian Massumi (Minneapolis: University of Minnesota Press, 1984), pp. 81-82.

how we know, on a day-to-day basis we in fact *believe that we do know*. Even an adamant antifoundationalist like Richard Rorty, for instance, who vociferously eschews all predetermined criteria of "the real" or "the true," nevertheless insists that his views "are better" than opposing ones.[11] Similarly, Walter Fisher argues that, whatever our ability to justify our convictions at the bar of Enlightenment rationality, on a daily basis we regularly supply what we inevitably refer to as "good reasons" for what we believe.[12] The common thread between these two observations is that, in point of fact, we regularly do think we *know*, and we operate on the basis of that assumption regardless of modern-postmodern debates about epistemological foundations. "Knowledge," from this point of view, is less an entity to be grasped than it is the actuality of our perceptions, judgments, and justifications of the validity of our statements.

According to Rorty, this kind of knowledge arises from, and is sanctioned by, the community in which we live. Accepting its description of "reality," we live by its terms and "know" according to the parameters it sets. Knowledge, therefore, is inherently cultural and communal. Acknowledging a kinship to Rorty's brand of pragmatism in these matters, Ihab Hassan nevertheless posits a deeper source for our knowing than simply our sociocultural locations. Hassan speaks of the human capacity — even drive — to *make sense* of the world, the urge to offer ever more apt and accurate descriptions of our encounters with, and experience of, that thing we call "reality" regardless of the absence of external criteria by which to assess the validity of our attempts with any finality.[13] From this point of view, the problems of modernity stem not from its desire to make sense of its experiences, but rather from its obsession with proving its account indisputably over all others. Inversely, the failure of postmodernity arises in its facile wish to "stop making sense" altogether.

Seeking an alternative, Hassan turns to Nietzsche (in many respects the patron saint of postmodernism) and notes that while Nietzsche ex-

11. Richard Rorty, "Solidarity or Objectivity?," in *Post-Analytic Philosophy*, ed. John Rajchman and Cornel West (New York: Columbia University Press, 1985), p. 6.

12. See Walter Fisher, *Human Communication as Narration: Toward a Philosophy of Reason, Value, and Action* (Columbia: University of South Carolina Press, 1987), esp. pp. 105-23.

13. Hassan, *The Postmodern Turn*, pp. 191-211.

poses all human creations — including myth, religion, art, science, and philosophy — as fictions, he nevertheless recognizes their necessity and extols "life-enhancing" fictions over those that are "weak or pusillanimous fictions, images of our self-solicitude."[14] Thus, while we humans cannot at rock bottom prove the verity of our creations (hence, Nietzsche names them fictions), neither can we dispense with them. Fictions, from this Nietzschean point of view, are valued because they are useful, even essential, to our survival as sense-making creatures.

According to Hassan, Rorty and other contemporary postmodernists seriously underestimate the importance of belief, desire, and conviction to shape human conversation and action. For this reason, Hassan turns instead to the work of William James, one of the original pragmatists, who not only acknowledges but even celebrates the necessity of belief. At the conclusion of a series of lectures later collected and published under the title *A Pluralistic Universe,* James describes the inevitable role belief plays in all of our theoretical, logical, and practical constructions:

> In some of my lectures at Harvard I have spoken of what I call the 'faith-ladder,' as something quite different from the *sorites* of the logic books, yet seeming to have an analogous form. I think you will quickly recognize in yourselves, as I describe it, the mental process to which I give this name.
>
> A conception of the world arises in you somehow, no matter how. Is it true or not? you ask.
>
> It *might* be true somewhere, you say, for it is not self-contradictory.
>
> It *may* be true, you continue, even here and now.
>
> It is *fit* to be true, it would be *well if it were true,* it *ought* to be true, you presently feel.
>
> It *must* be true, something persuasive in you whispers next; and then — as a final result —
>
> It shall be *held as true,* you decide; it *shall be* as if true, for *you.* And your acting thus may in certain special cases be a means of making it securely true in the end.
>
> Not one step in this process is logical, and yet it is the way in

14. Hassan, *The Postmodern Turn,* p. 197.

36

which monists and pluralists alike espouse and hold fast to their visions. It is life exceeding logic, it is the practical reason for which the theoretic reason finds arguments after the conclusion is once there. In just this way do some of us hold to the unfinished pluralistic universe; in just this way do others hold to the timeless universe eternally complete.[15]

Following James's lead, Hassan wants not only to take belief seriously, but also to realize that it is belief from which all of our other creations derive. "Without belief," he writes, "we could not make sense." This does not, however, grant belief some kind of Kantian a priori status invulnerable to critique; it is always perspectival, dependent on one's cultural and social position, and therefore not only inherently limited but also inextricably related to the belief of others.[16] Nor does it portray belief as isolated cognition. Just as there is no entry into sensory experience apart from our sociohistorical location (therefore ruling out classic empiricism), so also is there no escape from experience into pure cognition (therefore mitigating against classic rationalism). Instead, we discover ourselves in a world where belief stands at the core of all our attempts to make sense of our experience, a capacity that is itself shaped by our experience.[17] For this reason, Hassan and James posit that beneath all of our "knowing" is "believing," and that this is true as much for postmodernists as modernists.[18]

This forceful emphasis on belief — even belief stemming from interpreted experience and not exempted from critique — inevitably raises the specter of *relativism*. If it's "beliefs all the way down," then we appear to vitiate all means by which to discern between rival beliefs. According to Rorty, however, such concerns are grossly misplaced: "'Rela-

---

15. William James, *A Pluralistic Universe* (Cambridge, Mass.: Harvard University Press, 1977 [1908]), p. 148; cited by Hassan, *The Postmodern Turn*, p. 207.

16. As James writes, "Our faith is faith in someone else's faith, and in the greatest matters this is most the case." *The Will to Believe and Human Immortality* (New York: Dover, 1956), p. 9; cited by Hassan, *The Postmodern Turn*, p. 207.

17. Thus, beliefs, as with all other assessments, "are the results of our interpreted experience." Van Huyssteen, *The Shaping of Rationality* (Grand Rapids: Eerdmans, 1999), p. 189. See also his *Essays in Postfoundationalist Theology*, pp. 15-21.

18. See John McGowan, *Postmodernism and Its Critics* (Ithaca, N.Y.: Cornell University Press, 1991), p. 24; and Calvin Schrag, *Resources for Rationality: A Response to the Postmodern Challenge* (Bloomington: Indiana University Press, 1992), p. 39.

tivism' is the view that every belief on a certain topic, or perhaps about *any* topic, is as good as every other. No one holds that view. Except for the occasional cooperative freshman, one cannot find anyone who says that two incompatible opinions on an important topic are equally good."[19] "Relativism," Rorty contends, is a "red herring," the projection of "realists" onto those who refuse to ground their convictions in any transcendent, a-historical standard.[20] At the very worst, as Rorty himself acknowledges, he may represent a kind of "metaphilosophical relativism" that entertains no pretensions to describe reality but instead contends only that there exist no definitive means by which to judge between incompatible philosophical systems.[21] According to Rorty, such an admission is simply a matter of refusing the false sanctuary of objectivist "realism," but it does not imply practical or ethical relativism. Barbara Hernstein Smith agrees, writing that the "relativism" of which she is charged

> is not a "position," not a "conviction," and not a set of "claims" about how certain things — reality, truth, meaning, reason, value, and so forth — really are. It is, rather, a general conceptual style . . . specifically played out here as (a) a conceptualization of the world as continuously changing, irreducibly various, and multiply configurable, (b) a corresponding tendency to find cognitively distasteful, unsatisfactory, or counterintuitive any conception of the world as fixed and integral and/or as having objectively determinate properties, and (c) a corresponding disinclination or inability to use terms such as "reality," "truth," "meaning," "reason," or "value" as glossed by . . . objectivist conceptions.[22]

Neither Rorty nor Smith feels disinclined to articulate, defend, or act on their convictions, the inevitable state of the "true relativist." Rather, they reject the comfort of lodging those convictions in some predetermined, idealized standard of reality or truth, preferring in-

19. Richard Rorty, *The Consequences of Pragmatism* (Minneapolis: University of Minnesota Press, 1982), p. 166.
20. Rorty, "Solidarity or Objectivity?" pp. 12-13.
21. Rorty, *Consequences of Pragmatism*, p. 167.
22. Barbara Hernstein Smith, *Contingencies of Value: Alternative Perspectives in Critical Theory* (Cambridge, Mass.: Harvard University Press, 1988), p. 151.

stead to ground them in the immediate and historical situations and communities from which they arise.

Even if we have addressed the charge of relativism adequately, however, our very response raises another question, that of *fideism*. Here, the terrain grows more difficult. According to Wentzel van Huyssteen, whereas nonfoundationalism argues that "all of our beliefs together form part of a groundless web of interrelated beliefs," fideism implies "an uncritical, almost blind commitment to a basic set of beliefs."[23] But whereas van Huyssteen distinguishes cleanly between nonfoundationalism and fideism, I would contend that all forms of nonfoundationalism — to the degree that they surrender claims to proving their position by extrinsic criteria — are to some degree ineluctably fideistic. As Michael Polanyi writes, "any inquiry into our ultimate beliefs" to some extent "must be intentionally circular."[24] But circularity does not rule out the possibility for constructive critique, for making responsible judgments between competing beliefs, or for avoiding a plunge into abject subjectivism (which, as Polanyi reminds us, is different from "personal knowledge").[25]

The question, in my opinion, is therefore not whether we can escape fideism altogether but whether we stand for a *maximal* or *minimal* fideism. Whereas a minimal — or what I will also call a *critical* — fideism places its convictions in the public arena for critical scrutiny and evaluation, maximal fideism refuses to enter into cross-contextual conversation either from disinterest or because it believes such conversation cannot take place. For this reason, maximal fideism is marked by what van Huyssteen describes as "its complete inability to explain why we choose some viewpoints, some language games, or some networks of belief over others, and why we believe that some in fact offer better and more plausible explanations than others."[26]

Rorty at times exhibits what appears to be a maximal fideism. He contends, for instance, that while he cannot be charged with relativism, he can be accused of "ethnocentrism," an allegation he gladly admits:

23. van Huyssteen, *Essays in Postfoundationalist Theology*, p. 3. See also Terrence W. Tilley, "Incommensurability, Intratextuality, and Fideism," *Modern Theology* 5 (1989): 95.

24. Michael Polanyi, *Personal Knowledge: Towards a Post-Critical Philosophy* (Chicago: University of Chicago Press, 1962), p. 300.

25. See Polanyi, *Personal Knowledge*, pp. 300-303.

26. van Huyssteen, *Essays in Postfoundationalist Theology*, p. 26.

To be ethnocentric is to divide the human race into the people to whom one must justify one's beliefs and the others. The first group — one's *ethnos* — comprises those who share enough of one's beliefs to make fruitful conversation possible. In this sense, everybody is ethnocentric when engaged in actual debate, no matter how much realist rhetoric about objectivity he produces in his study.[27]

As Barbara Hernstein Smith observes, however, such an assessment not only overestimates the homogeneity of communities but also represents a disquieting option: "The sort of dilemma that could, at the end of the twentieth century, be thought to require a reflective human being to embrace any kind of ethnocentrism must, I think, be examined closely, as must also the nature of that ethnocentrism itself."[28]

What I advocate in response to the maximal fideism of Rorty and others is a critical fideism that, while it cannot prove the truth of its ultimate claims, nevertheless seeks to make a case in the public arena for their utility and soundness. The task at hand, therefore, is to identify the means by which to make such a case.

Of the several options that avail themselves, postmodern theorists often seize upon *justification* first. At issue in justification is not the external verity of one's claims but rather their internal consistency and coherency. The criteria used to assess claims from this point of view are those of categorical adequacy, assessing whether the claims prove adequate to the categories of meaning and validity as established by the overall system. In this way one avoids the appeal to external, extra-textual, or extra-systemic standards and looks instead to the internal logic of the system in question for legitimation.[29]

Precisely as a criterion based solely on internal considerations, however, justification cannot save us from the lonely provincialism of maximal fideism. It is a useful first step, but no more. For this reason, I

27. Rorty, "Solidarity or Objectivity?" p. 13. At other points, however, he appears far more interested in "conversation"; see *Philosophy and the Mirror of Nature* (Princeton: Princeton University Press, 1980 [1979]), pp. 389-94.

28. Smith, *Contingencies of Value*, p. 169.

29. See Ronald F. Thiemann's *Revelation and Theology: The Gospel as Narrated Promise* (Notre Dame: University of Notre Dame Press, 1985), pp. 71-91; George A. Lindbeck, *The Nature of Doctrine: Religion and Theology in a Postliberal Age* (Philadelphia: Westminster Press, 1984), pp. 47-52; Smith, *Contingencies of Value*, pp. 173-79.

want to move beyond the issue of justification to that of critical judgment. I do so with some trepidation, as the very ideas of "critique" and "judgment" are at the heart of postmodern complaints against modernity. Jean François Lyotard, for instance, observes that all criteria are inevitably bound to the communities that exercise them. Because they are legitimated by the narratives that produce them, Lyotard argues, they are inherently unable to critique themselves.[30]

In his book *The Resources of Rationality,* Calvin Schrag seeks to overcome criticisms similar to those of Lyotard and reinvigorate the idea of critique. He begins by describing the Greek concept of *krinō* (κρίνω), from which our words "criteria" and "critique" stem: "*Krinō,* for the Greeks . . . had to do with the capacity to distinguish, separate, sort out, and discriminate, but it also involved the volitional and actional comportment of assessing, deciding, and choosing."[31] The family of "senses in *krinō,*" Schrag continues, "was still present in the Latin rendering of *krinō* as *cernō,* the etymological root of the English *discern.*" *Cernō,* like *krinō,* is an action, judgment in practice. But then something happened:

> In the philosophical grammar of modernity . . . this praxis-oriented discernment was taken up into an epistemological quest for certainty, facilitating the slide of *cernō* into *certō.* The rich polysemy in the rhetoric of *cernō* as discernment became sedimented and confined within the bounds of certainty. . . . The closely related notions of "critique" and "criterion" simply became fellow travelers in the quest for certainty.[32]

Schrag seeks to reclaim "critique" understood as discernment *(krinō/cernō),* by viewing it, once again, as a practice of the community rather than a predetermined standard, in this way avoiding its foundationalist underpinnings. Schrag seeks to formulate what he therefore names "praxial" critique by means of "transversal interplay," the intersecting and overlapping of a variety of components and constituents of any given community that force presuppositions to the

---

30. Jean François Lyotard, *The Postmodern Condition,* p. 20. See also Schrag, *Resources for Rationality,* pp. 55-57.

31. Schrag, *Resources for Rationality,* p. 60.

32. Schrag, *Resources for Rationality,* p. 61.

forefront of the discussion, offer alternative points of view, and call into question predetermined conclusions. While thus locating criteria for judgment firmly in the historical and temporal situation of the concrete community, Schrag also employs the inherent diversity of any given community to rule against the devolution of praxial critique into mere custom or tradition.[33]

To put it another way, Schrag's view of "transversal interplay" greatly expands what we mean by "community." Here we return to Barbara Hernstein Smith's objections to Rorty's ethnocentrism, objections that center around two poles. First, according to Smith, Rorty — as with many postmodernists — greatly overestimates the homogeneity of any community: "Rorty ignores the mobility, multiple forms of contact, and numerous levels and modes of contemporary life and forgets, accordingly, that contemporary communities are not only internally complex and highly differentiated but also continuously and rapidly reconfigured."[34] Second, in turning toward his *ethnos*, Rorty looks to the wrong place for the justification of his beliefs: "what will matter with regard to *justifying* our beliefs are not those people whose beliefs we already share but, rather, those whose attitudes and actions in relation to our beliefs (which perhaps they do not share) have *consequences* for us."[35]

Thus, even within the communities to which we are historically and temporally bound there exists sufficient diversity by which to create a climate of critique that neither (1) appeals to an a-historical, idealized standard nor (2) is inherently and hopelessly parochial. By entering into conversation with others, that is, we discover the means to reclaim the practical and critical uses of discernment. While we do not and cannot escape the historical situatedness of our communities, we nevertheless can, according to van Huyssteen, "reach beyond the walls of our own epistemic communities in cross-contextual, cross-cultural, and cross-disciplinary conversation." This type of conversation "respects authentic pluralism — it does not force us all to share the same assumptions, but it finds ways we can talk with one another and criticize our traditions while standing in them."[36] Such cross-contextual

33. Schrag, *Resources for Rationality,* pp. 64-65.
34. Smith, *Contingencies of Value,* p. 168.
35. Smith, *Contingencies of Value,* p. 169.
36. van Huyssteen, *Essays in Postfoundationalist Theology,* p. 38.

conversation, then, yields the critical means by which to shield us from the charge of maximal fideism.

Because I began this discussion by trying to find a way around the modernist-postmodernist dichotomy over epistemological foundations, I want to be clear of the more nuanced relationship to foundations that a postfoundational, critically fideistic program entails. On the one hand, this proposal rejects traditional foundationalism on the grounds that it unacceptably privileges some particularistic viewpoint as a universally valid criterion for knowing. At the same time, however, it suspects that one cannot get by without some form of foundationalism, however weak.[37] (That is, even cries that there are no foundations sound — and function! — curiously like foundational statements.) Thus, postfoundationalism accepts penultimate foundations as ineluctably necessary for constructive thought while simultaneously insisting that no such assumptions remain beyond the pale of critical review, revision, and even reversal. Therefore, while it admits the contextual nature of all its defining presuppositions, it also seeks "to point creatively beyond the confines of the local community, group, or culture" through vigorous intercultural conversation.[38]

By rejecting (1) modernist foundationalism and its privileging of supposedly universal criteria of truth and meaning as well as (2) postmodern antifoundationalism and its retreat into ethnocentrism, we may then return to the distinct apprehensions of each partner in the modernist-postmodernist standoff. In a postfoundationalist stance, the acceptance of penultimate foundations should keep at bay, if not banish, fear of chaos.[39] Similarly, by refusing to exempt even its operative, or penultimate, foundational assumptions from critique — in fact, by seeking out such critique — postfoundationalism at least guards

---

37. Even Jacques Derrida writes, speaking of "transcendental signs" in terms similar to those with which we have described foundations: "But we cannot do without the concept of the sign, for we cannot give up this metaphysical complicity without also giving up the critique we are directing against this complicity." *Writing and Difference,* trans. with an introduction and additional note by Alan Bass (Chicago: University of Chicago Press, 1978), p. 281.

38. van Huyssteen, *Essays in Postfoundationalist Theology,* p. 4.

39. As Derrida has observed, the striking thing about the relationship between "structure" and "center" is that even though the "centers" regularly change, the structure remains (*Writing and Difference,* p. 280).

against, if not prohibits, the possibility of creating a totalizing hegemonic view of knowledge and epistemology.

The next logical step in the argument I have constructed would be to describe in greater detail the type of, and rules for, the critical conversation to which I have appealed. At this point, however, we immediately confront postmodernist objections to language's ability to refer beyond itself and therefore the very possibility of the kind of critical conversation I have been advocating. For this reason, we necessarily turn next to address the question of the limitation of language.

Adequate Translation

As with the issue of epistemic foundations, when considering the impasse over the nature and capacity of language, it will again be helpful to note that, whatever the distinctiveness of the stance of each combatant, modernists and postmodernists agree about the question: Does language have the capacity to represent, or refer to, anything beyond itself? Modernists contend that language depicts reality with some degree of precision, whereas postmodernists counter that language cannot refer beyond itself and that reality, consequently, is a sociosymbolic construction.

The gravity of this debate for my project is clear. If language creates its own entirely distinct "reality," then each language will project an utterly different world and the prospect for communication across cultural-linguistic divides diminishes significantly. Because of the challenge a sociosymbolic, or cultural-linguistic, view poses for this project (and, indeed, many other current philosophical and theological programs), it may prove useful to provide an extended illustration of one in action. To do so, I will examine perhaps the most creative and generative theological program of the last quarter-century, the postliberalism associated with George Lindbeck and other members of the "Yale school."

In his seminal 1984 work, *The Nature of Doctrine*, Lindbeck heralded the advent of postliberalism by describing the character and task of theology in terms tailored for postmodern times. In response to postmodernity's rejection of philosophical "first principles," Lindbeck offered a nonfoundational, cultural-linguistic model of religion. In response to postmodernity's sociosymbolic, or aesthetic, view of reality, Lindbeck proposed an intratextual, self-referential understanding of theology.

As its name implies, postliberalism seeks especially to reverse the common (liberal) assumption that a religion brings to symbolic expression primal (and primary) human experience. Lindbeck argues instead that a religion represents "a kind of cultural and/or linguistic framework or medium that shapes the entirety of life and thought." A religion, he asserts, is similar

> to an idiom that makes possible the description of realities, the formulation of beliefs, and the experiencing of inner attitudes, feelings, and sentiments. Like a culture or language, it is a communal phenomenon that shapes the subjectivities of individuals rather than being primarily a manifestation of those subjectivities.[40]

Because diverse religions constitute "different idioms for construing reality, expressing experience, and ordering life," one cannot locate religious "meaning" anywhere beyond the bounds of the religious discourse taking place within the specific tradition. For this reason, Lindbeck proffers an "intratextual" (or "intrasemiotic") approach to religion and theology that looks no further for the meaning of religious discourse than to the cultural-linguistic system in which a particular statement is embedded. As Lindbeck contends, because a religion is an entirely self-referential symbol system,

> Meaning is constituted by the uses of a specific language rather than being distinguishable from it. Thus the proper way to determine what "God" signifies, for example, is by examining how the word operates within a religion and thereby shapes reality and experience rather than by first establishing its propositional or experiential meaning and reinterpreting or reformulating its uses accordingly.[41]

At the heart of the postliberal proposal, therefore, rests the assertion that different cultural-linguistic traditions represent distinct, even

40. Lindbeck, *The Nature of Doctrine*, p. 33.
41. Lindbeck, *The Nature of Doctrine*, p. 114.

unique entities that prove ultimately to be incommensurable with each other.[42]

Many of the creative implications of such a view for theology have been both significant and salutary. Freed from the defensive task of justifying faith-claims at the bar of public standards of reasonableness, theologians instead discern the patterns of meaning-making inherent in their faith community and enable their fellow believers to speak their faith more "fluently." Undeterred by charges of "universal relativism" (akin to those we examined above), postliberal theologians are more concerned with — and usually more apt at — combating the "internal relativism" that incapacitates members of a particular group from participating in their own social structures.[43] Rather than occupying themselves with academic apologetics, they concentrate instead on the "upbuilding" of the body by entering into a program of intentional and explicit religious catechesis.[44]

However commendable these gains may be, the postliberal emphasis on the internal meaningfulness and uniqueness of distinct traditions nevertheless negates the possibility for the kind of critical conversation I have been advocating. Conversation assumes either (1) that all speakers share the same language, (2) that participants can translate their distinct claims into the idiom of their conversation partners, or (3) that participants can learn each other's languages sufficiently to speak with one another. Postliberals reject all three assumptions. First, taking very seriously the productive capacity of language, they deny any claims that we all "speak the same language." Second, because the meaning of every thought, word, and claim cannot be experienced out of its cultural-linguistic context, translation becomes nearly impossible. Since there is no universal or value-free idiom (like existentialist philosophy or a condition of ultimate need), translation is therefore also not an option. Third, because postliberals stress the utter distinctiveness of each cultural-linguistic system, they also rule out the possibility that participants can master each other's languages. As Lindbeck

---

42. See Lindbeck, "The Gospel's Uniqueness: Election and Untranslatability," *Modern Theology* 13 (1997): 423-50.

43. See Lindbeck, *The Nature of Doctrine*, pp. 133-34.

44. Lindbeck, *The Nature of Doctrine*, pp. 132-33; See Charles Campbell, *Preaching Jesus: New Directions for Homiletics in Hans Frei's Postliberal Theology* (Grand Rapids: Eerdmans, 1997), pp. 221-57.

writes, "genuine bilingualism (not to mention mastery of many religious languages) is so rare and difficult as to leave basically intact the barrier to extramural communication posed by untranslatability in religious matters. Those for whom conversation is the key to solving interreligious problems are likely to be disappointed."[45] Ultimately, one can evaluate a tradition, he suggests, only from the inside: "the logic of coming to believe, because it is like that of learning a language, has little room for argument, but once one has learned to speak the language of faith, argument becomes possible."[46]

While I agree with postliberals that we do not all speak the same language and that there is no common, neutral tongue available to us, I nevertheless contend that Lindbeck and others have misread the question of translation based on their conflation of the *incommensurability* of distinct cultural-linguistic systems with their potential *incomparability*. For example, because the Christian understanding of heaven and the Buddhist understanding of Nirvana are two entirely discrete conceptions, we would be accurate in describing them as ultimately *incommensurable;* that is, they are not merely different ways of saying the same thing. This does not necessarily imply, however, that the two discrete conceptions are *incomparable;* that is, a Christian may come to a sympathetic understanding of the Buddhist's position, and vice versa.

Lindbeck's apparent conflation of these two terms is not an uncommon error. Both admirers and critics of Thomas Kuhn alike, for instance, often read his statements about the incommensurability of paradigms to imply a correlative incomparability. Kuhn himself, however, disavowed such a conclusion altogether.[47] In fact, Kuhn viewed conversation between distinct paradigms — and the inevitable process of translation such conversation entailed — as an important part of the scientific program.[48]

What, then, leads some of those who claim Kuhn to disavow conversation between traditions? In her book, *Theories of Culture,* Kathryn

45. Lindbeck, "Uniqueness," p. 427; cf. *The Nature of Doctrine,* p. 129.

46. Lindbeck, *The Nature of Doctrine,* p. 132.

47. Thomas Kuhn, "Reflections on My Critics," in *Criticism and the Growth of Knowledge,* 3rd ed., ed. Imre Lakatos and Alan Musgrave (Cambridge: Cambridge University Press, 1970), p. 267.

48. See Thomas S. Kuhn, *The Structure of Scientific Revolutions,* 2nd ed. (Chicago: University of Chicago Press, 1970), pp. 198-204.

Tanner suggests that postliberals and other maximal fideists overestimate the *integrity* of cultural-linguistic traditions.[49] In particular, by conceiving of them in sharply bounded, entirely self-referential, and mutually exclusive terms, postliberalism overstates the case of a given culture's particularity and consequent untranslatability. In contrast, Tanner advocates perceiving cultures as "self-contradictory and entirely fissured wholes," whose identities rest as much on external comparison as internal coherence.[50] As a consequence, Tanner contends, "cultural identity," is always a "hybrid, relational affair," affirming "what one is" partly in relation to "what one is not."[51] In fact, as Tanner writes, any distinct tradition or way of life "is essentially parasitic; it has to establish relations with other ways of life, it has to take from them, in order to be one itself."[52]

Tanner's position is reminiscent of Barbara Hernstein Smith's critique of Rorty's sense of the homogeneity of a given community. Drawing on Clifford Geertz's assessment of community as an "enormous collage," Smith writes,

> What Rorty's (and other current) invocations of community miss and obscure, is that at any given time as well as over the course of anyone's life history, *each of us* is a member of many, shifting communities, each of which establishes, for *each* of its members, multiple social identities, multiple principles of identification with other people, and, accordingly, a collage or grab-bag of allegiances, beliefs, and sets of motives.[53]

For this reason, she continues, "Recognition of this situation requires a conception of 'community' and an image of individual social life and

49. Kathryn Tanner, *Theories of Culture* (Minneapolis: Fortress Press, 1997), pp. 107-19.

50. Tanner, *Theories of Culture*, p. 57. As Michael Root similarly writes, "religions or other comprehensive cultural systems are not such closed, non-overlapping realities" as postliberal theology at points suggests. "That cultures could be so utterly different that communication becomes in principle impossible is unthinkable. (What reason could there be to call the encountered reality a culture?)" "Truth, Relativism, and Postliberal Theology," *Dialog* 25 (1986): 178.

51. Tanner, *Theories of Culture*, p. 57.

52. Tanner, *Theories of Culture*, p. 113.

53. Smith, *Contingencies of Value*, p. 168.

mental life that is considerably richer, more subtly differentiated, and more dynamic than that articulated by contemporary communitarians."[54] Only to the degree that one overestimates the integrity and/or homogeneity of a given culture or community can one rule out the possibility of cross-cultural conversation.

In this regard, maximal fideists fail to take their own convictions seriously enough. That is, while they depend upon structuralist insights into the relationality of all meaning, they limit the level at which those insights function.[55] Let me explain. At the heart of structuralism rests the conviction that all "meaning" arises from the interplay of signs in a semiotic system. While maximal fideists grant this, they fail to see that just as words relate to other words within a semiotic system for their meaning, so also do whole systems rely on other distinct systems by which similarly to be defined.

Taking language as an example, I would note not only that there is no such thing as a "private language" (as Wittgenstein observed), but also that there is no such thing as a single, solitary language either. Rather, we can speak of "English" meaningfully only when we realize that there are other languages (French, Swahili, Finnish) that are *not* English. Admittedly, one can grow up speaking English unaware of these options, but a person (usually a young child) doing so does not refer to what he or she is doing as "speaking English" (for it makes no sense to do so). Further, even the most immature study of English reveals that it is not only distinct from other languages (to the point of calling it "unique"), but also dependent on many of these other options in terms of both grammar and vocabulary. (Hence the tradition of encouraging students to study a "foreign" language in order to grasp English better.)

It is therefore difficult to overestimate the level of interdependence between cultural-linguistic systems (religious, scientific, ethnic, or otherwise) that, while incommensurable in terms of their grounding pre-

54. Smith, *Contingencies of Value*, p. 168. She continues, "Indeed, the current invocation of 'community' as a replacement for 'objective reality' is not only a problematic gesture but an empty one. Where it is not (as it seems to be in Rorty's case) a conceptual retreat and apparent move toward socio-political isolationism, it is usually a form of neo-objectivism" (pp. 168-69).

55. See Mary McClintock Fulkerson, *Changing the Subject: Women's Discourses and Feminist Theology* (Minneapolis: Fortress Press, 1994), pp. 158-64.

suppositions, nevertheless are related to each other in a larger pattern of identification and signification.[56] In fact, far from closing off distinct systems from each other, structuralism constantly opens them up, as every time one entity — word, sentence, language — encounters another, another potential level of meaning and identification emerges from this novel interaction.

Richard Bernstein draws a similar conclusion from his study of Kuhn's sense of incommensurability:

> The "truth" of the incommensurability thesis is not closure but *openness*. For at their best, Kuhn and Feyerabend show us that we can understand the ways in which there are incommensurable paradigms, forms of life, and traditions and that we can understand what is distinctive about them without imposing beliefs, categories, and classifications that are so well entrenched in our language games that we fail to appreciate their limited perspective. Furthermore, in and through the process of subtle, multiple comparison and contrast, we not only come to understand the alien phenomenon that we are studying but better come to understand ourselves.[57]

Such a view not only mitigates against maximally fideistic assertions of the "untranslatability" of various cultural-linguistic systems, it also provides the means by which to move toward actual conversation. In particular, one recognizes that the boundaries between distinct traditions are far more "porous" than maximal fideists have suggested. This, in turn, prompts the pragmatic realization that conversation between traditions is already happening and, in fact, happens all the time as cultures ineluctably understand themselves in relation to each other. Such "happenstance" or "ordinary" conversation not only rules against the "untranslatability" of distinct cultural-linguistic systems, it also provides the basis for more intentional and self-reflective efforts at critical dialogue. By starting not at the central and defining differences

---

56. Lindbeck himself unwittingly testifies to this by clarifying his own position in contrast to two other incommensurable models of religions, actually naming and defining his proposal in relation to that which he rejects (post*liberal*)!

57. Bernstein, *Beyond Objectivism and Relativism*, pp. 91-92. Bernstein continues, "This openness of understanding and communication goes beyond disputes about the development of the natural sciences; it is fundamental to all understanding" (p. 92).

between traditions but rather at the overlapping and shared borders between them, participants create the terrain upon which they can later erect more meaningful and critical interaction. While such an approach cannot guarantee some universal common ground or neutral court of adjudication, it at least redeems conversation between distinct cultural-linguistic systems from being an entirely unpredictable, ad hoc, or insignificant affair.

This type of "borderlands" approach to cultural identity suggests far greater room for translation, and therefore critical conversation, than maximal fideists acknowledge, primarily by shifting the emphasis of attention from exclusive to inclusive components of distinct cultures.[58] Whereas maximal fideists focus on the ultimate incommensurability of distinct traditions, and therefore their essential unintelligibility,[59] I would suggest paying equal attention to those penultimate elements that are necessarily shared between traditions as they encounter each other and identify themselves in relation to one another.

In this way, while not sacrificing the particular identity of distinct traditions, we may discover the possibility of a "relative intelligibility" between traditions. While such translation is never "without remainder," it nevertheless can be conducted meaningfully and, in fact, arises from encountering and taking seriously those very differences in another culture or tradition that create for us in the first place what Thomas Kuhn describes as a "communication breakdown."[60] Suggesting a process by which translation might occur, Kuhn writes,

> Taking the differences between their own intra- and inter-group discourse as itself a subject for study, they can first attempt to discover the terms and locutions that, used unproblematically within each community, are nevertheless foci of trouble for inter-group discussion. . . . If they can sufficiently refrain from explaining anomalous behavior as the consequence of mere error or madness, they may in time become very good predictors of each other's behavior.[61]

58. Tanner, *Theories of Culture*, pp. 108-9.
59. See Lindbeck, "Uniqueness," pp. 423ff.
60. As Kuhn writes, "what the participants in a communication breakdown can do is recognize each other as members of different language communities and then become translators" (*The Structure of Scientific Revolutions*, p. 202).
61. Kuhn, *The Structure of Scientific Revolutions*, p. 202.

The payoff of such labor, as Kuhn describes, is that it "allows the participants in a communication breakdown to experience vicariously something of the merits and defects of each other's points of view," thereby providing the critical distance absent from maximal fideism.[62]

Such critical conversation is by no means easy. As Kuhn observes, because it involves the possibility of persuasion and even conversion (which is always, from Kuhn's point of view, to some degree *against* one's will), "for most people translation is a threatening process."[63] If pursued diligently, however, it yields, if neither perfect translation nor translation into some supposedly neutral and common tongue, at least an "adequate" translation that makes critical reflection, comparison, and conversation possible.

Dialogical Realism

The previous section entailed a necessary exploration into the question of linguistic referentiality so as to determine the possibility for conversation beyond the confines of our immediate cultural-linguistic domains. Having established not simply that such conversation is possible, but that it happens all the time, we can now approach again the question of whether we are warranted in speaking about a reality that transcends the limitations of our distinct cultural-linguistic traditions. As with the other conflicts we have monitored, the impasse over the nature of reality is thoroughly entrenched: modernists declare that reality exists "out there" waiting to be discovered and described, while postmodernists avow that reality is nothing more than a social construction, the projection of our desires, power plays, and language games onto the canvas of our communal interactions.

Once again, I suggest that we resist the urge to enter the metaphysical fray, reject the existing dichotomy, and step back for a more pragmatic assessment of our ordinary practices. If we suspend ultimate

---

62. Kuhn, *The Structure of Scientific Revolutions,* p. 202. While Kuhn sees this as translating *between* languages, not *into* some common tongue, he is clear that "to translate a theory or worldview into one's own language is not to make it one's own" (p. 204).

63. Kuhn, *The Structure of Scientific Revolutions,* pp. 203-4. As Kuhn also writes, "People deeply committed both to accuracy and felicity of expression find translation painful, and some cannot do it at all" ("Reflections," p. 267).

judgments about the "real" for even a moment, we realize that we *do*, in fact, talk about reality all the time. On any given day, we engage in numerous conversations ranging from grand discussions of love, loss, and the future to more mundane talk of arranging a car pool or ordering a sandwich from the deli, all with a remarkable confidence that our words refer beyond themselves adequately to describe reality.

Having acknowledged this, of course, we cannot ignore the degree to which language colors our expectations, creates and limits possibilities for constructing meaning, and vastly determines not only how we see but what we are willing even to look at.[64] To ignore the formative influence of language simply because we can execute the linguistic transactions of everyday life with a modest degree of success would be a betrayal; but to despair of a reality beyond our words and to deny existence to that which we have not ourselves experienced seems dishonest, and at times unconscionable. We find ourselves, then, in the middle, betwixt and between two unacceptable alternatives. Perhaps, however, the task is not to dissolve the tension but to learn to live within it with a modicum of courage. Donna Haraway, who began her career as a staunch postmodernist constructionist, isolates just this challenge:

> So, I think my problem and 'our' problem is how to have simultaneously an account of the radical historical contingency for all knowledge claims and knowing subjects, a critical practice for recognizing our own 'semiotic technologies' for making meanings, and a no-nonsense commitment to faithful accounts of the 'real' world, one that can be partially shared and friendly to earth-wide projects of finite freedom, adequate material abundance, modest meaning in suffering, and limited happiness.[65]

Haraway's strategy for moving in this direction revolves around what she describes as "situated knowledge."[66] Distinguished from "ob-

---

64. Hence, the aptness of Ralph Ellison's *Invisible Man*. To a society without the cultural-linguistic vocabulary to acknowledge the presence and personality of an African-American, Ellison's central character was for all intents and purposes invisible.

65. Haraway, *Simians, Cyborgs, and Women*, p. 187.

66. Mary Solberg appropriates this aspect of the work of Haraway and others and ties it to Luther's "theology of the cross" in her *Compelling Knowledge: A Feminist Proposal for an Epistemology of the Cross* (Albany: State University of New York Press, 1997).

jective knowledge" by its intentional acknowledgment of its socio-cultural position, "situated knowledge" professes to describe the "real" without appealing to foundationally guaranteed objectivity.[67] This type of knowledge admits its own position and passionate involvement in the act of knowing, and thereby denies itself the comfort of indisputable first truths.

Haraway contends that in order to speak of the "real" we must not only be *responsible* for our knowledge — admitting our perspective and prior commitments — but also accountable. For this reason, Haraway's "situated knowledge" relies upon the critiques of others, particularly those in a position to see the oppressive tactics of the dominant culture. She therefore privileges, not "being," the ideal of full presence, but "splitting," which she says "should be about heterogeneous multiplicities that are simultaneously necessary and incapable of being squashed into isomorphic slots or cumulative lists."[68] This entails that, while we attempt to identify *with* the "other," we dare not pretend *to be* the "other."[69] Maintaining this kind of thoroughgoing accountability is essential to Haraway's goal of offering "real" knowledge apart from a recourse to totalizing schemes, since "complete identification" with the other is not only a mythic ideal no less deceptive than "objectivity" but also allows the identifier the option of not actually conversing with those with whom he/she is identifying and in this way displacing "the other" once again.[70]

By these means Haraway hopes to escape the "mirror twins" of modernism and postmodernism, for while the totalizing knowledge of modernist foundationalism denies its *accountability* to all others, the relativistic anti-knowledge of postmodernist constructivism similarly denies its *responsibility* to all others.[71] Consequently, responsible descriptions of the "real" emerge not from the "discovery" of either some all-encompassing place to stand or its mirror opposite, the place from which to declare that there is no place, but rather from the "power-charged social relation of 'conversation.'"[72] According to Haraway, the

---

67. Haraway, *Simians, Cyborgs, and Women*, p. 191.
68. Haraway, *Simians, Cyborgs, and Women*, p. 193.
69. Haraway, *Simians, Cyborgs, and Women*, p. 193.
70. Haraway, *Simians, Cyborgs, and Women*, p. 191.
71. Haraway, *Simians, Cyborgs, and Women*, p. 191.
72. Haraway, *Simians, Cyborgs, and Women*, p. 198.

dynamic interplay between speaking from one's position (responsibility) and listening to the critique of others (accountability) leads to the kind of situated knowledge that emerges from critical conversation and, in turn, provides the possibility for speaking about the "real."

Haraway's desire to speak from one's own position with integrity while simultaneously listening to the "other" bears a marked resemblance to the interplay between *participation* and *distanciation* that Calvin Schrag adopts in the hope of realizing his goal of praxial critique.[73] Schrag borrows this language of participation and distanciation from Paul Ricoeur, who inherited the concepts from Gadamer. But where Gadamer saw "participatory belonging" and "alienating distanciation" as implacably opposed alternatives, Ricoeur sees a creative tension that becomes fundamental to the task of interpreting written texts.[74] In fact, according to Ricoeur, only by seizing upon the "productive notion" of distanciation can one "appropriate" — from the German *Aneignung,* to make one's own — the text and make its interpretation an event.[75]

In Schrag's use, participation implies an acceptance of the *prejudgments* operative in our communal existence:

> These prejudgments display our inherence in a linguistic community, our involvement and participation in a world of delivered and changing social practices. There is no discernment without these prejudgments. It is by virtue of them that one is installed in the world in such a manner that one is already oriented toward an understanding of it.[76]

Left alone, however, participation quickly "congeals into traditionalism and conservatism, paving the way to a tyranny of custom."[77]

---

73. Schrag, *Resources for Rationality,* pp. 62-67.

74. Paul Ricoeur, "The Hermeneutical Function of Distanciation," *Hermeneutics and the Social Sciences: Essays on Language, Action and Interpretation,* ed., trans., and introduced by John B. Thompson (Cambridge: Cambridge University Press, 1981), p. 131.

75. Ricoeur, "The Hermeneutical Function of Distanciation," p. 143. While Ricoeur here is admittedly talking about the interpretation of written texts, he suggests a far wider application in his essay, "The Model of the Text: Meaningful Action Considered as a Text," in *Hermeneutics and the Social Sciences,* pp. 197-221.

76. Schrag, *Resources for Rationality,* p. 64.

77. Schrag, *Resources for Rationality,* p. 65.

Distanciation is the creative and tensive countermove necessary to check such a process:

> As there is no discernment decontextualized from the background of prejudgments, habits, and skills that inform our participation in the communal world, so also there is no discernment apart from a placing of those prejudgments, habits of thought, and action into question. The activation of such questioning requires the performance of distanciation, a stepping-back, as it were, to discern what it is that has been going on behind our backs. It is this performance of distanciation that provides the distinctively "critical" moment of rationality as praxial critique.[78]

The interplay of participation and distanciation yields the possibility of attaining Schrag's goal of discernment as *krino/cerno*, leading to what Ricoeur names "appropriation."

In Schrag's appropriation of Ricoeur, I find the resources to conduct a meaningful, critical conversation that avoids the isolationism and impotence of maximal fideism while refusing to surrender to modernist totalities. Having abandoned our pursuit for (or, conversely, campaign against) the "real," we discover that from the "power-charged social relation of conversation" emerges, if not ultimate reality, at least a useful semblance we might describe as postfoundational "realism."

This is not, to be sure, the kind of "reality" dreamt of by our modernist forebears. It is instead what Mikhail Bakhtin calls a "dialogic" understanding of reality that, at best, evinces what van Huyssteen describes as a "weak," "pragmatic," or "limited" form of realism.[79] It is a "realism" that honors the limitations of our knowing imposed by our sociohistorical situation without despairing that those limits are insurmountable. As van Huyssteen writes,

> Critical realism in theology . . . makes a proposal about the provisionality, but also the reliability, of our theological knowledge. Without losing the validity of the fact that all of our knowledge is al-

---

78. Schrag, *Resources for Rationality*, p. 64.

79. Mikhail M. Bakhtin, "Discourse in the Novel," *The Dialogic Imagination: Four Essays*, ed. Michael Holquist (Austin: University of Texas Press, 1981), pp. 259-422; van Huyssteen, *The Shaping of Rationality*, pp. 215-21.

ways socially contextualized, critical realists — with good reasons, but not on compelling grounds — claim reference for their tentative proposals.[80]

The goals of such "realism" are therefore appropriately modest: "In a pragmatic or weak form of critical realism . . . the focus is only on the very limited epistemological conviction that what we are provisionally conceptualizing somehow really exists." But in its modesty it has the potential to be of some practical use. As van Huyssteen continues, "What is at stake in this postfoundationalist model of rationality is . . . not so much the existence or not of the 'real world' . . . but the status of our knowledge about it."[81] And, we might add, our ability to speak of it with integrity.

Recalling our particular interest in speech brings us back again to Ricoeur's notion of appropriation, which he describes as the interpretive analogue to an "answer" in spoken dialogue.[82] According to Ricoeur, the interpretation becomes an event — becomes actualized — only when it is "appropriated" by the interpreter. This is not to suggest that the interpreter now "owns" the text or its meaning, but rather that the interpreter has "entered into" the interpreted meaning of the text — and therefore is open to being changed by it — via the interplay of participation and distanciation.[83]

This dynamic interplay stems, in turn, from Ricoeur's stance against the Romanticist dichotomy between "understanding" and "explanation." Whereas in Romanticist hermeneutics one sought first to "understand" the text and then to "explain" it, Ricoeur argues that while one cannot explain apart from some understanding, by the act of explaining one comes to more full understanding, thereby setting off a dialectic of understanding and explanation.[84]

Similarly, appropriation for Ricoeur is not the end of the process, but only another beginning, as appropriation begets a new level of participation that calls for the act of distanciation in order to appropriate/

---

80. van Huyssteen, *Essays in Postfoundationalist Theology,* p. 43.

81. van Huyssteen, *The Shaping of Rationality,* p. 215.

82. Paul Ricoeur, "Appropriation," in *Hermeneutics and the Social Sciences,* p. 185.

83. Ricoeur, "Appropriation," p. 192.

84. Paul Ricoeur, *Interpretation Theory: Discourse on the Surplus of Meaning* (Fort Worth: Texas Christian University Press, 1976), pp. 71-88.

participate once again. Schrag notes the same dynamic when he underscores not only the "dialectics of participation and distanciation,"[85] but also the central role of *articulation* to any kind of rational understanding. Only by speaking (or writing) one's present grasp of a situation/idea can one enter into more full understanding.[86]

This brings us back to the importance of conversation as metaphor for life in the postmodern world. As Richard Rorty writes, "If we see knowing not as having an essence, to be described by scientists or philosophers, but rather as a right, by current standards, to believe, then we are well on the way to seeing *conversation* as the ultimate context within which knowledge is to be understood."[87] At the end of this brief study, we are perhaps in a better position to perceive that the closest thing to "reality" we can lay claim to is, according to van Huyssteen, not simply a "weak" realism, but an inherently interactional, relational, and even transactional one.[88] Stressing the importance of conversation to the degree that I have, I choose to speak of it as the "dialogical realism" that emerges from critical conversation. While such a dialogical version of reality may not reflect the permanence sought by modernist foundationalists, it nevertheless offers enough stability for speakers and hearers to meet, converse, and form consensus about their common life and thereby avoid the deafening silence of postmodern maximal fideism. As Dennis Olson writes,

> In a sea of conflicting dialogues and voices which is constitutive of every localized and particularized context, rhetors can make provisional, temporary but adequate arguments about truth and value to a given audience or interpretive community that is persuaded by the character and competency of the speaker, the cogency of the argu-

85. Schrag, *Resources for Rationality*, p. 65.
86. Schrag, *Resources for Rationality*, pp. 76-77.
87. Rorty, *Philosophy and the Mirror of Nature*, p. 389.
88. "The high degree of personal involvement in theological theorizing not only reveals the relational character of our being in the world, but epistemologically implies the mediated and interpretive character of all religious commitment, which certainly is no irrational retreat to commitment, but on the contrary reveals the committed nature of all rational thought, and thus the fiduciary rootedness of all rationality" (van Huyssteen, *Essays in Postfoundationalist Theology*, p. 44). See also his *The Shaping of Rationality*, pp. 197-221.

ments, and the artfulness by which the argument or appeal is made.[89]

To be sure, conversation that leads to such dialogical realism and occasional consensus is not easy. As David Tracy suggests, the arduousness of the task makes reflection with Jürgen Habermas on "ideal speech situations" imperative.[90] The danger in such reflection, however, is to assume — also with Habermas — that one needs to establish definitively the epistemological grounds for such criteria to validate it. In this regard, I agree with Rorty's characterization of the postmodern complaint that the problem with Habermas is not that he offers a metanarrative of emancipation (one which in a number of respects Rorty and others endorse), but that, preoccupied by metaphysical questions, Habermas feels the need to legitimize it on foundational grounds. Not content "to let the narratives which hold our culture together do their stuff," he ends up "scratching where it does not itch."[91]

If one follows Rorty's recommendation to adopt a more "assertive" approach — engaging in conversation without establishing its epistemological and metaphysical warrants first — one soon discovers with David Tracy that the "hard rules" of conversation quickly surface.[92] In particular, we come back to three governing stipulations.

First, conversation demands that we speak. We need, that is, to acknowledge and own our sociocultural position and thereby speak of our

89. Dennis Olson, "Biblical Theology as Provisional Monologization: A Dialogue with Childs, Brueggemann, and Bakhtin," *Biblical Interpretation* 6 (1998): 171-72.

90. David Tracy, *Plurality and Ambiguity: Hermeneutics, Religion, Hope* (San Francisco: Harper & Row, 1987), p. 26. See, especially, Jürgen Habermas, *Theory of Communicative Action*, vols. 1 and 2, trans. Thomas McCarthy (Boston: Beacon Press, 1984, 1987); and *Moral Consciousness and Communicative Action*, trans. C. Lenhardt and S. Nicholsen (Cambridge, Mass.: MIT Press, 1990).

91. Richard Rorty, "Habermas and Lyotard on Postmodernity," in *Habermas and Modernity*, ed. and with an intro. by Richard J. Bernstein (Cambridge, Mass.: MIT Press, 1985), p. 164. See also Nicholas Rescher, *Pluralism: Against the Demand for Consensus* (Oxford: Clarendon, 1993).

92. Tracy offers a "generic" summary of Habermas's position apart from an epistemological foundation: "Say only what you mean; say it as accurately as you can; listen to and respect what the other says, however different or other; be willing to correct or defend your opinion if challenged by the conversation partner; be willing to argue if necessary, to confront if demanded, to endure the necessary conflict, to change your mind if the evidence suggests it" (Tracy, *Plurality and Ambiguity*, p. 19).

beliefs with both integrity and responsibility, even as we recognize that all of our speech is a "provisional monologue" in the larger dialogue.[93] This entails that we value the tradition(s) and community(ies) from which we come without removing them from critical scrutiny. Second, conversation also requires that we listen. That is, we need to hear the critical feedback to our speech — the counter beliefs, opinions, affirmations, and corrections — and allow the speech of others to call into question our own.[94] This necessitates that we value the "other."[95] Third, conversation implies that this speaking and listening is an ongoing, active, dynamic process. Hence, Bakhtin speaks of the *dialogic* nature of reality; Ricoeur speaks of the *dialectical* movement of participation and distanciation to appropriation that leads back again to participation and so forth; and Calvin Schrag describes praxial critique as an ongoing *performance* of discernment (participation and distanciation) and articulation (speaking one's discernment) that may lead to disclosure (a new, fuller understanding) which itself beckons for further discernment.[96]

There is, then, an inherently "to-and-fro-*ness*" to our life in this world,[97] as we "shuttle back and forth" while "rebuilding our ship at sea."[98] For ultimately we realize that "reality" — such as it is — is never simply "out there" or "in here" but rather is constituted through our interaction with others as together we seek to discern it.[99] Admittedly, such a proposal does not yield everything we might want to say about "real-

93. See Olson, "Biblical Theology as Provisional Monologization," pp. 172-80.

94. This listening can be a result of "active engagement" with another or the "overhearing" that happens through our interaction with countless others in everyday life. See Richard Robert Osmer, "Practical Theology as Argument, Rhetoric, and Conversation," *Princeton Seminary Bulletin* 18, no. 1 (1997): 61-67.

95. See David Tracy, "Theology and the Many Faces of Postmodernity," *Theology Today* 51 (1994): 104-14; and Wendy Farley, *Eros for the Other: Retaining Truth in a Pluralistic World* (University Park: Pennsylvania State University Press, 1996).

96. Bakhtin, "Discourse in the Novel," in *The Dialogic Imagination*, pp. 259-422. Ricoeur, "The Hermeneutical Function of Distanciation," p. 134; "Appropriation," p. 186. Schrag, *Resources of Rationality*, pp. 76-89.

97. *Hin und Her* in the German. See Ricoeur's appropriation of Gadamer, "Appropriation," p. 186.

98. The imagery and language are borrowed from Kai Nielson, "Searching for an Emancipatory Perspective: Wide Reflective Equilibrium and the Hermeneutical Circle," in *Anti-foundationalism and Practical Reasoning*, ed. Evan Simpson (Edmonton, Alberta: Academic Press, 1987), p. 148; as cited in Schrag, *Resources for Rationality*, p. 177.

99. Tracy, *Plurality and Ambiguity*, p. 48.

ity," but given our concern to avoid either the modernist penchant for totalizing or the postmodernist surrender to silence, it seems to offer all we can say. In the end, I believe, we will discover that it is enough.[100]

Conversation and Confession

From this study of the importance of articulating one's beliefs in order to approach a conversational, or dialogical, realism, we discover — perhaps to our surprise — that in the postmodern world there may actually be *greater* room for religious belief and speech than in the modern.[101] For with the deconstruction of the rationalist hegemony of the Enlightenment, faith and reason are less likely to be portrayed as implacable foes. In fact, as we have seen, belief — particularly as that which makes sense of our interpreted experience — becomes an essential ingredient to our knowing. Faith and reason thereby each occupy their own distinct domain, and each has a complementary role to play, as faith provides the starting point for all rational thought, while rationality supplies the possibility for discernment and fuller appropriation of faith.[102]

On the far side of the postmodern turn, we discover that postmodernity does not spell the end of the world, or the end of speech, or even the end of truth. Rather, it drives us to embrace what Mary McClintock Fulkerson describes as a "ragged" kind of truth, a truth that is never complete, "its future literally open."[103] From this point of view, the paralysis that postmodernity invites and the crisis it bespeaks are only real to the extent that one accepts the terms of modernity and

100. See Ihab Hassan, *The Postmodern Turn*, p. 208; and David Tracy, *Plurality and Ambiguity*, p. 61.

101. As Mary-John Mananzan observes, in the turn of Ludwig Wittgenstein from the logical positivism of the *Tractatus Logico-Philosophicus* to the linguistic analysis of *Philosophical Investigations*, the possibility for religious speech is reborn. See *The Language Game of Confessing One's Belief: A Wittgensteinian-Austinian Approach to the Linguistic Analysis of Creedal Statements* (Tübingen: Max Niemeyer Verlag, 1974), pp. 10, 48-49.

102. On the relationship between faith and reason, see Diogenes Allen, *Christian Belief in a Postmodern World: The Full Wealth of Conviction* (Louisville: Westminster/John Knox Press, 1989), pp. 128-64; and Mary Solberg, *Compelling Knowledge: A Feminist Proposal for an Epistemology of the Cross*, pp. 55-94.

103. Fulkerson, *Changing the Subject*, p. 376.

demands the deceptive security it promises. Those who have chosen instead to live in and with the tension of uncertainty — supported as it were, by grace alone — are free, free to believe, to speak, and to act on the basis of their convictions.[104] Ultimately, therefore, what we surrender is not truth, but the ability to prove truth; not speech, but the right to have the last word; not faith, but unambiguous certainty; not hope, but a future secured by modernist foundationalism. Indeed, it is the very openness of the future that calls for faith, faith akin to that described in the Letter to the Hebrews as "the assurance of things hoped for, the conviction of things not seen" (11:1). In this sense, postmodernity renders Christians a tremendous service by clarifying the essential nature of our faith, as we realize and recall that Christian claims can rest upon *no* ultimate foundation, not even that of nonfoundationalism. Rather, Christianity exists solely by confession, the conviction and assertion of revealed truth apart from any appeal to another criterion; we live, that is, always by faith alone.

But if postmodernism in this way clarifies for Christians the nature of faith, Christians, in turn, offer postmodernists the means by which to move beyond merely deconstructive critique to constructive assertion. From the vantage point of the postfoundational understanding of theology and faith I have outlined, the question is ultimately not whether we *can* speak our faith, but *how*. How, that is, shall we describe the speech that gives voice to faith's deepest convictions? What will be its character? What kind of language, finally, best supplies the categories necessary to facilitate the critical conversation that is essential to life — and that includes the life of faith! — in our postmodern world?

Framing the question in this manner calls to mind one practice from the Christian tradition that seems to me to bear the greatest potential to serve us. That practice is "confession," the articulation of faith's deepest convictions; and it offers, in my opinion, the best chance for speaking into the postmodern whirlwind and in this way reaping it.

104. As Fulkerson reminds us, "Not having such foundations does not mean that we cannot believe what we confess and act on it" (*Changing the Subject,* p. 376). Or, to put it another way, "one can be an epistemological nihilist — that is, problematize knowledge — without simultaneously being an alethiological nihilist — that is, denying that there is truth" (pp. 372-73).

CHAPTER 3

Confessing the Faith

Thus far in this project, I have argued that, whatever its distinct challenges, postmodernity pushes Christians to live more fully by faith alone; that is, to live apart from rationally guaranteed foundations. Further, I have contended that within the Christian tradition lie the resources for overcoming the major weakness of postmodern thought through offering the means by which to speak of truth and reality with integrity and entering into critical conversation with those within and outside of our immediate communities. At the end of the last chapter, I suggested that the Christian practice of "confession" offers itself as a way by which to describe such speech in our postmodern context in that confession signifies articulating one's most deeply held convictions. It is the task of this chapter to examine more carefully this classic Christian practice so as to reclaim confession as a timely way to understand not simply speech, but also and especially Christian preaching, in a postmodern world.

In seeking to use confession to describe preaching, however, I must undertake self-consciously a project of reclamation, as confession can be understood in a variety of ways: criminals confess their crimes, penitents their sins, believers their faith, and lovers their passion, while each of us at one time or another has probably confessed doubt, dismay, surprise, and a whole range of other deeply felt emotions. It will therefore be important to describe clearly how confession has functioned as a distinctly Christian term and practice. Further, even if we seize exclusively upon its ecclesial use, confession lends itself to describing more than just preaching, or even speaking, the faith.[1] Throughout the church's history many have confessed their faith not only through their speech, but also and especially through their deeds.[2] Preaching, then, is one specific *type* of confession. Finally, "confession" has not figured as a significant homiletical term. For these reasons, I attempt in this chapter to describe and reclaim "confession" as a distinct Christian term and practice so as to develop it in later chapters especially for homiletical use.

I will execute this reclamation in three moves. In the first, I conduct a study of the Greek word for "confession," ὁμολογέω, in the New Testament, seeking not so much to define it as to trace its semantic use and function in the life and literature of the early church. In the second major section of this chapter, I discuss three recent theological attempts to claim confession as a viable and important concept in the postmodern age. In the third, I make use of the linguistic analyses of J. L. Austin, John R. Searle, and Mikhail Bakhtin to describe confession more fully as a particular speech act in order to clarify my use of the term and anticipate several possible confusions over it.

Ὁμολογέω in the New Testament

Both following and deviating from patterns of secular use, New Testament occurrences of ὁμολογέω and the family of words stemming from it can be divided along semantic lines into six general categories.[3] While these cannot be drawn with complete precision, and at times overlap, they nevertheless offer a useful guide to the nuanced way in which the New Testament authors employ the word.[4]

1. In this regard, it is worth remembering that while those who were persecuted and tortured for the faith and died were called "martyrs," those who were persecuted and tortured and lived were called "confessors."

2. See the sixth chapter ("Christian Confession as Word, Deed, and Stance") of Douglas John Hall's *Confessing the Faith,* vol. 3 of *Christian Theology in a North American Context* (Minneapolis: Fortress Press, 1996), pp. 343-404.

3. The entire family includes the related forms of ὁμολογέω (33 times) and the compounds ἐξομολογέω (10) and ἀνθωμολογέω (1).

4. Lexicons differ somewhat in their divisions, most following declension patterns and classifying them in relation to similarities to secular occurrences first, and then according to more specifically religious and Christian use. Although these works will in-

The first three of our six categories occur least frequently and stem from ὁμολογέω and its compounds, ἐξομολογέω and ἀνθωμολογέω. First, there is the sense of "promising," "swearing," or "making an oath," used in a fashion akin to the secular Greek, as in Matthew 14:7, where Herod swears (ὡμολόγησεν) to give Herodias's daughter whatever she wants; in Acts 7:17, referring to God's promise (ὡμολόγησεν) to Abraham; and in Luke 22:6, when Judas agrees (ἐξωμολόγησεν) to betray Jesus.

Second, the term can also refer to public penitential confession, here reflecting a more Semitic and cultic background, as in 1 John 1:9, ἐὰν ὁμολογῶμεν τὰς ἁμαρτίας ἡμῶν ("If we confess our sins . . .");[5] Matthew 3:6 and Mark 1:5, both referring to the confession of sins (ἐξομολογούμενοι τὰς ἁμαρτίας) made in response to the teaching of John the Baptist and accompanied by baptism; and James 5:16, where believers are encouraged to confess their sins to one another (ἐξομολογεῖσθε οὖν ἀλλήλοις τὰς ἁμαρτίας) and pray for one another. This sense also occurs, although lacking τὰς ἁμαρτίας, in Acts 19:18, πολλοί . . . ἐξομολογούμενοι καὶ ἀναγγέλλοντες τὰς πράξεις αὐτῶν ("many . . . confessed and disclosed their practices"), and at Romans 14:11, καὶ πᾶσα γλῶσσα ἐξομολογήσεται τῷ θεῷ ("and every tongue will confess to God").[6] The act of contrition implied in all these cases comes from acknowledging that one stands before the Holy God.

---

form my discussion significantly, I am interested less in a strict lexical division and more in a "semantic" division that will help us derive the general senses in which the word is employed in the New Testament. Cf. *A Greek-English Lexicon of the New Testament,* Walter Bauer, William F. Arndt, F. Wilbur Gingrich, and Frederick W. Danker (Chicago: University of Chicago Press, 1979 [1957]), s.v. "ὁμολογέω" (hereafter, *BAGD*); Otfried Hofius, "ὁμολογέω," *Exegetical Dictionary of the New Testament,* vol. 2, ed. Horst Balz and Gerhard Schneider (Grand Rapids: Eerdmans, 1991), pp. 514-17; Otto Michel, "ὁμολογέω," *Theological Dictionary of the New Testament,* vol. 5, ed. Gerhard Kittel and Gerhard Friedrich, trans. Geoffrey W. Bromiley (Grand Rapids: Eerdmans, 1967), pp. 199-220 (hereafter, as in this case, *TDNT,* 5:199-220).

5. Unless noted parenthetically, Scripture quotations are taken from the New Revised Standard Version (NRSV).

6. The NRSV and the Jerusalem Bible (JB) translate this phrase to mean "will give praise to God." This reading is supported by Paul's clear reference in this verse to Isaiah 45:23, the consistent LXX use of ἐξομολογήσεται τῷ θεῷ as "giving thanks" or "praise," and Paul's use of the same word in Philippians 2:11 and Romans 15:9. Given the immediate context of Paul's warning about eschatological judgment, however, it

Third, from this sense of "confessing" or "acknowledging" one's sins in the presence of God arose the more common use of ἐξομολογέω as "giving glory," "thanks," or "praise" to almighty God, as in Matthew 11:25 and Luke 10:21, where Jesus offers a prayer of thanksgiving (Ἐξομολογοῦμαι).[7] A liturgical influence is more evident in Philippians 2:11 and Romans 15:9, where the phrase "to God" is added, indicating clearly the doxological content of these prayers.[8] In Luke 2:38, ἀνθωμολογεῖτο τῷ θεῷ (the singular instance of the word) serves much the same purpose, as may ὁμολογούντων in Hebrews 13:15.[9]

The fourth through sixth semantic categories comprise words stemming directly only from ὁμολογέω; they appear more frequently and are of greater interest to this project. As a verb, the word often means "to acknowledge as true," "affirm," "admit," and "openly declare." In Acts 24:14, Paul "admits" (ὁμολογῶ) that he worships the God of the Jews; in Acts 23:8, the Pharisees, in distinction to the Sadducees, "acknowledge" (ὁμολογοῦσιν) the resurrection; in Hebrews 11:13 the author speaks of the wandering Israelites as those who "confessed (ὁμολογήσαντες) that they were strangers and foreigners on earth"; and the author of Titus rebukes those who "profess" (ὁμολογοῦσιν) to know God but deny God by their actions (1:16).[10] This use bears a resemblance to ὁμολογέω as it was used in secular society as a term of the Greek court, a function that lends these instances an "official," even "legal" overtone.[11]

This sense becomes more pronounced in Matthew 7:23 and Revela-

---

seems more probable that Paul is allowing the root ὁμολογέω to give what is normally a prayer of thanksgiving a more penitential sense; hence, the New English Bible's (NEB) "acknowledge" is better. See Joseph Fitzmyer, *Romans* (New York: Doubleday, 1993), p. 692.

7. See *BAGD*, s.v. "ἐξομολογέω."

8. Michel, "Ὁμολογέω," pp. 213-14.

9. This last use is more ambiguous, as the author of Hebrews more often employs ὁμολογέω with reference to liturgical/doctrinal formulae, but given the similarity in structure and sense to the LXX translation of the Psalms of "thanksgiving" (ἐξομολογεῖν) (e.g., Ps. 6:6, 9:12, etc.), "thanks" seems a very possible translation. See *BAGD*, p. 568.

10. 1 Tim. 3:16 employs an adverbial form of the same, ὁμολογουμένως, "confessedly," or "admittedly."

11. See Günther Bornkamm, "'ὁμολογέω', zur Geschichte eines politischen Begriffes," *Hermes, Zeitschrift für classische Philologie* 71 (1936): 377-93.

tion 3:5, both related to eschatological judgment. In the former, Jesus warns that he "will declare" (ὁμολογήσω) that he "does not know" those who do not do the will of God, even though they may call him "Lord"; and in the latter he promises that he will "confess" (ὁμολογήσω) or "acknowledge" (JB, NEB) before God the names of those who persevere. Even more striking is the case of John 1:20, where the narrator takes pains to pronounce (twice!) that John the Baptist "confessed" (ὡμολόγησεν) to those sent from Jerusalem to question him that he is "not the Messiah." In John's use the term is enlarged to encompass not only legal acknowledgment before the official representatives of Judaism, but also an implicit "negative" confession of Jesus, as John the Baptist "confessed, and did not deny, but confessed, 'I am not the Messiah.'" This confession prepares the way for his later declaration that, "Among you stands one whom you do not know, the one who is coming after me," and his consequent identification a day later of Jesus as this "one" (26b-27, 29-30).[12]

The link between ὁμολογέω as an official acknowledgment and Jesus as the one acknowledged becomes explicit in our fifth category, where secular Greek usage is overlaid with a more distinctly Hebraic sense to convey a binding religious confession.[13] In Matthew 10:32-33 and Luke 12:8-9, each evangelist couples Jesus' descriptions of the persecution to come with a warning of eschatological rewards and punishments: "Everyone therefore who acknowledges (ὁμολογήσει) me before others, I will acknowledge (ὁμολογήσω) before my Father in heaven; but whoever denies (ἀρνήσηται) me before others, I also will deny (ἀρνήσομαι) before my Father in heaven."[14] Here, and as will increasingly be the case, the meaning of ὁμολογέω is heightened by contrasting it with its opposite, the equally forceful ἀρνέομαι.[15]

It is in this more "official" capacity that ὁμολογεῖν (confessing)

12. C. K. Barrett, *The Gospel According to St. John,* 2nd ed. (Philadelphia: Westminster Press, 1978), p. 172.

13. The more distinctly religious affirmations are often marked by the accusative of the person (1 John 2:23; 4:3) or thing (1 Tim. 6:12), double accusative (John 9:22; Rom. 10:9), accusative and infinitive, or with an oti-clause (1 John 4:15).

14. Matt. 10:32 and Luke 12:8 show a particularly Semitic influence employing the dative (confessing to someone), a use foreign to secular Greek. See Hofius, "ὁμολογέω," *Exegetical Dictionary of the New Testament,* 2:514-15; BAGD, s.v. ὁμολογέω.

15. Michel, "ὁμολογέω," *TDNT* 5:210-11; BAGD, s.v. ἀρνέομαι.

bears a marked resemblance to μαρτυρεῖν (witnessing).[16] Both convey the sense of speaking of God's revelation from personal experience.[17] Such speech has authoritative standing throughout the New Testament. Luke appeals in the introduction to "those who were from the beginning eyewitnesses (αὐτόπται) and servants of the word" (1:2), and the "second" conclusion of John names the "beloved disciple" as the one "testifying (μαρτυρῶν) to these things" (21:24). Paul grounds his apostolic authority in the fact that he has seen the Lord (ἑώρακα) (1 Cor. 9:1; cf. 15:8), and in Acts 23:11 he receives instructions in a night vision to bear witness (μαρτυρῆσαι) to Christ in Rome. Again and again, experiencing God's revelation personally leads inevitably to authentic and authoritative speech: "We declare to you what was from the beginning, what we have heard, what we have seen with our eyes, what we have looked at and touched with our hands, concerning the word of life" (1 John 1:1; see also 2 Cor. 4:13).[18]

On many occasions, "confession" signifies not merely official acknowledgment, but rather a binding, even contractual relationship of mutual fidelity,[19] the breaking of which assumes enmity and disavowal.[20] In these instances, to make a confession of Jesus has ultimate consequences; this, in a double sense. First, confessing Christ proves to be eschatologically decisive; this is most clear in the eschatological warnings of Matthew, Luke, and Revelation 3:5 (as we have seen) and will be significant also in Romans 10:9-10 (as we will see below). Second,

16. See Michel, "ὁμολογέω," *TDNT* 5:212 n. 40. This is especially true in the Johannine writings; see Hermann Strathmann, "μάρτυς κτλ," *TDNT* 4:497-99.

17. "Seen from the standpoint of faith this content [of the Gospel] is a fact. God has established it. But it is a fact of a higher order which cannot be observed and attested like other facts of earthly occurrence. If the witness refers to this, it becomes the witness to revealed and believed truth. The factual witness in the popular sense becomes evangelistic confession" (Strathmann, "μάρτυς," p. 497).

18. As Otto Michel writes, "New insights are yielded by the very fact that primitive Christian proclamation (κήρυγμα) and teaching (διδαχή) are described and depicted as confessing (ὁμολογεῖν) and witnessing (μαρτυρεῖν). All such terms as κηρύσσειν, εὐαγγελίζεσθαι, ὁμολογεῖν, μαρτυρεῖν have a proclamatory character which expresses a commitment and an obligation, a bond and a claim" ("ὁμολογέω," *TDNT* 5:212).

19. See Günther Bornkamm, "Das Bekenntnis im Hebraerbrief," *Theologische Blätter* 21 (1942): 58.

20. This becomes even more pronounced, as we will see, in the later NT writings. See 1 John 2:22, where those who deny are designated ψεύστης (liars) and ἀντίχριστος.

confession aligns one with Jesus and therefore draws the hostility of his opponents, as "in openly confessing the authority of Jesus, one takes His side in the battle of spirits."[21]

The Fourth Gospel, in particular, vividly portrays the "here-and-now" consequences of confessing Christ. In John 9:22 the reader learns that confessing Jesus "to be the Christ" (ὁμολογήσῃ Χριστόν) merits expulsion from the synagogue, and in John 12:42 fear of the same silences many of those who believe. Most scholars agree that these verses reflect the "apologetic" rather than "historical" interests of the author, as "it is almost unbelievable that during Jesus' lifetime a formal excommunication was leveled against those who followed him."[22] The passages function, therefore, as words of encouragement to later believers, who can no longer remain disciples of Jesus and faithful Jews, to confess their faith. By at least the time John writes, therefore, confessing Christ has become the hallmark of genuine faith[23] and the dividing line between those who acknowledge Jesus as the messiah and those who do not.[24]

C. K. Barrett notes the striking similarity between the content of the confession in John 9:22 and that of Romans 10:9-10, which he takes to indicate the widespread prevalence of a normative Christian confession.[25] This brings us to our sixth and final sense of ὁμολογέω, that which implies acknowledging the lordship of Christ and participating in the fellowship of believers by affirming a specific tradition.

Romans 10:9-10 stands at the center of scholarly interest in this regard: "If you confess with your lips that Jesus is Lord and believe in your heart that God raised him from the dead, you will be saved. For one believes with the heart and so is justified, and one confesses with the mouth and so is saved."[26] In these verses Paul not only discloses the li-

---

21. Michel, "ὁμολογέω," *TDNT* 5:212. For this reason, as we will see, confession will often designate not just authoritative speech, but also testimony made under duress.

22. Raymond Brown, *The Gospel According to John (I–XII)* (New York: Doubleday, 1966), p. 380. See C. K. Barrett, *John,* p. 137.

23. Rudolf Bultmann, *The Gospel of John,* trans. G. R. Beasley-Murray, R. W. N. Hoare, and J. K. Riches (Philadelphia: Westminster Press, 1971), p. 454.

24. Hans Freiherr von Campenhausen, "Das Bekenntnis im Urchristentum," *Zeitschrift für die Neutestamentliche Wissenschaft* 63 (1972): 211.

25. Barrett, *John,* p. 361.

26. See Anders Nygren, *Commentary on Romans,* trans. Carl C. Rasmussen (Philadelphia: Muhlenberg Press, 1949), p. 383; C. E. B. Cranfield, *A Critical and Exegetical Commentary on the Epistle to the Romans,* 2 vols. (Edinburgh: T. & T. Clark, 1975, 1979), p. 527; Ernst

turgical form of the earliest Christian confession, κύριον Ἰησοῦν ("Jesus is Lord"), but also its theological thrust, that Jesus is Lord because he is the one whom God raised from the dead (cf. Mark 16:6; 1 Cor. 15:3-5).

In verses 5-13 of this chapter, Paul is moving to the climax and close of the central argument of his letter: that one is justified not by works of the law, but through faith. Having just asserted in verse 4 that "Christ is the end (τέλος) of the law," Paul moves immediately in verses 5-10 to establish this conclusion on the basis of Scripture:[27]

> Moses writes concerning the righteousness that comes from the law, that "the person who does these things will live by them." But the righteousness that comes from faith says, "Do not say in your heart, 'Who will ascend into heaven?'" (that is, to bring Christ down) "or 'Who will descend into the abyss?'" (that is, to bring Christ up from the dead). But what does it say? "The Word is near you, on your lips and in your heart" (that is, the word of faith that we proclaim); because if you confess with your lips that Jesus is Lord and believe in your heart that God raised him from the dead, you will be saved. For one believes with the heart and so is justified, and one confesses with the mouth and so is saved.

First quoting Leviticus 18:5 as representing the demand of the law for perfect fulfillment — a demand Paul has already demonstrated is impossible (ch. 3) — Paul then moves in verses 6-10 to deduce support for his conclusion from another passage central to the Jewish understanding of the relationship between righteousness and the law, Deuteronomy 30:11-14:

> Surely this commandment that I am commanding you today is not too hard for you, nor is it too far away. It is not in heaven, that you should say, "Who will go up to heaven for us, and get it for us that we may hear it and observe it?" Neither is it beyond the sea, that you should say, "Who will cross to the other side of the sea for us, and get it for us that we may hear it and observe it?" No, the word is very near to you; it is in your mouth and in your heart for you to observe.

Käsemann, *Commentary on Romans*, trans. Geoffrey W. Bromiley (Grand Rapids: Eerdmans, 1980), p. 291; Fitzmyer, *Romans*, p. 591.

27. See Cranfield, *Romans*, p. 521; Fitzmyer, *Romans*, p. 587.

Paul interprets these verses as attesting that those who live by faith (1:17), in distinction to those who live by the law, realize not only the impossibility of fulfilling the law, but also that Christ has already accomplished this through his death and resurrection.[28] In verse 8 Paul therefore applies the Deuteronomic assurance that "the word is near you" to the "word of faith" (ῥῆμα τῆς πίστεως) — the gospel of righteousness by grace through faith — that Paul proclaimed and the Romans now believe and confess.

These verses summarize much of what we have already discerned in our study and suggest four implications regarding the significance of the early Christian use of confession. First, Paul's allusion to what virtually all scholars agree is an early baptismal formula not only reinforces his earlier assertion that in baptism the believer is joined to Christ's death and resurrection (6:5-11), it also lends faith and confession equal status with baptism, as "one believes with the heart and so is justified and one confesses with the mouth and so is saved."[29] It is probably not the case that Paul refers here only to this particular affirmation (or other liturgical formulas), but rather that the baptismal credo summarizes the essential content of all articulations of the faith through which believers acknowledge Christ as Lord and by which they are incorporated into God's salvific plan.[30] In this way, confession is eschatologically decisive, as the act of baptism is fully realized only through faithful confession.[31]

Second, the early Christians perceived in Jesus and his cross and resurrection God's decisive intervention in the world; hence the double significance of according Jesus the title "Lord."[32] On the one hand, κύριος is

28. Hence Paul's "mishradic" interpretation, reading Deuteronomy 30:12-13 "with" Ps. 107:26 in light of his Christian confession.

29. C. K. Barrett, *The Epistle to the Romans* (New York: Harper & Row, 1957), p. 200; Cranfield, *Romans*, p. 527; Käsemann, *Romans*, p. 291.

30. Rudolf Bultmann, *Theology of the New Testament*, 2 vols., trans. Kendrick Grobel (New York: Charles Scribner's Sons, 1951, 1955), 1:314-16 (hereafter, *TNT*); Fitzmyer, *Romans*, pp. 591-92.

31. Hofius, "ὁμολογέω," *Exegetical Dictionary of the New Testament*, 2:516; Fitzmyer, *Romans*, pp. 592-93.

32. We need not settle the dispute of which context — Hellenistic or Semitic — exercised greater influence on the development of the early confession. Given the letter's interest in the relationship between Jewish and Gentile Christians and the very location of the church to which it was sent, we can safely assume both meanings were heard. See

the word used in the LXX for the Tetragrammaton. According to C. E. B. Cranfield, this indicates that "for Paul the confession that Jesus is Lord meant the acknowledgment that Jesus shares the name and nature, the holiness, the authority, power, majesty and eternity of the one and only true God."[33] At the same time, κύριος is the appellation reserved for the Emperor. In the pluralistic world of first-century Greco-Roman society, it became increasingly important that the early Christians confess that Jesus is not just *one* Lord among many, but rather that he is *the* Lord, "the image of the invisible God" (Col. 1:15), the one "that disarmed the rulers and authorities and made a public example of them, triumphing over them in it" (Col. 2:15; see 1 Pet. 3:22).[34] Such a confession of Christ's cosmic lordship and identification with the God of Israel extends back into the earliest Christian tradition, as evidenced by its presence in the early hymn that Paul incorporates into his letter to the Philippians: "God also highly exalted him and gave him the name above every other name, that at the name of Jesus every knee should bend, in heaven and on earth and under the earth, and every tongue should confess that Jesus Christ is Lord to the glory of God the Father" (2:9-11). To confess the crucified and risen Christ is therefore to acknowledge his lordship over every aspect of one's life and, indeed, over all the world.[35]

Third, the early Christian creeds are without exception explicitly christocentric. As Oscar Cullmann writes,

> In the earliest times, Christians regarded the confession of Christ as the essential of their faith. Faith in God was self-evident, and it they held in common with the Jews. When the centre of the Christian proclamation was to be affirmed, it seemed enough to give an exact expression of faith in Christ. The Old Testament, which alone

---

Vernon H. Neufeld, *The Earliest Christian Confessions* (Grand Rapids: Eerdmans, 1963), pp. 142-44.

33. Cranfield, *Romans*, p. 529.

34. As Barrett writes, "In the non-Jewish world, 'Christ' (Χριστός) was unintelligible, and speedily became (as it already is in the Pauline epistles) scarcely more than a proper name. The notion of divine kingship (more or less bound up with Messiahship) was now expressed by Greek-speaking Jews and Gentiles alike by the term Lord (κύριος)" (*Romans*, p. 201). See also Oscar Cullmann, *The Earliest Christian Confessions*, trans. J. K. S. Reid (London: Lutterworth, 1949), pp. 59-62.

35. Fitzmyer, *Romans*, pp. 592-93. This is precisely the claim that will prove so costly to those later Christians who refused to accord such recognition to Caesar.

formed Holy Scripture for the earliest community, had also to be read in light of this confession. A close connection exists between this Christocentric perspective and the fact that most of the New Testament confessions are purely Christological. Proclamation of Christ is the *starting point of every Christian confession.*[36]

Further, they looked not simply to Jesus, but particularly to God's activity in Jesus' cross and resurrection for *the* hermeneutical key to explicate their scriptures (the Old Testament), their faith, and the significance of Jesus' life and ministry.[37] As Jaroslav Pelikan explains,

> The followers of Jesus came very early to the conclusion that he had lived in order to die, that his death was not the interruption of his life at all but its ultimate purpose. Even by the most generous reading, the Gospels give us information about less than a hundred days in the life of Jesus; but for the last two or three days of his life, they provide a detailed, almost hour-by-hour scenario. And the climax of that scenario is the account of Good Friday and of his three hours on the cross. The Apostles' Creed and the Nicene Creed recognized this when they moved directly from his birth "from the Virgin Mary" to his crucifixion "under Pontius Pilate." What was said of the thane of Cawdor in Macbeth was true preeminently of Jesus: "Nothing in his life/Became him like the leaving it."[38]

When the early Christians reduced the faith to its bare essentials, that is, they focused neither on Jesus' teaching nor his miracles, but rather on his crucifixion "under Pontius Pilate" and God's raising him from the dead "on the third day . . . in accordance with the Scriptures."[39]

---

36. Cullman, *Confessions,* pp. 38-39.

37. See Cullmann, *Confessions,* pp. 11-17.

38. Jaroslav Pelikan, *Jesus Through the Centuries: His Place in the History of Culture* (New Haven: Yale University Press, 1985), p. 95.

39. This single-minded focus on the cross-resurrection kerygma, combined with recent evidence that indicates that the gospels did not arise from communities struggling with gnosticism, may help to refute Ernst Käsemann's hypothesis that the gospel narratives were used to ground and save the kerygma against gnostic abuse and lend support to Bultmann's reply that, in fact, the kerygma was used to redeem otherwise insignificant "sources" about Jesus' life. See Bultmann, "The Primitive Christian and the Historical Jesus," in *The Historical Jesus and the Kerygmatic Christ: Essays on the New Quest of the His-*

Hence, Paul does not come "preaching Jesus," but rather proclaiming "Christ crucified" (1 Cor. 1:23; 15:3-5).[40] Both the preaching and teaching of the early church testify that the central confession of Christ's death and resurrection *made sense* of everything else dealing with Christianity.

Finally, these verses reveal the interpenetrating and mutually dependent relationship between faith (πίστις) and confession. Intellectual assent is not enough; as James writes, even the demons believe in God (2:19). Rather, authentic faith leads to confession, to verbal testimony that "Jesus is Lord." In fact, *faith finds its full actualization only in its articulation.* For this reason Paul stresses the unity of the believing heart and confessing mouth (Rom. 10:10); conversely, and as the Fourth Evangelist testifies, silent lips betray the faithful heart (see John 12:42).[41] Confession is dependent on faith in that it springs from faith: "But just as we have the same spirit of faith that is in accordance with scripture — 'I believed, and so I spoke' — we also believe, and so we speak" (2 Cor. 4:13). At the same time, faith is dependent on confession — for it is the word of faith confessed that leads to belief. Indeed, as Bultmann writes, faith is always "faith in" something, namely, the crucified and risen Lord, Jesus Christ, as confessed by the church.[42] Ultimately there is no spoken word of faith — no kerygma — that is not at its core confession.[43] Faith and confession, then, are inextricably bound together, as confession is faith articulated and actualized to the end of creating confessing faith.[44]

---

torical Jesus, trans. and ed. Carl E. Braaten and Roy A. Harrisville (New York: Abingdon Press, 1964), pp. 15-42.

40. The centrality of the kerygma is confirmed not only by the place it occupies in the earliest traditions and confessions of the church (see Phil. 2:1-11; 1 Cor. 12:3; 1 Cor. 15:3-8), but also by its standing in Paul's teaching and preaching (see 1 Cor. 2:1ff.; 1 Cor. 15:1-3). See Cullmann, *Confessions,* p. 23.

41. See Ernst Haenchen, *John 2: A Commentary on the Gospel of John Chapters 7–21,* trans. Robert W. Funk (Philadelphia: Fortress Press, 1984), p. 101; Bultmann, *The Gospel of John,* pp. 452-54.

42. Bultmann, *TNT* 1:317, 2:239; "πιστεύω κτλ," *TDNT* 6:209. On "faith in," see further, James F. Kay, *Christus Praesens: A Reconsideration of Rudolf Bultmann's Christology* (Grand Rapids: Eerdmans, 1994), pp. 49-50 n. 56, p. 69 n. 31.

43. Käsemann, *Romans,* p. 290. It is striking that when C. H. Dodd offers his "summary" of the kerygma of "the Apostolic preaching," he outlines nearly point by point the early *homologia* that evolved into the Apostles' Creed. *The Apostolic Preaching and Its Development* (New York: Harper & Brothers, 1962), p. 17.

44. Bultmann, "πιστεύω," *TDNT* 6:209; *TNT* 1:318.

By the time of Paul, "confessing" had come to describe an established practice central to the church's identity, as persons joined and maintained fellowship with the company of believers by articulating their faith that Jesus is the Lord, the one whom God raised from the dead. In the post-Pauline New Testament literature, ὁμολογέω further develops as an "ecclesial" term in at least two ways. First, in the form of a noun (ὁμολογία), it comes to function more clearly as a recognized liturgical and/or doctrinal summary of the good news of God's activity in Christ. Second, "confessing" (ὁμολογεῖν) comes to specify affirming particular doctrinal tenets about the nature of Christ that distinguish "orthodox" from "heretical" teaching. Both lines of development merit our attention.

First, as a noun, ὁμολογία increasingly acts as an "official" summary of the gospel. As Vernon Neufeld writes, "the homologia represented the agreement or consensus in which the Christian community was united, that core of essential conviction and belief to which Christians subscribed and openly testified."[45] While this use becomes particularly evident in the later New Testament writings, however, it may date back at least to Paul's ministry. In 2 Corinthians 9:13 Paul tells believers that, through their gift to the Jerusalem church, they are glorifying God through their obedience to the confession (ὁμολογίας) of the gospel of Christ.[46]

In Hebrews, this sense of confession becomes more prominent. In 3:1, the author speaks of Jesus as "the apostle and high priest of our confession" (τῆς ὁμολογίας ἡμῶν). Readers are encouraged to "hold fast" (κρατῶμεν) to this confession (4:14), also called "the confession of our hope" (ὁμολογίαν τῆς ἐλπίδος) (10:23).[47] From repeated references to Jesus

---

45. Neufeld, *The Earliest Christian Confessions,* p. 20.

46. Michel, "ὁμολογέω," *TDNT* 5:215. Other readings are possible. Bultmann renders it simply as "acknowledging," *The Second Letter to the Corinthians,* ed. Erich Dinkler, trans. Roy A. Harrisville (Minneapolis: Augsburg Press, 1985), p. 258. Hans Dieter Betz takes it as a contractual legal agreement drawn up between the congregation at Corinth and the leadership of the church at Jerusalem. See *2 Corinthians 8 and 9: A Commentary on Two Administrative Letters of the Apostle Paul,* ed. George W. MacRae (Philadelphia: Fortress Press, 1985), pp. 122-24.

47. There are two other instances of the word in Hebrews. In 11:13 it is a verb and understood as "acknowledged": "they confessed they were strangers and foreigners on earth." In 13:15, a verb again, it probably carries the sense of "giving thanks" or "praise": "Through him, then, let us continually offer a sacrifice of praise to God, that is, the fruit

as τὸν υἱὸν τοῦ θεοῦ, "the Son of God" (1:1-4; 4:14; 6:6; 10:29) and ἀρχιερεύς, "high priest" (2:17; 4:14-16; 5:10; 6:20; 9:11-28), we can surmise that the confession affirmed Christ's unique role as the eternal Son (1:1-5) who through his self-sacrifice "once and for all" (7:27) mediated a new covenantal relationship (ch. 8) between God and the people of God.[48] But whether "confession" in these instances is taken to be the common creed of the community at worship (Käsemann),[49] a specific baptismal ritual (Moffatt, Bornkamm),[50] the believer's subjective confession of faith (Rengstorf),[51] or a set body of teachings (Buchanan)[52] is probably beyond recovery.[53] From 6:1-3 we can at least be confident that the believers to whom the letter was addressed were already versed in the basics of the Christian faith, of which this confession was a central part (see 5:12).

A similar use occurs in 1 Timothy, where Timothy is urged to "Fight the good fight of the faith; take hold of eternal life, to which you were called and for which you made (confessed) the good confession before many witnesses" (καὶ ὡμολόγησας τὴν καλὴν ὁμολογίαν ἐνώπιον πολλῶν μαρτύρων) (6:12). The double use of confession is striking, probably referring to Timothy's verbal confession of some well-known tradition in public. As with the *Sitz im Leben* in Hebrews, it is difficult to identify precisely the occasion of Timothy's καλὴν ὁμολογίαν. Some think it refers to his ordination,[54] while others believe it is a baptismal confession;[55] still others think it may have been Timo-

---

of lips that give thanks to (ὁμολογούντων) his name." Given the prominence of ὁμολογία in the early portion of the letter, however, the author may have had a double entendre in mind.

48. See Hofius, "ὁμολογέω," *Exegetical Dictionary of the New Testament*, 2:516.

49. Ernst Käsemann, *The Wandering People of God*, trans. Roy A. Harrisville and Irving L. Sandberg (Minneapolis: Augsburg Press, 1984), pp. 167-74.

50. James Moffatt, *A Critical and Exegetical Commentary on the Epistle to the Hebrews* (Edinburgh: T. & T. Clark, 1957 [1924]), pp. 41, 146; Bornkamm, "Bekenntnis," pp. 188-93.

51. Karl Heinrich Rengstorf, "ἀπόστελλω," *TDNT* 1:423.

52. George Wesley Buchanan, *To the Hebrews: Translation, Comment, and Conclusions* (New York: Doubleday, 1972), p. 80.

53. Harold W. Attridge, *The Epistle to the Hebrews*, ed. Helmut Koester (Philadelphia: Fortress Press, 1989), p. 108.

54. See Michel, "ὁμολογέω," *TDNT* 5:216.

55. See Martin Dibelius and Hans Conzelmann, *The Pastoral Epistles*, trans. Philip Buttolph and Adela Yarbro, ed. Helmut Koester (Philadelphia: Fortress Press, 1972), p. 88.

thy's confession before secular authorities.[56] In any of these cases, Timothy is admonished to maintain fidelity to the tradition to which he publicly pledged himself, an exhortation probably occasioned by disturbances created by "false teachers" (1:3-4; 4:1-2).[57]

The second way in which ὁμολογέω develops as an "ecclesial" term appears most clearly in 1 John, where "confessing" shifts in meaning from a general acknowledgment of God's accomplishment in Christ (soteriology) to a more specific affirmation of, or assent to, particular doctrinal issues about Christ's person (Christology).[58] The letter appears to be addressed to a situation of internal conflict that revolves along two lines of dispute. The first centers on the assertion that Jesus Christ "has come in the flesh" (4:2) and therefore probably indicates a struggle with some strand of Docetic Gnosticism.[59] The second involves the connection between belief and practice: "Those who say, 'I love God,' and hate their brothers or sisters, are liars, for those who do not love a brother or sister whom they have seen, cannot love God whom they have not seen" (4:20).[60] Interestingly, only the former dispute is identified by verb forms of ὁμολογέω (2:23; 4:2, 3, 15), perhaps testifying to its identification with doctrinal issues.

Both of the trajectories just traced represent developments in use along two distinct lines. In the first, "confession" has been expanded from the basic sense of articulating one's primary identity as a believer in Jesus the resurrected Lord (for which Paul uses a creedal affirmation as an example) and has taken on a greater sense of catholicity as it becomes shorthand for recognized and more complex liturgical and/or

---

56. The strongest support for the latter is the parallelism the author draws between Timothy's confession and that of "Christ Jesus, who in his testimony before Pilate (confessed) the good confession" (6:13), which Cullmann takes to suggest a commonality of situations as well as confessions (*Confessions*, pp. 25-26). But this reference could as easily be a part of a creedal affirmation, not unlike that of the later "Apostles' Creed," in which case it more likely refers to a baptismal or ordination vow (Dibelius and Conzelmann, *Pastoral Epistles*, p. 88).

57. See Werner Georg Kümmel, *Introduction to the New Testament*, trans. Howard Clark Kee (Nashville: Abingdon Press, 1989 [1975]), pp. 378-80.

58. See von Campenhausen, "Bekenntnis," p. 239. This movement, already evident in the New Testament, presages the controversy over the nature of Christ that will dominate the next three centuries of Christianity.

59. Kümmel, *Introduction*, p. 441.

60. Kümmel, *Introduction*, p. 441.

doctrinal summaries of the gospel. In the second, "confession" is applied more precisely to particular doctrinal affirmations and used to settle situation-specific controversies regarding "orthodox" faith.

Amid this development, however, there is also great continuity, particularly in two significant areas which, taken together, describe the central place confession held in the early church. Detecting the relationship between these two related understandings of "confession" will allow me to offer a summary of its use in the New Testament and prepare the way for further study so as to develop it as a useful theological and homiletical term.

First, when ὁμολογέω is employed as a distinctly Christian term, it often implies "bearing witness" to Christ *through a tradition.* That is, "confession" regularly serves as a summary of the "essentials" of Christianity and in this way represents something akin to classic designations of the *fides quae creditur.* As such, it has tremendous doctrinal and hermeneutical significance in that the confession that "Jesus of Nazareth, who was crucified . . . has been raised" (Mark 16:6) summarizes the Christian pattern for making sense of the world. In short, in Christ's cross and resurrection believers discern the frame of reference by which to interpret every aspect of their life in this world. Because this pattern defines Christianity as a faith tradition, confession also implies being joined to a community of believers. From the basic affirmations that Jesus is κύριος and Χριστός to later and more complex liturgical and doctrinal formulations, one confesses in solidarity with the shared faith of the larger community. Even if made by a single believer, therefore, confession is never a solitary affair.

Second, ὁμολογέω, particularly in its verb forms, represents not merely a tradition of belief, but a tradition that is presently being *articulated.* As we have repeatedly seen, one activates and actualizes the tradition — that is, makes it a living tradition — only by articulating it. In this sense, confession stands as something like the *fides qua creditur.* Further, this act of articulating — confessing — is inherently *responsive,* both to the word of faith proclaimed *and* to the external circumstances necessitating it.[61] Indeed, it is striking to mark the degree to which

---

61. This sense of ὁμολογεῖν, as a response to the exigency of the circumstances, may lend us some means by which to distinguish it from its sibling activity, μαρτυρεῖν. For whereas "witnessing" is most often self-consciously evangelistic in purpose, "confess-

many of the instances of ὁμολογέω encourage articulating faith in situations of duress. This may already be evident in Paul, where the confessional affirmation, "Jesus is Lord," is contrasted with its opposite, "Jesus be cursed" (ἀνάθεμα) (1 Cor. 12:3), perhaps reflecting outward pressure to denounce Christian faith. Matthew and Luke warn of the need to confess during persecution, and in John confessing Jesus as the Christ merits expulsion from the synagogue (9:20; 12:42). The crisis occasioning Hebrews appears to be one of flagging faith, perhaps caused by a fear of further persecution.[62] In 1 John it is the threat of heresy and the tension of internal division and dispute; and whether one believes that the "good confession" that Timothy is said to have made refers to baptism before the congregation or testimony before the authorities, the current situation apparently warrants repeated exhortation (1 Tim. 1:3-20; 4:7-16; 6:11-16). Throughout the history of its use, "confession" applies not only to the call to bear witness to Christ, but to do so particularly during moments of greatest duress in response both to the word of faith and the present circumstances.[63]

---

ing" reflects a stalwart declaring of what one believes, not simply toward the end of evangelistic persuasion, but also and especially because the circumstances demand it (Strathmann, "μάρτυς," *TDNT* 4:497 n. 63). As Michel observes, "confession" is often a response to questioning, liturgical, juridical, or otherwise (Michel, "ὁμολογέω," *TDNT* 5:211). Similarly, the tradition aptly designates Peter's declaration in Matthew 16:16 a "confession," despite the absence of any form of ὁμολογέω. While we must not draw this distinction too sharply — confessing and witnessing are used in most instances nearly synonymously — it seems evident from the earliest writings (1 Cor. 12:3) to the latest (1 John), that in the New Testament "confession" denotes a crucial means by which to articulate and defend the faith of the community during times of duress.

62. See Attridge, *Hebrews*, pp. 10-13; and Kümmel, *Introduction*, pp. 389-92.

63. In his work on *The Earliest Christian Confessions*, Oscar Cullmann discerns similar emphases. Believing that confession animated the church from its outset, he outlines five situations that occasioned the use of confessions related to the primal one, "Jesus is Lord." The first two — baptism and public worship — are both liturgical and reflect the community gathered in their common confession of the Risen Lord as the articulation of the Christian tradition. The remaining three reflect different situations of duress: exorcism (struggles against demons), persecution (struggles with secular authorities), and polemic against heretics (struggles against false teachers) (Cullmann, *Confessions*, pp. 18-34; see Neufeld, *Earliest Christian Confessions*, pp. 142-46). While Cullmann has been faulted for overestimating the influence of Roman persecution on the development of the church's early confessions (see Bultmann's review of Oscar Cullmann, *Les premières confessions de foi chrétiennes*, in *Theologische Literaturzeitung* 74 [1949]: 40-42), he can at worst

For both of these reasons, the act of confessing Christ is assumed throughout the New Testament to be essential to the life of the believer and the church. It is eschatologically decisive, in that through confession believers most fully realize their baptismal union to Christ's death and resurrection and therefore have a full share in his victory over death (Matt. 10:32-33; Luke 12:8-9; Rom. 6:5-11; 8:12-18, 31-39; 10:5-17; 1 Cor. 1:18-25; Rev. 3:5). Further, to confess Christ is to proclaim that word that creates faith and prompts further confession (John 20:20-21; Rom. 10:5-17; 2 Cor. 4:13; 1 John 1:1-4). Finally, the community itself was founded upon confession (Matt. 16:13-20) and fulfills Christ's intentions for it by confessing (Matt. 28:18-20). In all these ways, confessing faith in the Risen Lord establishes and maintains both believer and believing community.

Because of the significance of ὁμολογέω in the New Testament writings to denote both (1) the essential Christian tradition and (2) the articulation and actualization of that tradition in response to the church's proclamation and its present circumstances, I think that it has great potential to serve preachers in a postmodern context. In order to continue to realize its potential, I move next to describe the recent re-emergence of confession as an important term in contemporary theology.

"Confession" in Recent Theology

In part because of the advent of form criticism and the dominance of the historical-critical method in biblical studies, "confession" emerged during the middle third of the twentieth century as an important term, as biblical scholars and historians devoted considerable energy to tracing the form, content, and use of the church's early confessions. This activity was paralleled by a renewed interest in the old Roman symbol, the Apostles' Creed, in Western theology. Karl Barth, Hans Küng, Helmut Thielicke, Gustav Wingren, and other "church theologians" explicated the Creed as a meaningful embodiment of the central Christian confes-

---

be said to have "read back" later developments into the apostolic age, as certainly the confessions of the church did take on increasing significance in relation to persecution and, later, to heresy.

sion, as a living pattern by which to understand both faith and world, and as the critical norm for Christian proclamation.[64] In addition, the courageous role played by the "Confessing Church" *(bekenntnis Kirche)* that resisted Nazi rule also spurred interest in the term.[65] Despite the interest of biblical scholars and theologians in the *content* of confession, however, little attention was devoted to the *act* of confession; that is, to what it means to "confess the faith" as such. For this reason, most of the studies of this era were mainly historical or formal; they did not take up "confessing" as a particular theological activity or category.[66]

This situation has changed dramatically over the last several decades, as a number of theological works have been issued taking up the activity of "confessing faith" as an important topic.[67] As most of these works testify, this turn in theological interest has been prompted largely by our increasingly pluralistic and postmodern context where the confession "Jesus is Lord" is made amid a diversity of competing confessions.[68] In this section, I wish to examine the use of "confession" in three recent theological works emerging from this context, each of which contributes to my project: Miroslav Volf's *After Our Likeness: The*

64. See Karl Barth, *Credo: A Presentation of the Chief Problems of Dogmatics with Reference to the Apostles' Creed,* trans. J. Strathearn McNab (London: Hodder and Stoughton, 1936) and *Dogmatics in Outline* (New York: Harper & Row, 1959); Hans Küng, *Credo: The Apostles' Creed Explained for Today* (New York: Doubleday, 1992); Gustaf Wingren, *Credo: The Christian View of Faith and Life,* trans. Edgar M. Carlson (Minneapolis: Augsburg Press, 1981).

65. See, for instance, Arthur C. Cochrane, *The Church's Confession Under Hitler* (Pittsburgh: Pickwick Press, 1976 [1962]).

66. While "confession" may be mentioned in lesser or greater detail by Barth, Brunner, Küng, Thielicke, Tillich, Wingren, and others, it nowhere occupies a significant position in a major theological treatise as a distinct activity that is crucial to the life of the church. (Barth, as we will see, has the most to say about this, although in his work also, attention to the *act* of confessing is secondary to the *content* of confession.)

67. Of the forty-five works held in the Princeton Theological Seminary Library with "Confessing" in their title, only three were written before 1970. While anecdotal, this evidence is nonetheless illustrative. Similarly, at the fiftieth anniversary of Barmen, several more clearly theological studies of the movement emerged that also sought to explore the nature of what it means to "confess the faith." See, for instance, Victoria Barnett, *For the Soul of the People: Protestant Protest Against Hitler* (New York: Oxford University Press, 1992).

68. Of the works just mentioned, the vast majority of them state a pluralistic, ecumenical, or postmodern context as prompting their study.

Church as the Image of the Trinity; B. A. Gerrish's *Saving and Secular Faith: An Invitation to Systematic Theology;* and Douglas John Hall's *Confessing the Faith,* the third volume of his *Christian Theology in a North American Context.* This survey is not meant to be an exhaustive theological treatment, either of the term itself or the context that has occasioned its reclamation; nor is my goal to evaluate the overall argument of these works.[69] Rather, I am principally interested in how each one locates "confessing" in the life of the church so as to garner from their work a keener appreciation for the way in which "confessing" is emerging as an important concept that may prove useful for reorienting preaching in our postmodern period.

Miroslav Volf, After Our Likeness

Miroslav Volf writes an ecumenical book in what he views as a pluralistic, post-ecumenical age.[70] He does so from twin convictions. First, he believes that the church is failing to transmit its faith successfully to either a new generation of Christians or non-believers.[71] Second, he believes that this failure is due in part to a fracturing of the church down individualistic and egalitarian lines on the one hand, and communal and hierarchical lines on the other. He seeks to address this problem by commencing a dialogue between a Free Church ecclesiology that stresses individual decision and participation and the episcopal traditions of the Roman Catholic and Greek Orthodox churches that stress communal identity.[72] His significant theological move is to explicate the relationship between "person" and "community" on the terms of

---

69. In each case, therefore, I will provide enough background to understand the use of "confession," explore that use in greater detail, and then only anticipate its function in the larger argument of their work.

70. Miroslav Volf, *After Our Likeness: The Church as the Image of the Trinity* (Grand Rapids: Eerdmans, 1998), p. 19.

71. Volf, *After Our Likeness,* pp. 15-18.

72. Volf, *After Our Likeness,* pp. 19-25. On the meaning of "episcopal," Volf further notes that "I am using the term 'episcopal tradition' to refer to that ecclesial tradition according to which the episcopal office possesses theological-dogmatic, and not merely ecclesiastical-practical significance. In the present text, it functions as an abbreviation for 'Catholic and Orthodox episcopal tradition'" (p. 133).

the perichoretic relationship of the members of the Trinity, thereby offering an alternative to the present dichotomy between the individualistic and communal models.[73]

In the first part of his book, Volf critically examines the ecclesiologies of Joseph (Cardinal) Ratzinger and John D. Zizioulas (titular bishop of Pergamum) from his own Free Church perspective. He is particularly interested in exploring the way each theologian deals with the topics of personhood, community, and Trinity so as to outline the main features of two influential episcopal ecclesiologies that, while distinct, nevertheless share a common concern for the centrality of the universal church. In the second part of his book, Volf offers a constructive proposal incorporating both Free Church emphases on individual participation and episcopal concerns about the importance of the community. His proposal begins by identifying what is minimally necessary for the church to be recognized as the church (ch. 3). He then progresses through considerations of the relationship between person and community (ch. 4), how one's view of the Trinity bears on this relationship (ch. 5), and the implications of his study for church structure (ch. 6). He ultimately concludes with a consideration of what is maximally desirable for the church to execute its mission fully (ch. 7).

Volf's discussion of "confession" takes up much of the third chapter, on the minimal "marks" of the church. External features, or marks, of the church are important, he argues, because while the church is that new creation created and sustained by the Spirit of Christ, it is difficult to ascertain the Spirit's presence directly. For this reason, the church's *identity* as God's eschatological creation does not necessarily provide for the church's *identification* as such:

> If one is to speak meaningfully about ecclesiality, one must know not only what the church is, but also how a concrete church can be iden-

---

73. "Both the episcopal and the original Free Church ecclesiological models proceed on the assumption that there is but one correct ecclesiology; God has revealed a certain structure for the church, and this one structure must accordingly be maintained for all time. By contrast, exegetes speak of the several ecclesial models one can find in the New Testament. I proceed on the simple systematic assumption that what was legitimate during the New Testament period cannot be illegitimate today" (Volf, *After Our Likeness*, p. 21; see also pp. x-xi).

tified externally as a church. . . . Hence, all Christian churches have understood the signs of ecclesiality to be externally perceivable and simultaneously necessary conditions or consequences of the ecclesially constitutive presence of the Spirit of Christ.[74]

While noting that both episcopal and Free Church traditions view the word, the sacraments, and the presence of the people as chief marks of the church, Volf underscores that they understand the participation of these elements differently. Because he believes episcopal traditions chiefly emphasize "what the church does" to mediate Christ's grace — particularly with regard to the role of bishops to validate the sacraments and signify the concrete relationship between individual congregations and the larger church — Volf describes the resulting ecclesiology as "objective." Because he perceives that Free Church theology stresses Christ's direct, unmediated presence in the life of each individual member and congregation, Volf describes this form of ecclesiology as "subjective." At almost every point of contention, he observes, these two positions are irreconcilable.[75] In response, his stated goal is to

> suggest an ecclesial model that does not subscribe to the exclusivity of the episcopal and early Free Church models, and according to which the church is constituted through a consistently communal occurrence in which the objective and subjective conditions of ecclesiality appear as two dimensions of a single process.[76]

Seeking therefore to describe the minimal elements or marks that must necessarily be present for a church to be recognized as the church, Volf looks to Matthew 18:20, "Where two or three are gathered in my name, I am there among them." Noting that this verse has played a pivotal role for discussions of the nature of the church from the time of Ignatius, Tertullian, and Cyprian, through the "first" Baptist, John Smyth, and into the present, he derives from this verse and tradition the following ecclesial principle: "*Where two or three are gathered in Christ's name, not only is Christ present among them, but a Christian church is there as well,* perhaps a bad church, a church that may well transgress

74. Volf, *After Our Likeness,* pp. 129-30.
75. Volf, *After Our Likeness,* pp. 130-34.
76. Volf, *After Our Likeness,* p. 135.

against love and truth, but a church nonetheless."[77] Phrased most simply, the church is that body of believers who gather in Christ's name.

This leads Volf to identify and discuss what he considers the two primary and interrelated elements of the church: it is, first, an *assembly* that, second, gathers *in Christ's name*. His discussion of confession bears particularly upon the latter half of this designation:

> A church is an assembly, but an assembly is not yet a church. An indispensable condition of ecclesiality is that people assemble *in the name of Christ*. . . .
>
> The "name of Jesus Christ" unequivocally identifies the person around whom those in the church are gathering.[78]

Confession plays two critical roles in this "unequivocal identification." First, it proffers the content of the church's understanding of who Jesus is and what significance he holds: "one can relate to Jesus Christ only by believing something about him. The content of faith is necessary in order to distinguish Jesus Christ from 'another Jesus' and to distinguish his Spirit from 'another Spirit' (see 2 Cor. 11:4)."[79] Confession, then, supplies the "doctrinal specifications" of what the community believes and confesses about Jesus. Second, confession allows believers to identify with this content and, indeed, claim it as their own: "The purpose of the cognitive identification of Jesus Christ (correct doctrine) is personal identification with him. In so doing, [believers] attest that he is the 'determining ground' for their lives; in him they have found freedom, orientation, and power."[80] These two elements of faith come together most clearly in confession:

> Without personal identification with Jesus Christ, cognitive specification of who he is remains empty; without cognitive specification of who Jesus Christ is, however, personal identification with him is blind. In the act of *confessing faith*, this cognitive specification and personal identification coincide.[81]

---

77. Volf, *After Our Likeness*, p. 136.
78. Volf, *After Our Likeness*, p. 145.
79. Volf, *After Our Likeness*, p. 146.
80. Volf, *After Our Likeness*, p. 146.
81. Volf, *After Our Likeness*, p. 148.

Volf then specifies the three dimensions of confession that make it central to the life of the church. First, confession is *declarative,* in that it announces what the community believes about Jesus, thereby specifying the cognitive element of the faith. Second, confession is *performative,* in that it transforms cognitive assent into active commitment and thereby commits the confessor to the life and values of the community. Third, confession is also *social and public,* in that it (1) is made before others (communicative), (2) invites a response (invitational), and (3) binds the confessor to the larger confessing community (corporate).[82] It is for this last reason in particular that confessions are so often expressed in liturgical formulations; by saying together agreed-upon formulas articulating the community's convictions about Jesus, believers witness to their unity in Christ.

But, as Volf is clear, the activity of confessing Christian faith cannot "be reduced to the appropriation and public utterance of confessions; it merely acquires its most pregnant expressions in such confessions." In fact, as he continues,

> Every genuinely Christian speech act is, at least formally and implicitly, an act of confession. Thus, for example, a preacher can proclaim Christ as Lord only if the activity of proclamation is accompanied at least formally by the activity of confessing faith in him. Without confession accompanying and supporting the proclamation, there is no proclamation. By confessing faith in Christ through celebration of the sacraments, sermons, prayers, hymns, witnessing, and daily life, those gathered in the name of Christ speak the word of God both to each other and to the world. This public confession of faith in Christ through the pluriform speaking of the word is *the central constitutive mark of the church.* It is through this that the church lives as church and manifests itself externally as church. Although such confession is admittedly always a result or effect of the "word," just as faith, too, is a result or effect of the "word" (see Rom. 10:8-10), the "word" is proclaimed in no other way than this pluriform confessing. The confession of faith of one person leads to that of others, thereby constituting the church.[83]

82. Volf, *After Our Likeness,* pp. 149-50.
83. Volf, *After Our Likeness,* p. 150.

This understanding of the central, constitutive role of confession serves Volf's larger intent in two ways. First, it serves as a *criterion* by which to discern between what is *essential* and what is *beneficial* for the life of the church. Taking ordained office as an example, he writes,

> Since the only necessary intraecclesial condition of the constitutive presence of Christ for the church consists in people gathering in the name of Christ to profess faith in Christ before one another and before the world, the presence of Christ does not enter the church through the "narrow portals" of ordained office, but rather *through the dynamic life of the entire church.* The presence of Christ is not attested merely by the institution of office, but rather through the multidimensional confession of the entire assembly. In whatever way "office" may indeed be desirable for church life, either in apostolic succession or not, it is not necessary for ecclesiality. Ordained office belongs not to the *esse,* but rather to the *bene esse* of the church. This claim does not constitute any devaluation of the particular service of proclaiming God's word, but rather suggests that proclamation should be understood as a dimension of pluriform, communal confession of faith.[84]

The sacraments of baptism and the Lord's Supper, in contrast, are essential. Because (1) there has been no period of the church without them and (2) they mediate God's salvific grace, the sacraments are constitutive of the church.[85] But, Volf maintains, "the sacraments can be an indispensable condition of ecclesiality only if they are a form of the confession of faith and an expression of faith," which, he goes on to argue, they indeed are.[86]

Second, viewing confession as ecclesially essential also offers Volf a

---

84. Volf, *After Our Likeness,* p. 152.

85. On this basis, however, the question arises whether (1) there has ever been a time when there were no appointed leaders with responsibility as "stewards of the mysteries of God" (1 Cor. 4:1, KJV) and (2) whether the proclamation of the Word is in some way, if not dependent, then intimately related to such an office (see *Lutherans and Catholics in Dialogue VI: Teaching Authority and Infallibility in the Church,* ed. Paul C. Empie, T. Austin Murphy, and Joseph A. Burgess [Minneapolis: Augsburg, 1978]). The office itself, as with the sacraments, would be validated not by apostolic succession or other hierarchical models, but by its fidelity to the confession of faith in Christ's name.

86. Volf, *After Our Likeness,* p. 153.

unifying principle by which to understand the relation between individual congregations and the universal church. Taking "confession" in its broadest sense, he writes,

> The confession of faith . . . cannot be an idiosyncratic act of a local church. If this confession is constitutive for the church, then every church must be constituted by the *same* confession. Confession of faith not only distinguishes the church from the nonchurch, it simultaneously connects every church with all other churches.[87]

He makes this argument based on the assertion that the whole Christ is present through his Spirit in every church that confesses Christ's name. This, in turn, both guarantees the integrity of each congregation (it is the whole church) and unites it with every other congregation confessionally, if not officially.[88] In this way, "confession" offers Volf the core foundation upon which to construct his proposal for negotiating the relationship between both the individual and the community, on the one hand, and the individual congregation and universal church, on the other.

Volf's work is helpful in reclaiming "confession" as a viable and useful term in a postmodern age in three respects. First, as much as anyone writing today, he emphasizes the clear centrality of confession to the life of faith. Second, he realizes that *all* Christian speech is at heart confession, the assertion of the lordship of Jesus of Nazareth, the crucified and risen Christ. Third, when he describes the twin elements of confession, he does so in terms very similar to those I have discerned in the New Testament. "Cognitive specification" correlates very closely with what I have described as confession's role to summarize the "essential tradition," or *fides quae creditur,* of the Christian faith that lends believers a hermeneutical pattern and criterion for making sense of the world. Similarly, what Volf designates "personal identification" aligns closely with my sense that confession is also the articulation of the tradition, or *fides qua creditur,* that activates and actualizes it. While he does not develop either of these aspects fully enough to specify their use in relation to homiletics, he lays out a useful grid upon which to discuss Gerrish and Hall in more fully explicating these distinctions.

---

87. Volf, *After Our Likeness,* p. 154.
88. Volf, *After Our Likeness,* pp. 154-56.

B. A. *Gerrish,* Saving and Secular Faith

B. A. Gerrish organizes his six-chapter work *Saving and Secular Faith: An Invitation to Systematic Theology* around a series of questions about the nature and place of Christian faith: Can one discern a distinctly Christian (saving) understanding of faith? (ch. 1). How is this related to secular versions of the same? (ch. 2). Do we have good reason for having faith? (ch. 3). How do we come by the faith that we possess? (ch. 4). And how are secular and saving faith related to each other? (chs. 5-6). Addressing these questions, he suggests, will provide a meaningful and useful starting place for Christian systematic theology in our present pluralistic context.[89]

While my interest lies chiefly with Gerrish's exploration of "the confession of faith" in his fourth chapter, a brief overview of the first three chapters will enable us to appreciate more fully the function of "confession" in his overall project. Gerrish seeks to describe "saving" (or Christian) faith in chapter one. He begins by depicting biblical faith *(pistis)* as a combination of (1) belief in various cognitive propositions about Christ and (2) existential trust in Christ and therefore an appropriation of those propositions as true and meaningful for the believer. He then turns to Thomas Aquinas, Martin Luther, and John Calvin to offer a fuller description of saving faith. Without wanting to over-accentuate the differences between them, Gerrish borrows from Thomas a sense that faith is assent, an activity of the intellect, by which the believer is certain of the truth of the content of faith.[90] From Luther, he gains the sense that faith is also confidence, not merely *believing* things *about* God but also and chiefly *trusting in* God to care, support, and redeem God's children.[91] Turning to Calvin, Gerrish discerns that faith is also recognition, apprehending God's benevolent will through the revelation in

---

89. B. A. Gerrish, *Saving and Secular Faith: An Invitation to Systematic Theology* (Minneapolis: Augsburg Press, 1999), pp. ix-x, 50-53.

90. "Thomistic faith is an assent of the intellect that falls on the cognitive scale midway between scientific *knowledge* and mere *opinion.* All three are modes of assent to truths proposed, whereas *doubt* is withholding assent because you cannot make up your mind and choose between the available options. Faith differs from opinion because it is certain; and it differs from knowledge (in the strict sense) because its certainty is not derived from self-evident truth" (Gerrish, *Saving and Secular Faith,* p. 6).

91. Gerrish, *Saving and Secular Faith,* pp. 9-11.

Scripture and the believer's experience, and in this way "knowing" the truth of that revelation.[92] In sum, *"Saving faith is (1) perceiving one's experience under the image of divine benevolence* (fides) *and (2) a consequent living of one's life out of an attitude of confidence or trust* (fiducia)."[93]

Gerrish turns from his description of Christian saving faith to consider in his second chapter "secular" faith; that is, faith as understood by psychologists and scholars in comparative religion. Following the work of Wilfred Cantwell Smith, Viktor Frankl, and James Fowler, Gerrish discovers significant affinity between saving and secular faith, particularly with regard to two elements. The first is the necessity of trust; hence, fiduciary faith. The second is the way in which faith provides the framework in which one makes sense of experience in a meaningful way.[94] Gerrish describes the overlap between saving and secular faith as "generic faith": *"Generic faith is the perception of meaning and purpose in one's life through commitment to an object of ultimate loyalty in which one finds security."[95]*

In chapter three Gerrish moves from his historical (ch. 1) and psychological (ch. 2) considerations of faith to a more philosophical approach.[96] Given the omnipresent, if not necessarily universal, character of faith, he seeks to ascertain whether we can show good reasons for having faith; his interest, then, is in the philosophical justification of faith. Gerrish first tracks the devolution of the concept of the Reformation sense of "faith" from a reasonable and pious trust in God to the post-Enlightenment sense of faith as "accepting a quite stupendous claim because somebody else tells us to." Gerrish counters by pointing out that in every field of study there are some beliefs that, while not demonstrable, are nevertheless necessary.[97] In the rest of this chapter he examines the work of F. H. Jacobi and Friedrich Forberg to discuss the necessity of belief and the possibility for rational justification, if not verification, of our beliefs.[98]

92. Gerrish, *Saving and Secular Faith,* pp. 12-14.

93. Gerrish, *Saving and Secular Faith,* p. 14.

94. Gerrish, *Saving and Secular Faith,* pp. 18-32.

95. Gerrish, *Saving and Secular Faith,* p. 33. He adds that "Saving faith, as recognition plus confidence, is a particular instance of generic faith in this sense."

96. Gerrish, *Saving and Secular Faith,* pp. 34-35.

97. Gerrish, *Saving and Secular Faith,* p. 40.

98. Gerrish, *Saving and Secular Faith,* pp. 40-48. Gerrish here gives particular atten-

Having established the omnipresence and reasonableness of (secular) faith in general, and having described Christian (saving) faith in particular, Gerrish turns in his fourth chapter to the question of faith's transmission. Interested, as he writes, in this "sociological" aspect of faith, he investigates the nature and role of confessions of faith.[99] He begins by noting the irony that it was in part the intensity with which the Reformers sought to summarize and express the heart of the faith through their confessional documents that inevitably undermined the plausibility of creeds and confessions altogether:

> With Martin Luther and Ulrich Zwingli (1484-1531) begins the long decline into pluralism, which, along with secularization, weakens every claim to ecclesiastical authority; and a creed, by definition, claims authority as an official codification of Christian faith. Secularization reinforces skepticism about the dogmatic content of creeds; pluralism casts doubt over the very concept of a creed. For how can it seriously be imagined that any one of the rival statements of faith happens to coincide with the absolute truth of divine revelation?[100]

Amid this age of post-confessional pluralism, however, Gerrish contends that creeds and confessions are not anachronisms, but rather the means by which individual participants are socialized into their faith community. This is only true, however, to the degree that the church resists the temptation to see its confessions chiefly as "tests of orthodoxy" with which to weed out those with differing beliefs and instead reclaims them as instruments to "nurture and engender faith."[101]

Believing, particularly on the basis of his work in chapter two, that faith provides a pattern of perceiving and thinking that "construes the events of my daily experience as a meaningful sequence," Gerrish now adds that "it is in the community . . . that I first acquire the categories for seeing the pattern." Gleaning from the sociological,

---

tion to the related convictions that the world is "ordered" and "moral," convictions of what he will later describe as "elemental faith" (pp. 78-79).

99. Gerrish, *Saving and Secular Faith,* pp. x, 54-55.
100. Gerrish, *Saving and Secular Faith,* p. 49.
101. Gerrish, *Saving and Secular Faith,* pp. 50-53.

or cultural-linguistic, understanding of religious faith, Gerrish continues:

> Adopting a particular religious outlook is more like learning a language than passing a test; answering the questions put to me at my initiation or appointment to office testifies that the language of the community has in fact shaped the way I see myself. In short, having faith is being "socialized" — learning to think, speak, and act as the group does. The process is not a purely deliberate and rational one: I don't learn the rules by studying the grammar book, but much more from conversation in the group. On the other hand, learning the language is not like programming a machine; it calls for deliberate affirmation of the community's world of meaning as my world of meaning. Faith is born, the craving for meaning satisfied, as the individual learns to construe his or her existence in the light of the views and values that sustain the community.[102]

This leads to two convictions. First, faith is never faith in isolation. As both Friedrich Schleiermacher and Karl Barth affirmed, when it comes to faith, you have to belong somewhere, as patterns for making meaning (generic faith) are inevitably mediated through a community. Second, creeds and confessions are primary instruments of this socialization, "one of the devices by which the believing community maintains its world of meaning and so both reaffirms its own identity and confers identity on its individuals."[103]

From this point of view, confessing faith becomes critical to the community's ability to transmit its faith. As Gerrish writes, "The two main threats to the survival and health of the congregation are forgetfulness and disintegration." These phenomena, as Gerrish continues, "are closely related. Disintegration — the loss of a center — is the result of forgetting what it was that constituted the center in the first place." Confessions of faith serve first and foremost, therefore, to remind the community of who and what it is:

> Their primary use is not to smoke out heresy but, through constant recollection, to preserve identity. They prevent disintegration by maintaining a common language, a community of discourse, with-

102. Gerrish, *Saving and Secular Faith*, p. 54.
103. Gerrish, *Saving and Secular Faith*, pp. 55-56.

out which the fellowship would suffer group amnesia and might dissolve in a babel of discordant voices.[104]

In particular, "The Christian creeds rehearse the saving events on which the church is founded, the memory which sustains the church's identity."[105]

This insight into the "recollective" nature of confession leads Gerrish to explore the dimensions of what he describes as a "confessional identity." Noting that communal confessions of faith are expressed in a variety of forms beyond the liturgical formula (including hymns and other events that constitute and preserve the community's identity), Gerrish advocates an "open-confessionalism."

The difference between "open" and "closed" turns on whether a community accords to its primary confessional formulations a preeminent or universal standing. For instance, by sealing their shared commitments with the common confessional seal of the Book of Concord (1580), Lutherans established a closed confessionalism. Whatever comes after the Book of Concord by way of interpretation or addition cannot depart from the pattern of meaning articulated in that collection of confessions (including the ecumenical creeds) and be affirmed as "Lutheran." Reformed theologians, by contrast, neither gave any confession universal authority nor conferred overarching symbolic status on any set of confessions. They therefore established an "open confessionalism" that Gerrish maintains encourages greater tolerance for confessional pluralism.[106] Any Reformed confession of faith, therefore, is always a "provisional statement," open to, and indeed inviting, further reflection and correction.[107]

104. Gerrish, *Saving and Secular Faith*, p. 56.
105. Gerrish, *Saving and Secular Faith*, p. 57.
106. Gerrish, *Saving and Secular Faith*, pp. 60-61. I suspect that Gerrish overestimates the flexibility inherent in any confessional stance if those confessions are to maintain the identity and continuity of the community in question.
107. Gerrish, *Saving and Secular Faith*, p. 62. The question, I think, is not whether any new confession has "the last word" but whether all future confessions — whether as "official" formulations (church body constitutions, for instance) or "unofficial" expressions of faith (as in the preaching, teaching, worshiping, and singing of the church) — adhere materially to those confessions that constitute, define, and maintain the community in the first place. In this sense, central, formulated confessions — whether they are accorded official status or not — tend to be treated similarly to Scripture in that they

Having explored the historical, psychological, philosophical, and sociological dimensions of faith, Gerrish turns in his final two chapters to matters more explicitly theological. In particular, he hopes to accomplish two goals. First, he wants to offer his idea of the distinct but related conceptions of faith — which he describes as (1) elemental, (2) theistic (or creation), and (3) Christian (or redemption) faith — as the proper organizing principle for Christian systematic theology.[108] Second, he hopes to use his analysis of faith to address the "crisis of christology" currently facing the church concerning the significance of the person and work of Christ.[109] Believing that this crisis stems largely from the relativism and skepticism characteristic of our age, Gerrish proposes that the church can respond only with confession through which it seeks both to speak the truth and enter into meaningful dialogue:

> While genuine conversation is certainly inhibited by absolute and exclusive claims, there cannot be a conversation at all if the Christian has nothing to say, or no Savior to confess. Christians will begin the dialogue convinced that what has been given to them through Jesus Christ is for all humanity. But Jesus Christ may not be humanity's sole access to it; there is no way to know that in advance, before one has listened to the other parties in the conversation.[110]

It is in this respect that the church's confessions — and their continued confess*ing* — of God's decisive activity in Jesus Christ becomes most crucial. In the face of postmodern doubt and skepticism, confessing faith emerges not simply as the church's chief possession, but really as its *only* possession, as everything else that constitutes, maintains, and issues from the church is based on its confession. In the postmodern context, the church, as with all other institutions, can stand

are the hermeneutical lens through which the Scriptures are read. Having said that, all other instances of confession must in fact reflect the exigency of the circumstances occasioning them and are well regarded as provisional and (hopefully) timely, even as they seek to announce and interpret faithfully the "timeless" confession contained in the "symbolic books."

108. Gerrish, *Saving and Secular Faith*, p. 74. His proposal here owes most to Schleiermacher, although Calvin and Barth are also influential (pp. 77-83).

109. Gerrish, *Saving and Secular Faith*, p. 87.

110. Gerrish, *Saving and Secular Faith*, p. 102; see also pp. 87-94.

only upon its convictions, in this way learning, once again, to live by *faith alone*. Ultimately, the church is nothing other than that body that confesses faith in the Risen Christ. As Gerrish writes, taking the recent quest for the "historical Jesus" as his point of departure:

> Theological questers for the historical Jesus are not mistaken in seeking a historical anchorage for faith. The problem is that they look for it in the wrong place and hold faith captive to historical science, as the old doctrine of creation once held it captive to natural science. The historical anchorage is to be found in the life of the church, the confessing community in which the gospel is proclaimed — the body of Christ.[111]

Gerrish's study contributes to this project in several ways. Like Volf, Gerrish stresses the absolutely central position that confession holds in the life of the church and underscores the crucial role it may play in a postmodern age. At the same time, Gerrish explores in greater detail what Volf describes as "cognitive specification" and what I have termed confession's role as a summary of the essentials of the Christian faith, the *fides quae creditur*. In particular, he helps to illumine the degree to which the church's confessions claim to speak truthfully of the human condition and in this way offer a distinctive pattern for making sense of the world, a pattern into which the church invites all persons through its proclamation. Further, his treatment of confession evinces a distinct affinity for what I have described, adapting Ricoeur, as the participatory element of conversation. For only to the degree one can articulate a faith commitment about what one holds to be true, can one also offer that conviction as a response to present need, call it into question in relation to competing confessions, and ultimately appropriate it as a living tradition.

Douglas John Hall, Confessing the Faith

Confessing the Faith is the third in a three-volume work by Douglas John Hall entitled *Christian Theology in a North American Context*. In his first

---

111. Gerrish, *Saving and Secular Faith,* p. 104.

volume, *Thinking the Faith,* Hall takes up the theme of the nature of theology. In the second volume, *Professing the Faith,* he turns to explorations of anthropology and Christology. In his final volume he looks to the issues of ecclesiology, the doctrine of the church; missiology, the nature of the calling of the church as a confessing body; and eschatology, the character of the hope to which the church points. The volume is divided into four sections — one for each of these areas of emphasis and another one (Part II) devoted to the specific context of, and challenges facing, the church as a confessing body.[112] Of the three works considered here, Hall's represents by far the most ambitious — and, perhaps for that reason, diffuse — use of the term, as "confessing" becomes the major motif for understanding the activity of the church as the instrument of the Holy Spirit in the world. For this reason, it will be useful, first, to clarify how Hall uses the term; second, to trace briefly its impact in the four main sections of his work; and, third, to give a concrete example of Hall's sense of confession by looking to his understanding of preaching.

Hall does not so much offer a single definition of "confession" as he does provide a running commentary on what it is to "confess faith." He begins his description by underscoring the plethora of meanings associated with the English word "confess." Uniting all the many and varied uses of the word, he contends, is the strong sense that they all deal with what the speaker believes to be true: "To confess something is to own, avow, declare, reveal, or disclose what in the depths of the soul one considers truly to be the case."[113] In this sense, confession is communication about truth, or at least about what one believes to be true.

Two further elements of confession stem from this one. First, it is occasioned by outside circumstances. Confession, as we noted in our biblical treatment of the word, is most often offered in reply to some external cause. For this reason, "If anything is to be regarded as confessional, it is not only the internal condition of the confessor that must be considered (for example, the question of sincerity), but also the external circumstances in which the act is undertaken."[114] Second, and similarly, confession as communication is always public, offered by one

112. Douglas John Hall, *Confessing the Faith,* pp. 22-25.
113. Hall, *Confessing the Faith,* p. 8.
114. Hall, *Confessing the Faith,* p. 9.

person or group to another: "it belongs to the act of faith's confession that it wants to be heard by those round about."[115]

On both counts, confession is communication that is not only responsive and public, but also contextual. (In fact, even when it tries not to be, it is.)[116] Confession therefore calls for discernment: "Confessing the faith does not mean saying *everything*. It means 'saying' — whether with words, or deeds, or sighs too deep for either — the one thing that *needs* to be said, then and there."[117] But how does one determine what is the "one thing" needed to be said? Here Hall returns to his earlier judgment that confession is always in response to external circumstances, this time adding that it is response, in particular, to that which most threatens the world. As he writes,

> One important clue to the determination of obedient confession of the faith . . . is surely that it is necessarily related always to what the disciple community perceives as the most salient *danger* confronting the worldly context for which it has responsibility as stewards "of the mysteries of God" (1 Cor. 4:1). The "good news" (gospel) is formed over and against and in response to the "bad news" of the historical moment.[118]

Because it is speech to the world and for the world, Christian confession inherently is not defensive, but rather seeks to explain itself to those who will listen and to invite them into the faith to which it bears witness.[119] This is not to assert that confession finds its validation in its reception; the believer confesses truth regardless of whether she is believed.[120] Rather, it is to stress that confession refuses to adopt a coercive stance. Instead, it constantly risks public scorn, even rejection, and opens itself to a vulnerability modeled by its inspiration, the one "who, though he was in the form of God, did not consider equality with God as something to be exploited" (Phil. 2:6) and confessed with his life before Pilate and on the cross (1 Tim. 6:13).[121] Confession, in

115. Hall, *Confessing the Faith*, p. 9.
116. Hall, *Confessing the Faith*, p. 10.
117. Hall, *Confessing the Faith*, p. 11.
118. Hall, *Confessing the Faith*, p. 11.
119. Hall, *Confessing the Faith*, p. 12.
120. Hall, *Confessing the Faith*, p. 9.
121. Hall, *Confessing the Faith*, pp. 12-13.

short, is the church's public and contextual communication of its convictions about God's activity in Jesus Christ that is offered to and for the world in response to the present crisis of the world.

Hall concludes his commentary on "confessing" by turning to the "Barmen Declaration" of 1934. Barmen is instructive, he contends, for three reasons:

> first, it contemplated the received tradition with enough commitment and imagination to know that it could not remain at the professional level of detached reflection; second, it identified precisely that which was threatening the life of the world — and this despite the fact that in 1934 few in Germany, including Christians, regarded the program of the Nazi party as a worldly threat; and third, it thrust the "confessors" themselves into an active struggle against the evil thus named.[122]

Barmen is also important, Hall notes, because it illustrates that for confession to be contextual it must rule out, as well as affirm, particular, situation-specific options.[123] This becomes particularly clear in the *damnanus* ("we reject") clauses of the Declaration, where immediately after each affirmative element follows a resounding, "we reject the false doctrine. . . ." As Hall points out, both the affirmative and negative elements locate the confession in the particular time and place of its origin by naming those urgent circumstances that compelled it in the first place. It simply would not have been enough for those gathered at Barmen to assert in their first thesis that "Jesus Christ, as he is attested for us in Holy Scripture, is the one Word of God which we have to hear and which we have to trust and obey in life and in death." What Christian would affirm otherwise? When taken in *general,* the words are innocuous, offending no one in particular because they affirm nothing in particular. For this reason, those gathered at Barmen made the implications of their positive affirmation absolutely clear by ruling out specific negative options: "We reject the false doctrine, as though the Church could and would have to acknowledge as a source of its proclamation, apart from and besides this one Word of God, still other events and powers, figures and truths, as God's revelation." Only against the

---

122. Hall, *Confessing the Faith,* p. 13.
123. Hall, *Confessing the Faith,* p. 14.

backdrop of the contention of the "German Christians" that Hitler and his Reich were "persons and events" of similar standing to the revelation of Scripture did the positive affirmation of Christ as the "one Word" make sense and commit the confessors to a particular stand. Such is always the way with confession.[124]

Hall moves from his introductory commentary on "confessing faith" to a consideration of ecclesiology, the doctrine of the church. He construes the church as God's chosen means by which to announce the good news of God's activity in Christ to the world.[125] Confession, then, is not only the hallmark of the church, it is its chief purpose and its driving necessity.[126] If the church's thinking and professing do not lead to confessing, asserts Hall, they are "nothing" (1 Cor. 13). From this standpoint Hall not only affirms the four traditional "marks" of the church as taken from the third article of the Nicene Creed — "I believe in one holy, catholic, and apostolic church" — and the two "Protestant addenda" of word and sacrament, but also retrieves Luther's sense of a seventh mark, the mark of the cross; the mark, that is, of suffering.[127] Here Hall reclaims his conviction that confession is always made in response to the crisis of the world; therefore, true confession inevitably summons resistance and enmeshes the confessor in the travails of the world.[128]

In the second section of his book, Hall considers the context in which the church makes its confession today. He describes it as a period of disestablishment,[129] as the church leaves the era of Christendom and enters into a post-Christian diaspora.[130] Despite the crisis

---

124. See also Christopher Morse, *Not Every Spirit: A Dogmatics of Christian Disbelief* (Valley Forge, Pa.: Trinity Press International, 1994), pp. 34-38.

125. Hall, *Confessing the Faith*, p. 33.

126. Hall gleans three reasons for this from Karl Barth. First, because God loves the world the church confesses its faith of this love in Christ to the world. Second, the church confesses that it might correct itself from error and remain faithful to its Lord. Third, the church confesses because it knows itself to be responsible to the "here-and-now" (*Confessing the Faith*, pp. 36-37).

127. Hall, *Confessing the Faith*, pp. 70-86 (one, holy, catholic, and apostolic), pp. 86-90 (word and sacrament), and pp. 90-97 (cross).

128. Although Hall does not use the word, he aptly describes what Luther named *Anfechtung*, the existential struggle of the believer to trust in the benevolent God amid the adversity of worldly life.

129. Hall, *Confessing the Faith*, pp. 201-39.

130. Hall, *Confessing the Faith*, pp. 256-340.

this is occasioning for many "mainline" churches, Hall perceives in the present context an opportunity to reverse the steady decline the church has suffered in a world governed by convictions born of the Enlightenment. Christianity failed during the modern era, because, whereas modernism is governed by reason, Christianity "is at bottom a religion of faith and not reason."[131] As a consequence of the postmodern questioning of the rationalistic paradigm of modernity, Hall contends, Christians may have a chance to reinvigorate their chief doctrines, doctrines formulated to deal precisely with questions of doubt, meaning, and destiny. Justification by faith, for instance, "presupposes a context of extreme need, truly basic need — as one could appropriately say, a genuinely confessional context, when 'all other helpers fail and comforts flee.'"[132] Because modernity fled such circumstances, it robbed justification of its potency as direct address to human need. But, as Hall perceives, "The multifaceted crisis of our culture — and, for many Christians, particularly the insecurity created by the effective *disestablishment* of the Christian religion itself — may therefore be the occasion for grasping this central claim of the Reformation existentially and in original ways."[133]

In this situation of crisis and opportunity, Hall seeks to recall the church's resources for making its witness in his third section on "the forms of faith's confession." In particular, Hall first considers confession as a matter of word, deed, and stance, and then enters into a discussion of Christian ethics.[134] Also stemming from his sense of the crisis of the world, Hall concludes his work by exploring the hope that the church confesses and, simultaneously, prompts the church's confession.[135]

Having summarized Hall's conception of "confessing" and sketched its influence on his systematic work in this volume, I want to conclude this brief treatment by returning briefly to his discussion of preaching as one of the forms of confession. This will not only provide a concrete example of how he employs the term, but it will also lend itself to my own discussion of the same in subsequent chapters.

131. Hall, *Confessing the Faith,* p. 210.
132. Hall, *Confessing the Faith,* p. 278.
133. Hall, *Confessing the Faith,* p. 279.
134. Hall, *Confessing the Faith,* pp. 343-449. I will return to this section, particularly with regard to preaching, below.
135. Hall, *Confessing the Faith,* pp. 353-518.

Hall's treatment begins with a severe critique of the current state of preaching. According to Hall, preaching has been paralyzed by a lack of conviction in its message and confidence in its office and therefore has become captive to the entertainment age, pandering to the lowest common denominator of its audiences.[136] In response, Hall seeks to reclaim the "sacramental" nature of preaching, and therefore rehearses Reformation convictions about the primacy of the preached word in the life of the church in the hope of reversing the dismal trend in Protestant preaching and reclaiming a vibrant pulpit.[137]

At the center of his reclamation project is the conviction that preaching is authentic and salutary *confessio fidei*. While preaching is not the only form of confession, or even of confession as direct address, it nevertheless stands as one of its primary forms. According to Hall, preaching is nothing less than announcement of the kerygma, and kerygma is at heart always confession of God's gracious activity in Christ. Consequently,

> The first requirement of the preacher is to interpret the Scriptures, and the main thrust of the Scriptures, moralism in the history of Christianity not withstanding, is not the laying down of precepts and rules for living but the declaration of God's unmerited grace and love. Edification of the faithful, the building up of the Body of Christ, is certainly part of the intention of this act, as of all other aspects of worship; but it is not the primary function. First and foremost, preaching is confession.[138]

Tied closely to this sense of preaching is a reinvigorated sense of preachers as those who, in making their confession, speak for, with, and to the people gathered before them. Because preaching is confession, by its very nature,

> it is the confession of a particular human being, the preacher, but a human being whose very presence in that place, before that people, is representative. The preacher is before the people as one of them. . . . The preacher is also before the people as one sent

---

136. Hall, *Confessing the Faith,* pp. 348-51.
137. Hall, *Confessing the Faith,* pp. 351-60.
138. Hall, *Confessing the Faith,* p. 361.

(apostellein) to them: he or she represents before them the God who wills to bless them, too.[139]

Further, according to Hall, we should regard preaching as confessional because it reminds us of the intimate relationship between confession *of* the Word and belief *in* the Word. Preaching as confession is productive; it creates and sustains living faith, and because hearers are both faithful and faithless, they need to hear the Word confessed again and again that they might continue in faith. Simply because faith at its core "is an ongoing dialogue with doubt," preaching as confessing faith is central to the nurturing of "genuine faith."[140]

Like that of Volf and Gerrish, Hall's work offers several elements useful to my goal of reclaiming confession to describe preaching in a postmodern era. First, Hall stresses the assertive character of confession, its claim to speak the truth. Second, Hall describes confession as not only articulating the Christian tradition but articulating it in response to the current need of the world. In particular, confession is a word spoken in response to the radical skepticism and doubt of our age, not to silence or banish such doubts, but to live within them. In this sense, Hall helps to illumine confession as the dynamic articulation of the church's faith in response to the present circumstances in a manner akin to Ricoeur's sense of distanciation, in that the situation prompting confession (be it doubt or duress) is not to be overcome but rather is what prompts confession and therefore activates and actualizes faith. In this way, Hall offers a deeper analysis of confession as the means by which classic Christian affirmations are intentionally articulated in response both to the biblical promise that God loves the world and to the specific needs and crises of the age.

Taken together, Volf, Gerrish, and Hall affirm, augment, and extend my observations about the two main New Testament uses of "confession." In its first instance, "confession" designates a summary of the church's essential assertions concerning God's decisive activity in Jesus of Nazareth, the one crucified and raised from the dead. In the second, "confession" denotes articulating that faith as a living response both to this proclaimed word and to the current situation and crisis of the world.

139. Hall, *Confessing the Faith*, p. 361.
140. Hall, *Confessing the Faith*, p. 362.

Confessing as Act and Utterance

Before turning to develop "confession" as a homiletical term, I want to describe it as a specific "speech act" with reference to the linguistic analyses of J. L. Austin and John R. Searle and then to extend that understanding by means of Mikhail Bakhtin's description of speech "utterances." This will help not only to position confession in relation to other kinds of Christian speech but also to address several possible confusions or questions about employing "confession" as a homiletical term.

At the outset of his classic work, *How to Do Things with Words,* Austin distinguishes between constative and performative statements. Constatives describe "some state of affairs" and therefore can be judged as true or false, as in the statement, "It's raining outside."[141] Performatives, by comparison, are neither true nor false for they do not describe something but rather carry out an action, as when a bride or groom says "I do" in the context of a wedding; an official declares "I name this ship the 'Queen Elizabeth'" while christening a vessel; one person says to another, "I bet you fifty dollars the Yankees will win the pennant"; or a pastor says, "I baptize you in the Name of the Father and of the Son and of the Holy Spirit" during the baptismal liturgy.[142] Speech, in all of these cases, doesn't primarily describe an act but performs it. While distinguishing between these two types of speech, however, in the course of his study Austin argues that *all* language turns out upon closer examination to be performative.[143] All words, that is, ultimately "do something," as even describing some state of affairs or conveying some bit of information turns out to be what he calls a "speech act."[144]

For this reason, Austin further distinguishes between three distinct actions that statements execute. The *locutionary* act denotes the "meaning" that corresponds to the physical vocalizing of particular sounds; the *illocutionary* act names the force of what is said; and the *perlocutionary* act signifies the actual effect caused by saying something.

141. J. L. Austin, *How to Do Things with Words,* 2nd ed., ed. J. O. Urmson and Maria Sbisà (Cambridge, Mass.: Harvard University Press, 1975), pp. 1-4.

142. Austin, *How to Do Things with Words,* pp. 4-6.

143. Austin, *How to Do Things with Words,* p. 133.

144. Austin, *How to Do Things with Words,* p. 121.

Hence in the simple sentence, "I warned them of the impending thunderstorm," the locutionary element involves the descriptive content of the words and sounds of speech, the illocutionary denotes the speaker's intent "to warn" (as opposed to "describe," "promise," "command," etc.), and the perlocutionary element describes the impact of the words on the hearers (to be moved to action, disbelief, laughter, defiance, etc.).

Austin then narrows his focus to illocutionary acts, where speech is most clearly performative, and describes five loose, even fluid, categories of these.[145] While Mary-John Mananzan has described confessional, and particularly creedal, statements using Austin's categories to good effect, I wish at this point to turn to the work of one of Austin's heirs, John R. Searle, as he more clearly defines different types of illocutionary acts and examines them in greater detail.[146]

Searle also offers a "taxonomy" of five categories of illocutionary speech acts. "Assertives," according to Searle, "commit the speaker to something's being the case, to the truth of the expressed proposition," and are characterized by words such as "believe," "state," "contend," "hypothesize," and "suggest." "Directives" are attempts by the speaker to get the hearer to do something and include words like "order," "insist," "beg," "pray," "advise," "invite" and "command." "Commissives" (which overlap closely with Austin's category of the same name) commit the speaker to a certain course of action and include words like "promise," "intend," "covenant," "undertake," "pledge," "plan," "vow," and "guarantee." "Expressives" indicate the attitude or psychological state of the speaker and are characterized by words like "congratulate," "apologize," "deplore," "welcome," "thank," and so forth. "Declarations" are defined by their ability to bring about a correspondence between their propositional content and the actual state of affairs and therefore demand that extra-linguistic conventions are in place that guarantee the success of their utterance, such as a judicial system that vests judges with the power to declare guilt or innocence or a set of

145. Austin describes verdictives, exercitives, commissives, behabitives, and expositives (*How to Do Things with Words*, pp. 151-64).

146. See Mary-John Mananzan, *The Language Game of Confessing One's Belief: A Wittgensteinian-Austinian Approach to the Linguistic Analysis of Creedal Statements* (Tübingen: Max Niemeyer Verlag, 1974), pp. 109-10.

rules that allows an umpire to declare a player "out." They include actions like "naming," "hiring," and "designating."[147]

The move to Searle's terminology is important in that those theologians following Austin tend to describe confession as a commissive.[148] In Austin's terms, confession is commissive in that it, first, commits the speaker to a particular existential stance; second, makes a pledge to the hearer that the speaker does, indeed, believe what she says; and, third, seeks to engage the hearer by making a commitment, rather than by ordering or commanding.[149] In Searle's more precise taxonomy of speech acts, however, all three of these properties are more properly associated with assertives, statements about the truth. Describing confession as assertive rather than commissive not only highlights the promissory nature of confession (as assertives and commissives overlap at several points), but also addresses the question of truth more directly, thereby highlighting the utility of confession as a theological and homiletical term amid the doubt and skepticism of the postmodern age. As Gerrish and Hall both note, the church's confessions are essentially claims about truth, assertions about the way the world "really is."

Searle's taxonomy is also useful in that he suggests that each category of illocutionary acts implies within itself what he describes as an "appropriate response," a response, that is, that allows the conversation to continue.[150] In this sense, the appropriate response to an assertive is belief or disbelief; to a directive, obedience or disobedience; to a commissive, trust or mistrust; and so forth. While the perlocutionary response of the hearer cannot be determined by the speaker, the *character* of the perlocutionary act can indicate the success (or what Austin and Searle call the "felicity") of the performative utterance. This obser-

147. John R. Searle, *Expression and Meaning: Studies in the Theory of Speech Acts* (London: Cambridge University Press, 1979), pp. 12-20.

148. See Volf, *After Our Likeness*, p. 150; James Wm. McClendon, Jr., and James M. Smith, *Convictions: Defusing Religious Pluralism*, rev. ed. (Valley Forge, Pa.: Trinity Press International, 1994), pp. 62-74; Mananzan, *The Language Game of Confessing One's Belief*, pp. 109-10.

149. On "commissives," see Austin, *How to Do Things with Words*, pp. 151-64. See Volf, *After Our Likeness*, p. 150; James Wm. McClendon, Jr., and James M. Smith, *Convictions*, pp. 62-74.

150. Searle, *Expression and Meaning*, pp. 33-36.

vation highlights the fact that confession, as a speech act, is inherently relational; it seeks a response from the one spoken to. Further, it helps to clarify the type of response the speaker looks for and thereby assists the speaker in keeping the conversation going. For instance, when I confess "Christ is risen," I expect the hearers to respond (especially in a worship service during the Easter season), "He is risen indeed," or (perhaps more likely in private conversation), "I believe that's true," or "I don't believe Christ is risen and think the gospels are absolute fictions." Whatever my emotional disposition to these divergent replies, in both cases I have received an "in kind" response, one appropriate to the assertive nature of my confession. If, however, the hearer responds, "Risen from what?" or "the hills rise behind my house," the conversation stalls. In the case of the first response, the speaker has not understood me and I must clarify what I mean; in the case of the second, while the speaker may misunderstand me entirely, it may also be that the speaker simply refuses to engage me at the level of my assertion.

Adapting Searle's discussion of speech acts in this way corroborates several of the aspects of confession that I have already discerned. In particular, it highlights the usefulness of confession for those who desire to speak, and preach, of truth. In addition, it enables one to speak of truth *in a certain way*. A confession is not a directive, either in its strong form as a command or its weaker form as an invitation. That is, although one confessing desires that the hearer believe what is said, the primary point is not to get the hearer to do something, but rather to speak with integrity in a way that allows the hearer to respond. In fact, despite the clearly vested interest of the one who confesses, a confession — whether of love, sin, guilt, or some other sentiment — is not dependent on its reception by another for its validation. When one person confesses love to another, for instance, the validity of that sentiment is not dependent on its reciprocation. Although the lover desires affirmation from the beloved, and hence a reciprocal confession of love, the lover's sentiment is valid in and of itself; that is, whether affirmed or rejected, the lover knows the depth and character of his emotion. Similarly, in a "preached" confession of faith, although the preacher/confessor desires the affirmation of her hearers, the integrity and validity of the confession stands independent of its reception and reciprocation. This, I believe, ensures the integrity of preaching as an assertive, but noncoercive activity, as the hearer responds without having to shoulder the responsibility for the integrity of the preached message.

In this way, Searle's designation makes stronger the link between my discussion of the two elements of confession to Ricoeur's dialectic of participation and distanciation, as assertives both specify a cognitive proposition (cognitive specification/participation) and seek, but do not coerce, a response from the hearer (personal identification/distanciation). In some ways, in fact, describing confession in the terms of speech-act theory lends itself more easily to fostering a critical conversation of the faithful than Ricoeur's discussion in that speech-act theory addresses directly the issue of speech; that is, how we articulate our convictions about truth and reality in a way that others can hear, affirm, question, and perhaps appropriate so as to be prompted to confess in response, thereby enhancing the sermon's ability to foster a genuine "conversation among the faithful."

The utility of speech-act theory can be further extended by turning to the work of Mikhail Bakhtin. For where speech-act theory usually restricts itself to individual acts, sometimes without giving sufficient attention to the larger linguistic context, Bakhtin explores the significance not only of individual statements but also of the larger speech episode or utterance.[151] From this perspective, we can view preaching as one distinctive linguistic utterance in the larger dialogue of worship and, indeed, the life of faith. Preaching, then, is what Bakhtin might describe as a "provisional monologization." It is a monologue, in that one person undertakes an extended speech, but provisional, rather than final, in that it stems from listening and invites further speech in turn.[152] Preaching, that is, is neither a single word nor the final word; rather, it exists to prompt and nurture the larger conversation of the faithful.

By combining the insights of both Searle and Bakhtin, we may describe preaching as an assertive utterance, a provisional monologue that seeks, but will not coerce, a response of faith from those who hear

---

151. See Mikhail Bakhtin, "The Problem of Speech Genres," in *Speech Genres and Other Late Essays,* trans. Vern W. McGee, ed. Caryl Emerson and Michael Holquist (Austin: University of Texas Press, 1986), pp. 60-102.

152. Bakhtin, "The Problem of Speech Genres," esp. pp. 67-82. See also Dennis Olson, "Biblical Theology as Provisional Monologization: A Dialogue with Childs, Brueggemann, and Bakhtin," *Biblical Interpretation* 6 (1998): 171-80.

it. An additional advantage of this conception is that we may anticipate that a single assertive utterance will contain a variety of distinct speech acts, thereby freeing preachers to name, declare, judge, promise, and forgive in the context of their sermons, in this way faithfully replicating the variety of speech acts in the biblical witness itself.

Describing confession as a particular speech act and utterance may also help to clarify three possible misunderstandings about my use of it as a homiletical term. First, it helps to distinguish between confession as a "genre" and confession as an "activity" or "practice." The first describes confession as a literary convention, speaking specifically of the various liturgical and doctrinal formulas present in the New Testament and later church.[153] The second refers to the activity of speaking forth one's Christian convictions. As I move to consider the relationship of preaching to confessing faith, the latter instance of confession will move into the foreground. This is important to stress, as I am not advocating that the preacher merely repeat confessional formulas from the pulpit (although teaching, interpreting, and reappropriating those formulas may indeed be a fruitful confession to make). Rather, I seek to discern the means by which preachers can offer their sermons as vibrant, living, and faithful articulations of the classic Christian confession that "Jesus is Lord" in response to the present circumstances and need. That is, I am focusing on the ecclesial practice of sermonic confession.

Second, some readers may wonder how "preaching" can be truly conversational. While one could certainly contend that preaching has not always been a monologue or commend retrieving the "dialogue" sermon of a generation ago, I assume that much of the preaching in our churches will continue to be executed mainly by one voice at a time. In speaking of conversation in preaching, therefore, I am particularly interested in the nature of confession as a response (both to the proclaimed word and the world's need) *that seeks a response* from the hearers. That is, I am focusing on the preacher's role to confess faith in such a way so as to spark further conversation among the faithful. For this

153. These range, of course, well beyond those identified by ὁμολογέω, as many of the hymns, sayings, and references to Jesus as "Christ," "Lord," or both could very well be classified in the "confessional" genre. See Amos Wilder, who names story and various types of poetry as other vehicles (*Early Christian Rhetoric* [Cambridge, Mass.: Harvard University Press, 1971 (1964)], pp. 55-58, 102-17).

reason, I do not think that the sermon has to — or should try to — shoulder the whole load of the congregation's conversation. Not only is there the rest of the liturgy — which is inherently dialogical — but also the rest of the community's life. Therefore, I see preaching as an important, catalytic moment in the larger conversation of faith and will explore that modest role more fully in Chapter Six.

Third, I can imagine that for some readers "confession" is associated too strongly with a notion of "personal testimony" to be particularly helpful in the context of preaching during worship. Certainly there is indisputably a *personal* aspect of confession.[154] As Volf stresses, the believer is called not only to *know* the faith but also personally to *identify* with it.[155] In the language of Ricoeur, it is this kind of appropriation that makes an event of the encounter between the individual and the text/tradition.[156] Further, I would argue that it is *only* through this kind of appropriation that preachers come themselves to lively faith and therefore have something compelling to say. What Michael Polanyi writes of knowledge can be readily applied to faith: "The personal participation of the knower in the knowledge he believes himself to possess takes place within a flow of passion."[157] In this sense, preachers strive to confess what is at stake for them in the given readings and worship service in light of the present circumstances of their congregations.

But even as we admit the personal dimension of confession, we must hasten to remember that our biblical and theological study revealed that the faith preachers proclaim is never given apart from the community. Therefore, the faith confessed is the *common* faith, and preachers seek through their confessing to speak not only *to* the congregation (as one believer to others) but also *for* and *with* the commu-

---

154. On the "personal" versus the "subjective," see Michael Polanyi, *Personal Knowledge: Towards a Post-Critical Philosophy* (Chicago: University of Chicago Press, 1962), pp. 300-303.

155. Volf, *After Our Likeness*, p. 146.

156. Paul Ricoeur, "Appropriation," in *Hermeneutics and the Social Sciences: Essays on Language, Action and Interpretation*, ed., trans., and introduced by John B. Thompson (Cambridge: Cambridge University Press, 1981), p. 185. Appropriation, of course, is not possession, but rather, as Ricoeur reminds us, is more like being possessed by the text or tradition — entering into it, being open to it, and therefore the possibility for it to shape and change the one appropriating it (p. 192).

157. Polanyi, *Personal Knowledge*, p. 300.

nity, as preaching is but one part of the larger movement of corporate worship. (It is in this sense that preaching is always public and social.) Most simply, because confession, when it is used by Christians, always functions on some level as an encapsulation of the "essential gospel," no sermon can be individualistic (as opposed to personal) or unique; if so, it has ceased being a Christian sermon. From this perspective we can appreciate the significance of the Latin root for our word, *confitēri*, a compound derived from *com-* and *fatēri*, literally "to admit or acknowledge *together*."[158]

Further, it will help to recall the close link between Searle's descriptions of assertives and commissives in terms of binding the hearer and speaker together through the speaker's pledge to stand behind what he or she says.[159] This is not to imply that the preacher validates the message, as only God can do that, but rather to stress that through the sermon the preacher enters into relationship with those to whom she is confessing, and in this way fosters a fellowship of persons united by a shared confession.

Having described confession in biblical, theological, and linguistic terms as a term and practice that suits the postmodern context, it remains to describe how it may function homiletically. It is to this task that I turn in the next chapter.

---

158. This distinguishes my use of "confession" from a privatized version of the same, as in Johannes Bauer's work a century ago, which Karl Barth rightly criticizes. See Karl Barth, *Homiletics*, trans. Geoffrey W. Bromiley and Donald E. Daniels (Louisville: Westminster/John Knox Press, 1991), pp. 32-34.

159. In this sense, I agree with Mary-John Mananzan in comparing confession with "sacramental" speech that includes "pledges or vows." See *The Language Game of Confessing One's Faith*, pp. 109-10.

CHAPTER 4

Narrative Identity and
Critical Distance in Preaching

It may be helpful to retrace my argument thus far. I sought the means by which to speak — and preach — of truth with integrity amid the postmodern whirlwind; that is, to speak of truth without succumbing either to a modernist foundationalism that quickly becomes univocal, even hegemonic, speech or to a postmodern constructivism that seriously undermines, if not eliminates, the possibility for speaking of truth at all. I then contended that the best way to approach such a goal was by engaging in critical conversation, and I suggested that adopting and adapting Paul Ricoeur's sense of the ongoing dialectic of participation and distanciation toward appropriation and articulation would provide some level of dialogical realism that permits and encourages speaking of truth with integrity. Finally, I explored biblical, theological, and linguistic elements of "confession" and found it to be a useful term by which to think about preaching that encourages the conversation of the faithful by articulating and activating the Christian tradition (participation) in response to the current situation, while refusing to banish the ambiguity and doubt inherent in the life of faith by coercing a response from the hearer (distanciation). The goal of confession, ultimately, is that the hearer may believe the Word proclaimed, enter into the identity offered, and articulate and thereby actualize the tradition for him or herself (appropriation) through the power of the Holy Spirit.

In this chapter I draw from recent homiletical work to make a more

111

concrete proposal for preaching that simultaneously roots hearers in the tradition and encourages critical reflection and response that enables them to appropriate the tradition. To do this, I first consider Charles Campbell's proposal of a postliberal homiletic to describe the way in which the biblical narrative grounds believers in the Christian community and thus supplies a narrative and communal identity (participation). Criticizing Campbell's understanding of narrative at several important points, I nevertheless claim his sense of the narrative and communal identity of the hearers as an important element of a confessional homiletic. I then turn to Lucy Atkinson Rose's proposal of a postmodern, conversational understanding of preaching to discern the means by which to preserve the critical distance (distanciation) necessary for hearers to appropriate their identity and faith. While raising concerns that Rose's proposal risks the particularity of Christian identity through the diminished role it gives to Scripture and tradition, I nevertheless see in her interest both to invite all persons into a more vibrant confession of the faith and to preserve the integrity of the hearer's selfhood the means by which to safeguard the critical distance in which hearers may experience and appropriate the faith. While neither of these proposals is entirely new — Campbell's bears a marked resemblance to African American accounts of preaching and Rose's depends upon the work of Fred Craddock and other "inductive" and "narrative" preachers — each develops their position further than previously articulated in order to meet the postmodern challenge.[1]

After considering these two proposals, I will trace three homiletical implications of my proposal. I will first explore briefly several biblical and homiletical studies that strengthen my use of a dialectic between participation and distanciation; I will then highlight the need to view both the participatory and distanciatory elements of preaching as simultaneous elements of a confessional homiletic; finally, I will distinguish between the *words* of the preacher and the *work* of the Holy Spirit so as to emphasize the dynamic freedom of the God who speaks to us

---

1. On the African American sense of the "creative" power of preaching, see Dolan Hubbard, *The Sermon and the African American Literary Imagination* (Columbia: University of Missouri Press, 1994), pp. 12-22. On Craddock and the role of the hearer, see Fred Craddock, *As One without Authority*, 3rd ed. (Nashville: Abingdon Press, 1983 [1979]).

through Jesus Christ's cross and resurrection. In this way I hope to strengthen and extend my sense of the utility of describing preaching in a postmodern context as an act of "confessing Jesus Christ."

Postliberal Narrative and Christian Identity

Charles Campbell's *Preaching Jesus: New Directions for Homiletics in Hans Frei's Postliberal Theology* moves in essentially two directions, one critical and the other constructive. In the first, he offers a compelling critique of recent homiletical work by challenging what he perceives to be the modern, liberal theological presuppositions beneath contemporary narrative preaching, presuppositions that he argues are grounded in the Enlightenment and existentialist convictions positing the individual self and his or her experience as the criteria of meaning.[2] Such an orientation, Campbell argues, establishes anthropology and individual experience as the normative concerns, stipulates that the primary task of biblical interpretation and preaching is the "translation" of "meaning" or "self-understanding" from ancient thought-patterns into modern ones, and reduces the uniqueness and particularity of Jesus Christ to categories of general religious feeling.

Of these critiques, perhaps the most serious is the last, as Campbell charges that contemporary narrative preachers, in their effort to "correlate" the biblical story with that of their hearers, relinquish any claim to the uniqueness of God's saving action in Jesus Christ. Simply by proposing a "plight-to-solution" model in the well-intentioned desire to be "relevant," Campbell argues, contemporary narrative preachers are forced to define Jesus in terms of human need and equate salvation with generic categories of religious well-being.[3] The inherent danger of such an approach manifests itself in the eventual irrelevance of the particular Jew from Nazareth named Jesus, who inevitably takes

2. Charles Campbell, *Preaching Jesus: New Directions for Homiletics in Hans Frei's Postliberal Theology* (Grand Rapids: Eerdmans, 1997), pp. 122ff.

3. "Explanation takes the place of description or redescription in order to make the gospel 'meaningful' to modern human beings. In the process Christology becomes a function of soteriology, understood as freedom from existential anxiety. A general anthropology sets up the soteriological problem for which Christology becomes the solution. Jesus becomes a good existentialist" (Campbell, *Preaching Jesus*, p. 161).

a back seat to the more general and humanistic goals of "acceptance," "the good," "authentic life," and so forth, which he merely represents.[4]

Second, and more constructively, Campbell proposes Hans Frei's distinctive understanding of biblical narrative as an alternative to such an anthropologically driven approach to preaching. In particular, Campbell seeks to apply Frei's focus on the ascriptive logic of the gospel stories, his cultural-linguistic model of religion borrowed from George Lindbeck, and his later intratextual, communal hermeneutic to the task of preaching.[5] To appreciate Campbell's program, therefore, it will help to outline briefly Frei's own.

Frei advanced the major elements of his position in two books and several articles. In *The Eclipse of Biblical Narrative*, Frei tracks the turn in biblical hermeneutics and interpretation away from a narrative and literal reading of Scripture to a historical and critical one.[6] The result of such a shift was disastrous, Frei maintains, because "the depicted world and the real historical world began to be separated at once in thought and in sensibility."[7] For the first time in the history of the church, according to Frei, the primary task of biblical interpretation was no longer to read the text for the text's sake but to use it as a vehicle to reach through and behind it to its meaning.[8] The text, in such a construction, ultimately becomes dispensable, functioning only as the husk of "meaning."[9] Further, by this process text and reader are alienated, as

4. According to Campbell, Paul Tillich's sermon "You are Accepted" stands as an archetype of such sermons, betraying both their intentions and, from his point of view, their severe limitations (*Preaching Jesus,* pp. 40-44).

5. Campbell, *Preaching Jesus,* p. xiv.

6. A narrative and literal reading of Scripture (also called "pre-critical" and "realistic") entails three assumptions: (1) the narrative refers to and describes actual historical circumstances (it is non-symbolic); (2) the events in the biblical world/narrative are temporally sequential and therefore depict a single, cumulative story (the unity of the narrative); (3) the world depicted in the biblical narratives is the one and only real world and therefore embraces the reader's world. See Hans Frei, *The Eclipse of Biblical Narrative: A Study in Eighteenth and Nineteenth Century Hermeneutics* (New Haven: Yale University Press, 1974), pp. 2-3.

7. Frei, *Eclipse,* p. 5.

8. This seems, however, to ignore the tradition of allegorical interpretation that was influential, if not dominant, roughly from Origen to Luther. See Karlfried Froehlich, *Biblical Interpretation in the Early Church* (Philadelphia: Fortress Press, 1984); and Francis Schüssler Fiorenza, "The Crisis of Scriptural Authority," *Interpretation* 44 (1990): 357-58.

9. Witness, for instance, the atomization of the biblical text into sources, forms, additions, etc. Genesis is no longer a comprehensive narrative but rather J, E, P, and D; and

the text becomes an object to be used to achieve another end, that of uncovering the author's original intent. Following the lead of Erich Auerbach in *Mimesis,* Frei argues against this modern development by emphasizing the "history-like" or "realistic" character of the biblical narratives.[10] Closer to a historical novel than a doctrinal treatise, the biblical narrative can no longer be discarded in the quest for its meaning, because "narrative form and meaning are inseparable, precisely because in both cases meaning is in large part a function of the interaction of character and circumstances."[11]

In *The Identity of Jesus Christ,* Frei focuses on the particular New Testament gospel accounts to make a case for the unique and indispensable identity of Jesus Christ for Christian faith. The concerns of the two works are remarkably similar. In *Eclipse* Frei charges that the biblical narrative as a particular text has become superfluous. In *Identity,* he contends that the same has happened to the particular identity of Jesus. All too often in modern theology, Frei asserts, it is what Jesus *represents* — his meaning, self-understanding, or whatever — that is most significant, and therefore Jesus himself becomes historically unnecessary and is easily replaced by any of a host of "Christ figures."[12] In response, Frei makes two moves. First, he appropriates Gilbert Ryle's conception of human identity as the interaction of an agent's "intention" and "action."[13] Second, he adopts the literary-critical assertion that narrative renders the identity of its characters *through* the depiction of the events that they enact or are enacted upon them in the course of the narrative.[14] In short, Jesus "does what he means and means what he does."[15]

Matthew is no longer a unitary witness to Christ but a carefully constructed amalgam of Mark, "Q," and material peculiar to Matthew.

10. Erich Auerbach, *Mimesis: The Representation of Reality in Western Literature,* trans. Willard R. Trask (Princeton: Princeton University Press, 1953; Princeton Paperback Edition, 1974).

11. Frei, *Eclipse,* p. 280.

12. Hans Frei, *The Identity of Jesus Christ: The Hermeneutical Bases of Dogmatic Theology* (Philadelphia: Fortress Press, 1975), pp. 63-73.

13. Frei, *Identity,* pp. 41-44, 91-94.

14. Frei, *Identity,* pp. xvi, 47. Frei was particularly attracted to Henry James's questions, "What is character but the determination of incident? What is incident but the illustration of character?" ("The Art of Fiction," in *Partial Portraits* [London: Macmillan, 1888], cited in *Identity,* p. 88, and *Eclipse,* p. 14).

15. Frei, *Identity.*

By setting the terms in this fashion, Frei turns the tables on the historical-critical tradition by making the biblical narrative the crucial element to the hermeneutical enterprise by its function to render a reality that claims absolute reality and therefore cannot be correlated or translated but exists as *the* reality into which all others must be subsumed. As Auerbach observes, "Far from seeking, like Homer, merely to make us forget our own reality for a few hours, [the biblical narrative] seeks to overcome our reality: we are to fit our own life into its world, feel ourselves to be elements in its structure of universal history."[16] Similarly, Jesus cannot be extricated from the gospel narratives because to speak of him, or even of his personality or presence, apart from the narrative that renders his identity is not merely absurd but impossible. Whenever one does so, Frei maintains, one trades the particular identity of the Jesus who died on the cross in obedience to God's will, was raised again in triumph, and lives as the author of the Christian story, for an evanescent and thereby unreliable "Christ figure" or, worse, a shadowy projection of ourselves.

In this sense the biblical narrative is not primarily descriptive but *ascriptive,* in that it neither describes one reality among others nor refers to an independent meaning but actually renders a particular reality and stands as an entirely self-referential narrative. Further, Frei's argument not only establishes the identity of the principal character of the Christian narrative, Jesus Christ, as indissoluble, irreplaceable, and unsubstitutable, but it also binds his identity to the gospel story which renders it through its inseparable narrative juxtaposition of character and incidents.[17] Finally, Frei maintains that of all the events depicted in the gospels, the narrative of Jesus' death and ultimately his resurrection renders his identity most fully.[18] Only in the resurrection ac-

16. Auerbach, *Mimesis,* p. 15.

17. Hence Frei's sharp preference for "narrative" over "myth," since myth by its very nature precludes the unsubstitutability of its protagonist. See Frei, *Identity,* pp. 59, 63-66. See further, James F. Kay, "Myth or Narrative: 'New Testament and Mythology' Turns Fifty," *Theology Today* 48 (1991): 326-32.

18. "I have argued that Jesus' individual identity comes to focus directly in the passion-resurrection narrative rather than in the account of his person and teaching in his earlier ministry. It is in this final and climactic sequence that the storied Jesus is most of all himself, and there — unlike those earlier points at which we can get to his individual identity only ambiguously — we are confronted with him directly as the

counts, in fact, do we finally transcend all analogies to literature and encounter the factual or actual identity and presence of Jesus.[19]

In later essays, Frei begins to articulate his sense of Christianity as a distinct "cultural-linguistic" tradition, a position derived from that of his colleague at Yale, George Lindbeck.[20] This has two important implications for Frei's work. First, it places his concern for the biblical narrative into a larger cultural-linguistic framework that values the narrative not primarily for narrative's sake, but because it renders and guarantees the semiotic universe constituting the cultural-linguistic system in question.[21] Second, Frei expands his sense of interpretation to include not only the narrative itself but also the community and the history of its relationship with the narrative.[22]

In *Preaching Jesus*, Campbell appropriates several elements of Frei's theology to re-envision homiletics as a distinctly ecclesial affair. First, Campbell employs Frei's sense of the ascriptive logic of the gospel narratives to critique the contemporary use of narrative as narrow and misguided, emphasizing the structure of narrative in general rather than being bound to the particular content of the biblical story. In a postliberal homiletic, "narrative is important because it is the vehicle through which the gospels render the identity of Jesus of Nazareth, who has been raised from the dead and seeks today to form a people to follow his way."[23] This understanding guards against the devolution of

---

unsubstitutable individual who is what he does and undergoes and is manifested directly as who he is" (Frei, *Identity*, pp. 142-43).

19. Frei, *Identity*, pp. 145-46.

20. See, in particular, "Theology and the Interpretation of Narrative: Some Hermeneutical Considerations," a lecture presented in 1982 and published posthumously in *Theology and Narrative: Selected Essays*, ed. George Hunsinger and William C. Placher (New York: Oxford University Press, 1993), pp. 94-116; "The 'Literal Reading' of the Biblical Narrative: Does It Stretch or Will It Break?" in *The Bible and the Narrative Tradition*, ed. Frank McConnell (New York: Oxford University Press, 1986), pp. 36-77; and *Types of Christian Theology*, ed. George Hunsinger and William C. Placher (New Haven: Yale University Press, 1992), pp. 19-27.

21. See Campbell, *Preaching Jesus*, pp. 65-80.

22. As Campbell writes, "In his interpretation of biblical narrative, Frei turns from a general, literary approach based on the genre of realistic narrative to a particular 'communal hermeneutic' focused on the church's tradition of literal reading. His key categories become not text and interpreter, but Scripture and community" (*Preaching Jesus*, p. 77).

23. Campbell, *Preaching Jesus*, p. 289.

the sermon into an anthropological flight from plight to solution, as "the story of Jesus, not the particulars of human experience, is the fundamental reality and starting point."[24] The ascriptive logic of the biblical narrative, therefore, provides not merely the form but also, and essentially, the content of the sermon by reorienting preaching to its fundamental task of reenacting the biblical narrative and thereby rendering the unique and unsubstitutable identity and reality of the Jesus of the gospels in the presence of the gathered assembly. In this way only, Campbell argues, can narrative preaching resume with integrity its calling to preach Jesus.

Second, from this sense of the narrative's function to render identity stems Campbell's use of Frei's emphasis upon "intratextuality," by which he means that the narrative text makes a claim upon our "text" and the narrated or rendered reality incorporates our reality.[25] From this vantage point, the biblical reality and our reality are not equal partners engaged in mutual interaction with preaching serving as a thoroughfare between the two, as conceived by contemporary narrative homileticians. Rather, a postliberal understanding of narrative preaching follows that of postliberal biblical interpretation and seeks to render the biblical reality such that the fullness of our reality — including our language, identity, culture, and being — is absorbed into, and is understood on the terms of, the narrated, rendered reality of the Bible. As Frei explains,

> The direction in the flow of intratextual interpretation is that of absorbing the extratextual universe into the text, rather than the reverse (extratextual) direction. The literal sense is the paradigmatic form of such intratextual interpretation in the Christian community's use of Scripture: The literal ascription to Jesus of Nazareth of the stories connected with him is of such far-reaching import that it serves not only as the focus for inner-canonical typology but reshapes extratextual language in its manifold descriptive uses into a typological relation to these stories.[26]

24. Campbell, *Preaching Jesus*, p. 193.
25. Sharing this concern with Frei, George Lindbeck's work on "intratextuality" may help to illumine Frei's understanding and Campbell's appropriation of it. See his *The Nature of Doctrine: Religion and Theology in a Postliberal Age* (Philadelphia: Westminster Press, 1984), pp. 113-23.
26. Hans Frei, "The 'Literal Reading,'" p. 72.

Finally, as preachers absorb their hearers into the rendered reality of the biblical narrative and beckon them to reconceive themselves in light of this reality, they may also begin to train their people in the language of faith. Because religion, from this perspective, is most akin to a cultural-linguistic system, the life of faith can be conceived as one of learning and practicing the language of Christianity.[27] Appropriating this dimension of Frei's theology, Campbell encourages preachers not to translate but rather to teach, make use of, and inculcate believers in the church's "peculiar speech" so as to develop a community of faithful listeners and thereby build up the church. Because the church is Jesus' "indirect presence" in the world, believers are granted the possibility not only of joining their story to the biblical one but also of continuing that story by publicly enacting it in the worship of the congregation.[28] Thus, Campbell exhorts preachers to eschew the anti-communal tendencies of modern narrative preaching which focuses almost exclusively on the experience of the individual, and he encourages them to adopt instead Frei's more ecclesial and narratively faithful approach. For, "God in Jesus Christ is not simply the predicate of individual human experience or needs, but is an active subject building up a people to embody and witness to Jesus' presence in and for the world."[29]

In Charles Campbell's hands, the biblical narrative becomes a powerful tool with which to ground believers in their Christian faith. By interpreting the Scripture not in terms of what it "means" but by how it "builds up" the church; by offering typology, rather than translation, as the means by which to incorporate the current world into the biblical narrative; and by stressing the role of the preacher as a teacher and model of the Christian language, Campbell encourages preachers to inculturate their hearers into the Christian reality rendered by the biblical narrative.[30] As he writes,

27. Lindbeck, again, is instructive: "a religion can be viewed as a kind of cultural and/or linguistic framework or medium that shapes the entirety of life and thought." Therefore, "to become religious — no less than to become culturally or linguistically competent — is to interiorize a set of skills by practice and training. One learns how to feel, act, and think in conformity with a religious attitude that is, in its inner structure, far richer and more subtle than can be explicitly articulated" (Lindbeck, *Doctrine,* pp. 33, 35).

28. Campbell, *Preaching Jesus,* pp. 221-31.

29. Campbell, *Preaching Jesus,* p. 227.

30. On interpreting Scripture, see Campbell, *Preaching Jesus,* p. 230; on typology, pp. 250-57; on preacher as disciple, p. 236.

Sermons become the means through which the Christian community enters more deeply into its own distinctive speech, so that Christian ideas, beliefs, and experience become possible. Preaching seeks to recreate a universe of discourse and put the community in the middle of that world — instructing the hearers in the use of language by showing them how to use it.[31]

Campbell's goal that postliberal preaching "build up" the church resonates clearly with my own sense that one of the primary elements of confession is to join persons to the community of faith and root them in that communal identity.[32] In many respects, Campbell's work embodies the "sociological" role of confession articulated by B. A. Gerrish and that I have described as "participation." At bottom, Campbell wants preachers to reiterate and proclaim the biblical narrative so as to make it large and distinctive enough for their hearers to *live into,* that they may come to know themselves first and foremost as followers of that narrative's rendered character, Jesus Christ.

With appreciation for Campbell's intentions, I nevertheless harbor three significant concerns about his proposal, each related to an element of confession as developed above. The first regards his understanding of preaching in relation to faith; the second his view of narrative and its capacity to engender participation in the community of faith; and the third his failure to allow the critical distance necessary to appropriate the narrative identity offered.

As we have seen, for Campbell preaching is primarily an event aimed at "constituting a people."[33] While I share this interest, I fear that in his concern to protect preaching from the individualistic excesses of modernity he has severed the relationship between proclamation and a biblical understanding of faith. By appropriating Frei's theology, Campbell transforms faith into a "set of skills and practices within a distinctive, cultural-linguistic community."[34] Whatever the sociological or postmodern strengths of this move, it undercuts the biblical understanding of *pistis* as both personal assent *and* trust. Faith, to Campbell, is not about a relationship with Christ and Christ's body, the church; rather

31. Campbell, *Preaching Jesus,* p. 234.
32. Campbell, *Preaching Jesus,* pp. 221-31.
33. Campbell, *Preaching Jesus,* p. 224.
34. Campbell, *Preaching Jesus,* p. 145.

faith is construed in entirely sociological terms as those cultural and linguistic habits that constitute membership in a particular tradition. Faith, in this sense, is closer to the Aristotelian notion of virtue or *habitus* than it is to the biblical sense of trusting confidence.[35] Hence, in a postliberal homiletic, preaching is not about proclaiming the gospel by which the Holy Spirit creates faith, but rather is the means by which to inculturate participants more deeply in their tradition while training them in the habitual practices of their community.

At this point, we may profit by noting Barth's discussion of preaching's confessional nature and its relationship to faith. Also speaking of the importance of building up, or edifying the church, Barth clarifies that he is not primarily interested in preaching as edifying in "the sense of ongoing building, or building up, or integrating." Rather, Barth continues, "The point is that the church must be built afresh each time." For this reason, while Barth allows that pastors may preach so as to edify, educate, and train, he states unequivocally that "all such things are to be only the zeros after the one. Conformity to the confession is the one. Nothing must be subtracted from this nor anything put before it."[36] Preaching, to Barth, is the announcement *(epangelia)* of God's own Word to us in Jesus Christ.[37] That Word, as we have seen, is what creates faith and thereby constitutes the church, the body of Christ. Any preaching that seeks to build up that body through catechesis or other instruction must not overlook its need first to be "built up afresh" by proclaiming to it that Word by which the Holy Spirit creates faith.

Campbell's appropriation of Frei is manifestly inadequate to this central task of preaching. As James F. Kay notes, "However much realistic narratives render character identity, they do not, as such, function as 'performative utterances' by 'self-involving' agents."[38] In other

---

35. On *"habitus,"* see Edward Farley, *Theologia: The Fragmentation and Unity of Theological Education* (Philadelphia: Fortress Press, 1983), esp. pp. 29-48; and Heiko Augustinus Oberman, *The Harvest of Medieval Theology: Gabriel Biel and Late Medieval Nominalism* (Durham, N.C.: Labyrinth Press, 1983), esp. pp. 160-84.

36. Barth, *Homiletics,* trans. Geoffrey W. Bromiley and Donald E. Daniels (Louisville: Westminster/John Knox Press, 1991), pp. 65-66.

37. Barth, *Homiletics,* pp. 45-46.

38. James F. Kay, review of *Preaching Jesus,* by Charles Campbell, *Theology Today* 56 (1999): 404.

words, Campbell gives no account of how God speaks through the Bible or the preacher; how, in short, the Bible as a *creation* functions as the voice or authoritative word of the *Creator*. Ultimately, according to Campbell, preaching does not seek to address hearers with a living, dynamic word of the gospel that creates faith; rather, preaching executes a primarily catechetical and ethical function to train the mind, but not quicken the spirit, of the hearers.

My second concern revolves around Campbell's understanding of narrative. Following Frei, Campbell trusts that the biblical narrative unfailingly renders a stable semiotic "universe of discourse" into which hearers are invited.[39] The difficulty of Frei's proposal (and Campbell's appropriation of it) rests in establishing the "semiotic universe" of the Bible apart from all other semiotic universes and sealing off its ongoing development in relation to other historically and contextually conditioned semiotic systems. As Mary McClintock Fulkerson writes, a postliberal intratextual program "does not recognize that signifying practices cannot be completely controlled." Consequently,

> The desire to ensure that the grammatical rules are dominant allows their virtual removal from the process of ordinary semiosis. The power of a core biblical lexicon, the "world of the bible," to signify in one direction shows that certain textual unities have such force that they are not subject to the constraints of ordinary signifying processes. They do not participate in the instability of signification.[40]

Whereas the normal processes of signification — in which "any sign cannot make meaning independent of other signs" — grant readers or hearers a role in construing the "narrative world" rendered by the text in question, postliberal intratextuality seems to imply "a text that signifies in only one direction."[41]

Such a move creates a false dichotomy between the world "inside" the text and that "outside," ignoring the fact, as Fulkerson writes, "that the former does not exist without the latter."[42] In short, there is no

---

39. Campbell, *Preaching Jesus,* p. 234.

40. Mary McClintock Fulkerson, *Changing the Subject: Women's Discourses and Feminist Theology* (Minneapolis: Fortress Press, 1994), pp. 159-60.

41. Fulkerson, *Changing the Subject,* pp. 160-61.

42. Fulkerson, *Changing the Subject,* p. 161 n. 67.

"biblical universe" apart from that created by persons who live in a variety of overlapping cultural and linguistic systems, thereby creating multiple "biblical texts" that, while recognizably similar, are not identical. According to Regina M. Schwartz, Frei (and therefore Campbell) adopts a faulty sense of textualism that artificially bifurcates the worlds "inside" and "outside" the text:

> Our current understanding of textuality has broken down the distinction between these worlds. That does not mean that the Bible is privileged, that it can subsume a non-biblical world: we do not try to cram the world onto the pages of the Bible. Nor does it mean that some historical realm is privileged: we do not use the Bible to footnote the text of history. Rather, the pages of both are contiguous, and the categories themselves — biblical and non-biblical — have become obsolete.[43]

This highlights a question John McClure raises of Campbell's work: "Is the polarity between the biblical text and experience overstated?" By overemphasizing the priority of the text over experience, Campbell risks the same danger of the "liberals" he criticizes for subsuming the text under experience; namely, both liberals and postliberals risk losing "the many ways that text and experience are interwoven." McClure offers as a counterproposal the possibility that preachers should *both* "textualize experience," thereby inviting their hearers to see their lives on the terms of the biblical narrative, *and* "experientialize the text," thereby allowing current experience to illumine the meaning and ongoing significance of the text.[44]

From this point of view, translation between "the biblical story" and "our story" is not only possible, but absolutely necessary. For the words of the Bible only take on meaning when they are viewed *both* in relation to the narratives in which they are used *and* in relation to the common words of the hearers as they go about their daily lives. Campbell trusts that words receive their meaning only in relation to other words of the linguistic system in question; hence the need to allow the

---

43. Regina M. Schwartz, "Introduction: On Biblical Criticism," in *The Book and the Text*, ed. Regina M. Schwartz (Cambridge, Mass.: Blackwell, 1990), p. 11.

44. John McClure, review of *Preaching Jesus*, by Charles Campbell, *Journal for Preachers* 21, no. 2 (1998): 36.

biblical narratives to define their own terms in preaching.[45] Even if this is entirely true — and I suspect that Campbell, like Lindbeck, overestimates the stability and integrity of languages — one learns language not only by "immersion" but also by "association," that is, by connecting the signs of various "semiotic systems," whether linguistic or experiential. While I recognize the danger that a significant Christian word like "grace" may be lost if it is consistently replaced by "acceptance," as in Tillich's famous sermon, "You Are Accepted," I believe that such a risk is inevitable. For apart from the everyday words of "acceptance," "love," "gift," "kindness," "forgiveness," and others — as they function both inside and outside of the narrative — we have no capacity to understand "grace" in the first place.

Campbell's concern, I believe, is that the biblical word of "grace" shapes our understanding of "acceptance" and not the other way around. I agree, but I think this can happen only insofar as we trace that word's use in the biblical narratives *and* relate it analogically to other words from our various "linguistic fields." The key to such translation is that it be a two-way street, an ongoing and mutual affair. As McClure writes, it is the intention to "persuade experience to meet the text" while simultaneously seeking to "persuade the text to meet experience."[46] While this invites inevitable risks, there is no way to avoid them, as we translate — and therefore, as one of the shades of the meaning of the word implies, *betray* — our words all the time. When it comes to the use of narrative in preaching, then, I must argue against both Campbell's insistence that the preacher start always with biblical narrative *and* those who contend that we start always with the human "story." Rather, both kinds of narratives are necessary so as to mutually interpret each other, and neither must become a cipher for the other; artificial rules about the order of their appearance simply cannot guarantee this.

Writing in a similar vein, Karl Barth urged preachers to adopt *both* the "language of Canaan" *and* "the speech of Mr. Everyman." On the one hand, according to Barth, the church speaks in the language in which its confession has been formed, the language of the Bible and the Christian tradition, "for it has in history its own special history, its

45. Campbell, *Preaching Jesus,* pp. 233-36.
46. McClure, review of Campbell, p. 36 (italics omitted).

own special road. It speaks, when it confesses, in relationship to this special history." Apart from retaining its distinctive language, the church risks severing its tie to its own history and thereby sacrificing both its identity and its capacity for speech. As Barth warns, "Where the Christian Church does not venture to confess in its own language, it usually does not confess at all."[47] On the other hand, according to Barth, the church must also confess in the language of the world, as "not one of us is only a Christian; we are all also a bit of the world." Further, as Barth writes, "By the very nature of the Christian Church there is only one task, to make the Confession heard in the sphere of the world as well." In order to speak God's Word to the world, therefore, "There must be *translation,* for example, into the language of the newspaper. What we have to do is say in the common language of the world the same thing we say in the forms of Church language."[48] The language of Canaan and the language of the newspaper exist in a reciprocal relationship, the former preserving the distinct identity and character of the church's confession, and the latter lending it the means by which to be articulated in the world and fulfill its God-ordained purpose. To be faithful to their confession, therefore, preachers must learn to be bilingual.[49]

My third concern is related to this last one. Not only do I believe that Campbell's understanding of narrative is faulty — that is, I don't think language or narratives *work* the way he describes — even if his understanding of narrative were accurate, I do not think it would realize his goal of training Christians in the faith. For whereas Campbell understands his task in terms that I have described as participation, he allows no means for distanciation, or critical distance, by which hearers can really be encountered by, and appropriate, the narratives we preach. It is here that Campbell's sense of the ascriptive logic of Scripture and intratextual interpretation is not only faulty but, I think, wrongheaded in the first place. For the hearer that is "absorbed" by the text has no ability to engage in critical conversation by which to appropriate the biblical narratives for him or herself. This lack of space in which to ap-

---

47. Karl Barth, *Dogmatics in Outline* (New York: Harper & Row, 1959), p. 31.

48. Barth, *Dogmatics in Outline,* pp. 32-33.

49. I borrow this term from Deborah van Deusen Hunsinger. See her *Theology and Pastoral Counseling: A New Interdisciplinary Approach* (Grand Rapids: Eerdmans, 1995).

propriate the text limits, as Ricoeur pointed out, the ability of the hearer really to be encountered by the claims of the narrative, to enter into the text, or to be changed by it. Confession, recall, is decidedly assertive — making claims about the nature of reality — and therefore demands a response from the listener. Nevertheless, it is not coercive, as its integrity does not depend upon the affirmation of the hearer. My concern is that while Campbell's proposal may yield greater *adherence* to a tradition, and even more competent practice of it, his method of preaching cannot lead to greater *fidelity* understood as a dynamic trust and confidence.

For this reason, while I intend to retain the strengths of Campbell's association between the biblical narrative and communal identity, I will also seek the means by which to preach so as to preserve the space in which hearers may be encountered by the Spirit, be brought to faith, and in this way genuinely respond to the identity and truth-claims asserted and offered. Toward this end, I turn to consider a position that places a concern for the integrity of the hearer at the center of its enterprise.

Postmodern Conversation and Critical Distance

Few, if any, homileticians have given greater attention to the hearer's role in contemporary preaching than Lucy Atkinson Rose. In her *Sharing the Word: Preaching in the Roundtable Church,* Rose offers a conversational homiletic that seeks to be, as she describes, communal, nonhierarchical, personal, inclusive, and scriptural.[50] Her work begins with an appreciative survey and critique of the twentieth century's three dominant approaches to preaching, which she describes as "traditional" (characterized by the emphasis on "sacred rhetoric" that runs from Augustine to John A. Broadus), "kerygmatic" (influenced in her judgment particularly by C. H. Dodd and Karl Barth), and "transformational" (including those who seek to create for hearers an experience of the gospel, often called the "New Homiletic"). After describing these approaches, she analyzes each with respect to their understanding of sermonic purpose, content, language, and form. While she tracks encouraging shifts in all

50. Lucy Rose, *Sharing the Word: Preaching in the Roundtable Church* (Louisville: Westminster/John Knox, 1997), pp. ix, 112.

of these areas, she also points out less encouraging continuities in three distinct areas: (1) the implied gap between congregation and preacher, (2) a naïve confidence in the neutrality of language, and (3) uncritical assumptions about the universal quality of truth.[51] In order to overcome these limitations, Rose proposes a method of preaching she describes as "conversational."[52]

Throughout all three eras of preaching, according to Rose, homiletical theory presupposes a gap between the preacher and the congregation. This is easiest to see in "traditional" and "kerygmatic" preaching, where the preacher is charged with delivering "truth" and speaking "for God." But even in transformational preaching the relationship implied by the sermon is predominantly a one-way affair, as the preacher "creates" a transformative experience for the hearer who is still, by and large, a recipient. Such a gap perpetuates the separation of preacher and hearer "even while community and shared life are affirmed."[53]

By envisioning preaching as a "conversation," Rose seeks to eliminate this gap. Both the preacher and hearer, she reminds us, are members of one body of faith, the same priesthood of all believers. Ministers, according to Rose, are responsible for seeing that preaching *be* done, not necessarily responsible for *doing* all the preaching. When ministers *are* the primary preachers of their congregations, they should involve parishioners in the task of interpreting the texts through pre-sermon group study; seek to represent voices from throughout the congregation; and offer their sermons as open discourse, invitations to further dialogue.[54]

Rose detects another point of contact between the three approaches to preaching that dominated the twentieth century in a shared confidence in the "neutrality" of language as a medium by which to convey, alternatively, "truth," "the kerygma," or "experience." Contesting this position, Rose writes, "Language is powerful. It can create new worlds in consciousness. But it is also limited and participates in the sins and distortions of the generations and cultures that use and reshape it."[55]

51. Rose, *Sharing the Word*, pp. 89-91.
52. Rose, *Sharing the Word*, p. 4.
53. Rose, *Sharing the Word*, p. 90.
54. Rose, *Sharing the Word*, pp. 93-94.
55. Rose, *Sharing the Word*, p. 83.

As a consequence of the limitations of language, Rose advocates that we employ language that is intentionally *confessional* and *multivalent*. Sermonic language should be confessional in a double sense. First, because we admit that we imperfectly perceive God's revelation, we can only offer our sermons as "interpretations" of God's Word, as "gestures" toward divinity. In this sense, sermonic language should reflect a greater modesty about its ability to reflect "humanity's relationship to God and the eschatological reality that God is bringing into being" and be offered as a confession to the community that, in response, "tests our beliefs and practices."[56] Second, sermonic language is confessional in that it "should reflect the preacher's personal convictions." That is, "the language preachers choose should have so shaped their lives that it expresses the convictions out of which and into which they are living."[57] In addition to being confessional, sermonic language should be intentionally multivalent, capable of evoking multiple meanings. "Intentional," here, is key, as language is by nature multivalent. Believing that earlier emphases on "clarity" privilege the preacher's knowledge and experience over the hearer's, Rose urges preachers to use language that not only permits but also encourages hearers to find their own meaning. Employing this kind of language, Rose says, not only admits the inherent ambiguity and limitation of all language but also "spotlights the community of faith as opposed to the preacher."[58]

Rose's third area of concern rests in the unquestioned assumptions about "truth" shared by all of the preaching positions she has described. Because our knowledge of the world, ourselves, and God is distorted by human sin, we cannot and should not claim to know ultimate truth.[59] For this reason, Rose suggests that words like "truth," "kerygma," and "revelation" are no longer tenable, as by their exclusive claims they exclude too many voices from around the table and silence conversation.[60] Rather than claiming to proclaim the truth, Rose suggests instead that preaching "is about tentative interpretations, pro-

56. Rose, *Sharing the Word,* pp. 108-9.
57. Rose, *Sharing the Word,* p. 109.
58. Rose, *Sharing the Word,* p. 5 (clarity), pp. 109-10 (multivalence).
59. Rose, *Sharing the Word,* p. 99.
60. Because she believes that "Truth" is an "eschatological" reality only (*Sharing the Word,* p. 5), she calls for a "moratorium on truth" (p. 104).

posals that invite counterproposals, and the preacher's wagers as genuine convictions placed in conversation with the wagers of others."[61]

Preaching is an interpretation not only because we have limited knowledge, but also because we cannot escape our context, perspective, and self-interest; others, from different perspectives, will perceive matters differently. Similarly, describing sermons as proposals reminds both preachers and their hearers that they work within a "context of the unavailability of absolute truth." As Rose writes, "Determining preaching's content, therefore, is difficult. What might be liberating to one set of worshipers . . . might be oppressive to another."[62] While wanting in this way to underscore our limitations, Rose also seeks to highlight the degree to which preachers' beliefs inform their living; therefore, she calls preachers to view their sermons as wagers, "those convictions upon which they have staked their lives or those insights where their journey has found a temporary resting-place. These wagers they now offer to others in the conversation called preaching, publicly acknowledging that their own personal wagers are particular and limited."[63]

The dominant metaphor that Rose employs to describe her proposal is conversation. The central goal of such preaching, as she writes, is "to gather the community of faith around the Word where the central conversations of the church are refocused and fostered." She is clear, however, that by describing preaching as "conversation," she is not seeking to reinvigorate the "dialogue sermon" of the early seventies; rather, she asks that preaching be more like a conversation among friends, more representative of the diversity of those gathered in the pews and more inviting of their response. Reminding us that the root of "homily" is derived from the Greek word for "conversation" (ὁμιλέω), Rose contends that preaching should nurture the community's conversations about meaning in light of their life together and shared tradition. As she writes, "In conversational preaching, the sermonic conversation is grounded in solidarity — a shared identity as the believing people of God, a shared priesthood before God and within community, and shared tasks of discerning and proclaiming God's Word."[64]

61. Rose, *Sharing the Word,* p. 100.
62. Rose, *Sharing the Word,* pp. 100-101.
63. Rose, *Sharing the Word,* p. 101.
64. Rose, *Sharing the Word,* p. 95.

In seeking to describe conversational preaching, Rose asserts that preaching be both "personal" and "inclusive." Careful not to imply by her use of words such as "personal" or, even more suggestive, "autobiographical," that the sermon should be a series of "I" statements, she suggests that, like good fiction, sermons should flow from the actual life experience of the preacher.[65] Similarly, when she speaks of "inclusive" she does not call simply for a nod to the concerns and experiences of those often excluded from the homiletical table but rather seeks to promote sermons that actually arise from the life experience of the whole community. These two — personal and communal — are inherently related in that the preacher shares with the congregation a "modicum of faith and commitment within a community of faith" which is lived out in divergent ways and through a number of different interpretations, proposals, and wagers.[66] Hence, the truly personal sermon will welcome and incorporate the responses of the community and thereby also be inclusive.

Throughout her work, Rose evinces a concern to protect and nurture the integrity of the hearer that provides the critical space which I have argued is necessary to promote the "productive distanciation" by which the hearer can be really encountered by the Word and appropriate the faith confessed in the sermon and liturgy. By inviting preachers to admit both their limitations and their faith, eschew foundational language, and encourage a partnership with their hearers by preaching conversationally, Rose supplies and safeguards the critical space in which hearers can listen, reflect, question, reject, or affirm and appropriate what they have heard.

But while she therefore exemplifies noncoercive preaching that takes distanciation seriously, she simultaneously jeopardizes the sermon's ability to engender significant participation in a tradition. Preaching, to Rose, is not about proclaiming "truth" but rather discovering "meaning" in life. As Rose says, she seeks to

> challenge preachers and homiletical scholars to confront how unconsciously, and sometimes ruthlessly, the word *truth* is used to designate partisan interpretations and personal wagers. In place of the

65. Rose, *Sharing the Word*, pp. 124-27.
66. Rose, *Sharing the Word*, p. 128.

word *truth* with its all-too-often assumed link to objective reality, I suggest we use the word *meaning* with its link to commitment and discipleship.[67]

Hence, "More important than truth is meaning and the testimony of life's experiences."

The question, however, is what norms the community's experiences. Is there any norm, border, or control on the content of the sermon? Rose asks this question herself, and her response takes her more deeply into the question of the contextual, temporal, and even ephemeral nature of truth and its relationship to notions of the Word of God, kerygma, and gospel.[68] Borrowing from the work of L.-M. Dewailly and Maureen P. Carroll, Rose affirms that God's Word in its fullness remains hidden, a mystery. For this reason, the church turns to the Bible, seeking in its "multiplicity of 'word images'" a conversational, dialogical sense of a word that would otherwise remain "incomprehensible . . . this side of the eschaton."[69]

Because it is always a particular and concrete community that is engaged in dialogue with the biblical texts, the nature or content of "the Word" becomes a matter for the community to discern. Rose interprets and transforms "kerygma" to capture that communal sense of the "heart or core of the Word." As she makes clear, this interpretation has direct implications for preaching:

> My proposal is that in conversational preaching the *kerygma* is no longer the unchanging core of the gospel, grounded in the apostles' preaching as once-and-for-all revelation. Instead, the *kerygma* might designate a temporary formulation of a slice of God's activity in the world that is critical for the contemporary church and that is grounded in revelation as an ongoing conversation with God, the Word, and biblical texts. The *kerygma* for one generation in one corner of the church might be human freedom; it will be different in a different generation in a different corner of the church. Given this redescription of the *kerygma,* a part of the work of preaching as a communal, ecclesial activity becomes formulating and reformulat-

67. Rose, *Sharing the Word,* p. 104.
68. Rose, *Sharing the Word,* p. 99.
69. Rose, *Sharing the Word,* p. 103.

ing the *kerygma's* provisional content; that is discerning those dimensions of the Word that become correctives for the future as the distortions of the past and present come into focus.[70]

Aware that her proposal raises questions about the "validity" of any and all communal "wagers," Rose entertains two possibilities for norming the community's experience. The first is ecclesial and locates the preacher's wager within the confines of the broader community, the universal church. The second is biblical and looks to the text to norm the sermonic proposal. Rose, however, is suspicious of the need for such checks, asserting that the central question is not *what* controls the preaching, but *who,* and she suggests that it must be each and every community as it meets week in and week out to gather in faithful conversation that exercises control over the validity of its preaching.[71] As she writes, "Preaching's content will shift and shuffle until the eschaton. *Kerygmas* will rise and fall, only to rise and fall again. . . . The hope that preaching's content will remain faithful lies in the grace of God and the vitality of all the multiple ecclesial conversations."[72]

While Rose's confidence in conversation echoes my own, I nevertheless think that she misunderstands the dialectical nature of conversation and therefore emphasizes one element, the space and freedom in which to reflect critically and respond (distanciation), at the cost of the other, a shared communal identity (participation). Or, perhaps it would be more accurate to say that Rose *assumes* that shared identity and therefore gives little or no attention to establishing, nurturing, and maintaining the identity of the group gathered not simply as participants in a conversation about meaning, but as Christian participants. But, as B. A. Gerrish points out, social identity can be a fragile thing, always susceptible to disintegration or amnesia. For this reason he highlights the sociological, or what I have been describing as the

---

70. Rose, *Sharing the Word,* p. 103.

71. "For me, the critical issue in conversational preaching is not whether preaching meets some absolute standard of orthodoxy but whether sermonic interpretations, proposals, and wagers serve to foster all the central conversations of the church as the people of God, whether they upbuild the communities of faith in their local and global configurations (see 1 Cor. 14:12), and whether they respect and invite the voices of the silenced, the disenfranchised, the poor, and women" (*Sharing the Word,* p. 106).

72. Rose, *Sharing the Word,* pp. 106-7.

"participatory," function of confession.[73] Apart from some such sense of norms — not as measures of orthodoxy, but as communal identifiers — Rose's conversational preaching risks becoming indistinguishable from any other talk.

Further, Rose truncates confession by emphasizing only its role to articulate the faith here and now, missing or denying its sibling role to summarize the "essentials" of the Christian tradition. Such a view of preaching takes the hearer seriously only at the cost of the tradition in which the hearer stands and ends up privileging a noncoercive sermonic form over a recognizably Christian content, thereby sacrificing preaching's function to proclaim to persons a living word that may address them directly. Robbed of its assertive character, of its ability to advance propositions about truth and reality, confession ceases to be performative. Rather than *do* things, confession in Rose's hands merely describes the preacher's own experience, tentatively proposing — rather than asserting or declaring — possibilities for the hearers to consider. This not only runs contrary to the text itself, which is constantly making assertions, but it also substitutes secondary theological reflection for primary proclamation.[74] Ultimately, one is never addressed directly in Rose's version of preaching, and therefore the hearer cannot hope to enter into the confession of the church to claim it, appropriate it, and give it voice once again. Therefore, while I share both her eagerness to invite all the voices of the community to share in the conversation of the faithful and her concern to preserve the integrity of the hearer, I think that, without a stronger sense of preaching's role to engender a narrative and community identity, Rose's proposal risks surrendering the means by which to guarantee that it is a recognizably Christian conversation in which the community is engaged.

---

73. "Their primary use is . . . to preserve identity. They prevent disintegration by maintaining a common language, a community of discourse, without which the fellowship would suffer group amnesia and might dissolve in a babel of discordant voices." B. A. Gerrish, *Saving and Secular Faith: An Invitation to Systematic Theology* (Minneapolis: Augsburg Press, 1999), p. 56.

74. See Cornelius Plantinga, Jr., "Dancing the Edge of Mystery," *Books and Culture,* September/October 1999, p. 19.

Confessional Preaching

I have so far been arguing that the Christian practice of confession — understood both as the essentials of the Christian tradition and the assertive, but not coercive, articulation of that tradition in response to present circumstances — prompts a dynamic encounter with the Word through which hearers may affirm, question, and ultimately appropriate and articulate for themselves the Christian faith as a living tradition through the power of the Holy Spirit. I have also suggested that, understood in this fashion, the Christian practice of confession resonates with Paul Ricoeur's dialectic between participation and distanciation and thereby provides the means by which to engage in a critical conversation that grants one the ability to talk and preach about the "truth" with some measure of integrity and confidence. For this reason, I believe that understanding preaching as the task of "confessing Jesus Christ" offers a useful way to think about how to preach in a postmodern context. In order to give greater homiletical shape to these related suggestions, in this chapter I have examined two constructive homiletical proposals. In them I have found strong articulations of one of the two aspects of confession (or poles of the dialectic) at the expense of the other. Thus, while appreciating the strengths of each, I also claim that neither is sufficient in and of itself to offer an appropriate and faithful homiletic for a postmodern context. Rather, I contend that Charles Campbell's postliberal homiletic and Lucy Atkinson Rose's conversational homiletic need to be viewed and employed in relation to each other so as to realize both aspects of confession and produce a lively dialectic of participation and distanciation toward appropriation.

In this section, I will explore in greater detail three aspects of my proposal that will give greater shape to the claims I have made. First, and in order to strengthen the move from Ricoeur's discussion of participation and distanciation to homiletics, I point to the work of several scholars in biblical studies and homiletics who have suggested a similar relationship between identity and distance to the one I have outlined. Second, I will illustrate the degree to which the dialectic between confession as identity and confession as assertive, noncoercive articulation is not a temporal dialectic, but rather that the participation and distanciation of confessional preaching occur nearly simultaneously in the preaching event. Third, I will distinguish between the *words* of the preacher and the *work* of the Holy Spirit in order to make greater sense of, and appropriate more fully, the relationship between identity and distance with regard to Christian preaching. This work will prepare us to anticipate discussing the major conversation partners of the preacher, the biblical canon and the community of faith, in the final chapters of this project.

In his work on *The Poetics of Biblical Narrative*, Meier Sternberg suggests that the "gaps" of narratives are as important to reading them as is the "information" provided by those narratives.[75] Taking the story of David and Bathsheba as a paradigmatic example, Sternberg illustrates how the gaps that permeate all literary works not only engage readers by inviting them to actualize the meaning of the text through a process of interpretation ("gap-filling"), but also highlight the nature of the text itself as a literary work of art. Particularly in the case of complex, tightly woven narratives, gaps and ambiguities that refuse univocal resolution force readers to choose among possible interpretations (not necessarily once and for all, but in a particular reading), knowing that each choice highlights and simultaneously minimizes particular aspects of the text itself.[76] This both emphasizes the details that are provided and holds the reader accountable for construing them in a certain fashion. In this way, the indeterminacy of a text defies those who wish to possess it, and demands that those who read may only enter into it, interpret it, and thereby appropriate it and be changed by it.

Robert M. Fowler and R. Alan Culpepper demonstrate similar principles at work in their respective works on the Gospels of Mark and John. According to Fowler, while Mark certainly offers a good deal of straightforwardly "referential" information that grounds the narrative,

---

75. Meier Sternberg, *The Poetics of Biblical Narrative* (Bloomington: Indiana University Press, 1985), pp. 186-229.

76. "A simultaneous reading of a text from two unresolvable perspectives, with its constant movement between the rivals, not only enriches every doubled construct, actional or psychological. It inevitably makes for heightened perceptibility. It sharpens our awareness of the work's verbal art, foregrounds the modes of expression, and brings out the more subtle features of the represented events. Each detail assumes importance, deriving from the support or resistance it offers to the hypotheses and from the coincident pleasure afforded by its double reading. In short, the ambiguity calls attention to the literary texture as such" (Sternberg, *Poetics of Biblical Narrative*, pp. 227-28).

the "indirection" of Mark defies the reader's desire to obtain "objective knowledge" and seeks instead to teach the reader a "frame of mind" through its literary effect on the reader.[77] Similarly, Culpepper suggests that the plot and characterization of John confront the reader with distinct responses to Christ so that, in the climax of the gospel, when the reader is encountered by the Risen Christ through the confession of the narrator, the reader must respond with belief or disbelief.[78] Both the narratively rendered character of Jesus and the distance provided by the multiple options by which to respond to him make it possible for the reader to appropriate the confession of the text. On all these counts, the biblical literature (and, indeed, all great literature) provide both narrated information as well as the critical distance by which readers can appropriate that information.

Two homileticians have also recently offered proposals that resonate with my own to the degree that they highlight the need for sermons not only to offer narrative content and communal identity but also to safeguard the distance in which hearers can be encountered by, and appropriate, the message of the sermon. While neither theorist executes the move I suggest fully, they are at least promising indicators that we may be on the right track.

In her work, *Performing the Word,* Jana Childers notes that one of the similarities between preaching and theater is the necessity for distance:

> The role of distance is first of all a practical one; the performer and the audience must be separated from each other in order for the audience to see. Distance makes the sight lines work. . . . But distance in the theatre or in the worship service provides for more than physical ease. It creates a place for something to happen. It creates arena.[79]

The able actor or preacher uses this physical distance to "create a psychological or spiritual space" in which the audience can safely suspend its disbelief and make themselves vulnerable to the movement and po-

77. Robert M. Fowler, *Let the Reader Understand: Reader-Response Criticism and the Gospel of Mark* (Minneapolis: Fortress Press, 1991), pp. 222-27.

78. R. Alan Culpepper, *Anatomy of the Fourth Gospel: A Study in Literary Design* (Philadelphia: Fortress Press, 1983), pp. 145-48.

79. Jana Childers, *Performing the Word: Preaching as Theatre* (Nashville: Abingdon Press, 1998), p. 45.

tency of the drama enacted on the stage or in the pulpit. Hence, preaching, like good drama, involves a mix of identification and distance. As Childers writes, "preachers work to create a climate where the audience *may believe*. This ability to believe depends on getting the titrate just right — this much involvement, this much distance."[80] Because Childers's interest does not lie in this direction, she only mentions, but does not develop, this commonality between performance and preaching. Further, and as we will see below, it will prove crucial to avoid reading Childers and others as suggesting that the preacher's communicational devices are what creates (or precludes) faith, as that is the work of the Holy Spirit. Nevertheless, Childers's recognition of the need for dramatic involvement and critical distance is suggestive.

Writing in a similar vein, Robin R. Meyers adapts communication theory to suggest that preachers need to relocate the primary force of speaking from the speaker to the hearer.[81] Meyers contends, in fact, that rather than seek to persuade their hearers, preachers should aim to provide both the information and the distance by which hearers can persuade themselves.[82] This means, for Meyers, that preachers seek in the sermon preparation first to persuade themselves and then in their preaching offer evidence of what they have found persuasive to their hearers.[83] In order to achieve this, according to Meyers, the preacher strives for an authority of "appropriation" — "until the listener authenticates [the gospel] in his own experience, grasps it as true, and articulates it through the creation of new, self-generated messages, there is no authority per se in the original message."[84] While Meyers's own effort is hampered by the limited attention he gives to the biblical and theological content of the "message" — and the rhetorical demands that message may make — his recognition that hearers must appropriate the sermon for themselves is helpful.[85]

80. Childers, *Performing the Word*, p. 46.

81. Robin R. Meyers, *With Ears to Hear: Preaching as Self-Persuasion* (Cleveland: Pilgrim Press, 1993), p. 49.

82. Meyers, *With Ears to Hear*, p. 6.

83. Meyers, *With Ears to Hear*, p. 15.

84. Meyers, *With Ears to Hear*, p. 53.

85. For a critique of Meyers in terms of content and rhetorical "naïveté," see André Resner Jr., *Preacher and Cross: Person and Message in Theology and Rhetoric* (Grand Rapids: Eerdmans, 1999), pp. 75-80.

By referring briefly to both biblical and homiletical texts that suggest a similar dynamic to what I have described as narrative identity and critical distance, I hope to make my use of the dialectic between participation and distanciation more plausible and imaginable. Further, I hope that it helps to demonstrate the utility of "confession" as a homiletical term in a postmodern age. For "confession" is a single word that implies *simultaneously* (1) a grounding in a communal understanding of the gospel and (2) an articulation of that identity that does not demand from the hearer its own validation and therefore preserves the critical distance in which the hearer might appropriate the confession. This simultaneity is important, as I do not want to suggest that the dialectic I employ is a temporal one; that is, that one first grounds hearers in a narrative and then creates critical space in which they can evaluate it, and so on. Rather, I want to suggest a form of preaching that offers narrative identity and critical distance in roughly the same measure and at roughly the same time. To illustrate my desire, I want to highlight the dynamic quality of biblical interpretation and suggest that a similar dynamism also animates biblical, confessional preaching.

At the outset of his *Freud and Philosophy*, Paul Ricoeur makes a distinction between two types of hermeneutics that imply distinct, even opposing stances toward the text they seek to interpret. Employing the first, a reader approaches the text with utmost respect, regards it as a sacred symbol, takes its validity on faith, and seeks to listen to it conscientiously so as to discern the message it seeks to transmit. Employing the second, a reader approaches the text with suspicion, seeks to demystify its claims, to penetrate through its surface descriptions, and explain its "real" meaning by bringing external criteria to bear. Stating that there is no "general" or neutral hermeneutics, Ricoeur names the first approach a hermeneutics of *restoration* and calls the second a hermeneutics of *suspicion*.[86]

Much interpretation in the wake of Ricoeur's classification has set these two strategies at odds, claiming that they are intractably opposed approaches to a text or tradition.[87] In distinction to this assumption, I

86. Paul Ricoeur, *Freud and Philosophy: An Essay on Interpretation*, trans. Denis Savage (New Haven: Yale University Press, 1970), pp. 26-27.
87. Hans Frei, for instance, reclaims a hermeneutics of restoration and poses his

want to affirm with Walter Brueggemann that one can and must employ both strategies simultaneously when approaching the biblical text. Asserting that the entire textual process — its formation by the biblical authors and editors, its interpretation by exegetes and preachers, and its reception by present-day readers and hearers — is "always a mixture of faith and vested interest," Brueggemann contends that interpretation is necessarily a dynamic, and at times difficult, task. As he explains,

> To study "the social process" is to pay attention to this vexed combination. That the textual process is skewed by interest requires a hermeneutics of suspicion. That the textual process is an act of serious faith permits a hermeneutics of retrieval. Despite the identification of these two hermeneutics, the matter remains complicated and problematic because we cannot practice one hermeneutic and then the other. We cannot first sort out vested interest and then affirm faith, because vested interest and faith always come together and cannot be so nicely distinguished. We must simply recognize that the two always come together, even in the midst of our best efforts of discernment and criticism.[88]

That is, the Christian interpreter and preacher simultaneously *trusts* that God speaks through the biblical witness even while admitting — nay, expecting — that God's speech comes through human speech and therefore always suffers the incompleteness of human perception and distortion of human sin.

For this reason, there is no way to read — or preach! — the biblical texts faithfully apart from this paradoxical mixture of trust and suspicion. Unaware of the historical and contextual boundness of any speech, even biblical speech, a hermeneutics of restoration *alone* leads to a "hermeneutics of nostalgia" and posits an a-historical, a-contextual ideal

---

intratextual method of interpretation against the extratextual practices implied by a hermeneutics of suspicion (*Types of Christian Theology*, p. 12). Similarly, Richard B. Hays proposes a "hermeneutics of trust" over and against one of suspicion. "Salvation by Trust? Reading the Bible Faithfully," *The Christian Century* 114 (1997): 218-23.

88. Walter Brueggemann, "The Social Nature of the Biblical Text," in *Preaching as a Social Act: Theology and Practice*, ed. Arthur Van Seeters (Nashville: Abingdon Press, 1988), p. 131.

that cannot affect, let alone transform, the present-day reader.[89] Conversely, lacking even a modicum of trust in the text's integrity as, in some sense, "Word of God," a hermeneutics of suspicion *alone* leads to a "hermeneutics of alienation," where the bond between reader and text is irreparably severed.[90]

In a manner akin to that by which the interpreter comes to the texts wielding simultaneously a hermeneutics of restoration (or retrieval) and one of suspicion, the preacher also offers her confession of the meaning and import of the text to the gathered assembly in a way that both grounds hearers in a narrative, communal identity while simultaneously safeguarding the space in which they can appropriate, rather than merely give their assent to, the gospel proclaimed. Confession, that is, is not "either/or," either identity or distance, but inevitably and necessarily both/and, both offering of a communal identity and maintaining the distance in which to appropriate it. By my affirmation and criticism of both Charles Campbell's postliberal narrative and Lucy Atkinson Rose's postmodern conversation, I hope to identify for preachers distinct elements of the sermonic confession that, in order to be confession, must be employed together.

Finally, and before moving to the concrete implications of a confessional homiletic for the preparation of sermons, it is also important to note that I have focused this discussion primarily on the preacher's confession rather than on the hearer's response. In doing so I make a conscious distinction between the *words* of the preacher and the *work* of the Holy Spirit. In the end, and as the Apostle Paul testifies, the question of why some hearers are moved to faith and others are not can only be consigned to the mystery and providence of God. Similarly, as not only Paul, but also Augustine, Luther, and others have argued, faith itself is a gift of grace, without which fallen humans cannot believe.[91]

---

89. I borrow and adapt the term "nostalgia" from Barbara Hernstein Smith's critique of what she describes as Alasdair MacIntyre's "axiologically nostalgic meditation on the decline of moral discourse and practice in modern times." *Contingencies of Value: Alternative Perspectives in Critical Theory* (Cambridge, Mass.: Harvard University Press, 1988), p. 86.

90. Although I disagree strongly with the way he has employed it, I borrow and adapt the term "hermeneutics of alienation" from Leander Keck, *The Church Confident* (Nashville: Abingdon Press, 1993), p. 60.

91. With regard to Paul, see Rom. 9-11; for Augustine, see *On the Predestination of the*

This may help to explain why, upon hearing the biblical text read or preached, we often do not feel "invited" to "choose" whether we believe it, but rather compelled to recognize that which we have already come to believe or doubt.[92] As Thomas Kuhn notes, because conversion overturns the neat order we have imposed upon, and use to make sense of, our world, it regularly happens essentially *against* our will and most often in spite of us, not because of us.[93] And yet, the decision for — or, perhaps better, the acceptance of — the new reality to which one is converted is certainly not coerced, but instead is prompted or compelled by the encounter with the Word. Coming to faith, like falling in love, certainly involves one's participation, but nevertheless is rarely if ever experienced as simply a volitional act. Rather, in coming to faith and falling in love there is a sense of being out of control, even overwhelmed, by something larger than oneself. Curiously, even inexplicably, in such circumstances one is free, but not free; neither coerced, nor in control; an active participant, yet passive recipient. Such is the mystery of God's election.

Hence, the critical distance for which I advocate is not primarily the space in which a supposedly autonomous or neutral hearer can "choose" between different belief-options, but rather the space in which a lively encounter between Word and hearer can take place through the power of the Holy Spirit. Productive distanciation, therefore, not only protects the integrity of the hearer (which seems essential if we are to speak of living faith, not mindless adherence, and of love, not rape), but also provides the arena in which the hearer and Spirit-driven-Word dance. If either the hearer is absorbed by the Word (as in Campbell) or there is no definite Word (as in Rose), the likelihood of such an encounter is diminished.

Saints, trans. R. E. Wallis, in *Basic Writings of Saint Augustine*, vol. 1, ed. Whitney J. Oates (New York: Random House, 1948), pp. 777-817; for Luther, see *The Bondage of the Will* (1525), in *Luther's Works*, American edition, 55 vols., ed. Jaroslav Pelikan and Helmut T. Lehman (St. Louis and Philadelphia: Concordia Publishing House and Fortress Press, 1955ff.) (Hereafter cited as *LW.*)

92. In this sense, as Rudolf Bultmann indicates in his comments on John 3:18, is Jesus the *Revealer*, not only of God but also of the human heart, as the eschatological judgment which Christ not simply represents or brings, but actually *is*, makes "manifest what [one] is." Bultmann, *The Gospel of John*, trans. G. R. Beasley-Murray, R. W. N. Hoare, and J. K. Riches (Philadelphia: Westminster Press, 1971).

93. Thomas Kuhn, *The Structure of Scientific Revolutions*, 2nd ed. (Chicago: University of Chicago Press, 1970), pp. 198-204.

By focusing on the preacher's responsibility to take care for both proclaiming to hearers a narrative identity and safeguarding their critical distance, I therefore do not seek to "explain" the power of the gospel to bring persons to faith, but rather to suggest the means by which to leave open the space in which the hearer can be encountered in all of her integrity by the living and active Word, come to faith through the Holy Spirit, and appropriate as her own the message and identity proclaimed. As I will describe in greater detail in Chapter Six, I take my cue for this proposal from God's own self-disclosure in the "Word made flesh," Jesus the Christ. For in Jesus Christ, and most particularly in his cross and resurrection, one encounters a word that has been accurately described as "summons," "demand," and "promise," even as it simultaneously is unmistakably — and, in fact, painfully — noncoercive. That is, in the "weak" word of the crucified and risen Christ, one encounters God's most eloquent and compelling utterance.[94]

With this in mind, and in moving toward the final chapters of this project, it will be helpful to note that preachers occupy a unique role in relation to confessing faith in the weekly worship service as they are both recipients of confession and confessors. This is true not only in terms of the dialogical nature of worship — where the preacher speaks and listens to the congregation, both confessing and hearing in turn their confession of faith — but also in view of the preacher's stance between canon and community, both receiving the confession of the text and articulating a confession to the congregation.

In one way, this is precisely the way confession works in the life of all believers, as confession seeks to prompt belief that leads to future confession in both the worship service and their life in the world. While affirming this aspect of "the ministry of all the baptized," it is also important to recognize that the preacher has been set apart by the community to engage both canon and community so as to prompt, focus, and nurture the conversation of faith by publicly "confessing Christ." To accomplish this, preachers play two roles or, perhaps better, are involved in two conversations. First, they are involved in a conversation

94. See James F. Kay, *Christus Praesens: A Reconsideration of Rudolf Bultmann's Christology* (Grand Rapids: Eerdmans, 1994), pp. 111-17. This suggests an interesting conception of the Trinity, where God the Father is the one who speaks (the *deus loquens*), God the Son the vulnerable word spoken, and God the Holy Spirit the one who effects hearing of that word unto faith.

with the text by which they hope to hear the text's confession and thereby be prompted to their own confessing of faith through the sermon. Second, they are then involved with the corresponding conversation with the congregation through their sermon whereby they hope their confession draws their hearers more deeply into the Christian conversation. They therefore approach each conversation with a slightly different concern. In the first (with the text), the elements of participation and distanciation govern their exegesis; in the second (with the congregation), those same elements govern their sermon preparation, as they seek both to confess in response to their listening to the text *and* encourage further conversation and confession in their hearers. To clarify these distinct conversations, and offer some practical guidance in how to negotiate them, Chapter Five investigates the preacher's conversation with the text, and Chapter Six explores the preacher's conversation with the congregation.

CHAPTER 5

Confession and the Biblical Canon

Throughout this work, I have contended that preaching plays one distinctive role in the larger life and conversation of the faithful: to proclaim the gospel in a way that both grounds hearers in a narrative, communal identity while simultaneously preserving the space in which they are able not simply to listen to, but also be encountered by and appropriate, the gospel proclaimed. I have reclaimed the Christian word "confession" to describe this kind of postfoundational preaching because it has functioned biblically and theologically in two important ways. First, it functions as a summary of the "essential" Christian tradition, offering a communal identity and pattern for making sense of the world; in this capacity, we may describe confession as the *fides quae creditur*. Second, confession functions to describe the practice of articulating that faith (and thereby activating and even actualizing that tradition) in response both to the proclamation of the word and the present circumstances and needs of the hearer and world in such a way that it prompts faith or disbelief in the hearers; in this respect, we may liken confession to the *fides qua creditur*.

Let me say it again: Preaching plays *one* role in the larger conversation of the faithful. It is important to retain the singularity of this conviction for three reasons. First, it guards against preachers expecting too much from their sermons. Even the best preaching cannot by itself sustain a community of faith. There are many other components, in the liturgy and common life of the community and in their shared ministry in and to the world, that also contribute to this conversation. Preaching plays one role, even an essential role, but one nonetheless.

Second, keeping in mind a more modest goal for preaching helps to remind us that we offer our sermons in service to a larger cause, the conversation of the faithful that is kindled by a dynamic encounter with the living Word of God through the power of the Holy Spirit. In this respect, saying that preaching plays one primary role does not in any way diminish, but in fact enhances, the importance of the preaching office and, further, clarifies its purpose, as we perceive that preaching performs a crucial, catalytic function for the community by prompting, focusing, shaping, and nurturing the larger conversation of faith by which the community lives.

Third, preaching understood as confessing faith in Jesus Christ so as to prompt and nurture the conversation of the faithful provides a guide for preparing properly "confessional" sermons. In the final two chapters of this project, therefore, I want to explore the impact of a "confessional homiletic" on the two principal conversation partners with whom the preacher interacts, looking at the biblical canon in this chapter and the gathered, worshiping community of faith in the next.

The Biblical Canon as "Witness"

I have argued that in the context of postmodern doubt we are called to confess, rather than attempt to prove, what we believe to be the truth. On one level this is a modest proposal, simply a rethinking of the role of our speech and proclamation about "truth" and "reality" in light of the current context. At another level, however, this is a tremendously immodest assertion. For postmodernity does not simply claim that for the past fifty years or so it has been difficult to maintain the certainty for which modernity strove; rather, it contends that modernist certainty was *from the outset* illusory, deceptive, and very often destructive. In a similar way, I am not only claiming that confession *happens to be* a useful way to think about speaking and preaching in this era, but rather that the postmodern turn has done us the service of reminding us that *all* speech about truth and reality *has always been* a matter of confession, even when speakers have claimed otherwise.

From this vantage point, I contend that we recognize the Bible fundamentally as a collection of *confessions*, of *testimony*, of *claims* and *assertions* that purport to speak of truth and reality both accurately and

146

with integrity. In a number of books on the subject, biblical scholar
Walter Brueggemann has advanced a similar claim:

> I wish to propose that *the rhetorical practice among exiles given in scripture is best understood as testimony,* that is, utterance by alleged first-person witnesses who offer an account of experience that depends solely upon the trustworthiness of the witnesses, but that cannot appeal for verification either to agreed-upon *metaphysics* or to external *historical data.*[1]

Brueggemann designates the Bible as testimony for two main reasons. The first is eminently pragmatic: we approach the Bible as persons who have no recourse to the events it names.[2] We are, therefore, dependent on the biblical texts if we seek to come to any conclusions about the "truth" of their subject matter and claims.

The second reason for speaking of Scripture as testimony is that it speaks of itself that way. In this regard, Brueggemann points to central passages from "second" Isaiah, where Israel is called to bear witness to the Lord's sovereignty to all the world, and takes the following passage as paradigmatic:

> Bring forth the people who are blind, yet have eyes,
>   who are deaf, yet have ears!
> Let all the nations gather together,
>   and let the peoples assemble.
> Who among them declared this,
>   and foretold to us the former things?
> Let them bring their witnesses to justify them,
>   and let them say, "It is true."
> You are my witnesses, says the Lord,
>   and my servant whom I have chosen,
> so that you may know and believe me
>   and understand that I am he.
> Before me no god was formed,

---

1. Walter Brueggemann, *Cadences of Home: Preaching Among Exiles* (Louisville: Westminster/John Knox Press, 1997), p. 44.

2. Walter Brueggemann, *Theology of the Old Testament: Testimony, Dispute, Advocacy* (Minneapolis: Fortress Press, 1997), p. 117.

> nor shall there be any after me.
> I, I am the Lord,
>   and besides me there is no savior.
> I declared and saved and proclaimed,
>   when there was no strange god among you;
>   and you are my witnesses, says the Lord.
> I am God, and also henceforth I am he;
>   there is no one who can deliver from my hand;
>   I work and who can hinder it?
>
> (43:8-13; comp. 44:8; 48:6, 20)[3]

Brueggemann's assessment of Scripture as testimony directs his work down two distinct paths. First, it leads him to reject historical-criticism as the proper method of biblical study and to pursue a rhetorical interpretation instead. Whatever "may" have occurred in Israel's history is beyond our reach and therefore unimportant: "What we have available to us is the speech of this community." For this reason, historical concerns are secondary considerations, at best. He continues,

> Note well that in focusing on speech, we tend to bracket out all questions of historicity. We are not asking, "What happened?" but "What is said?" To inquire into the historicity of the text is a legitimate enterprise, but it does not, I suggest, belong to the work of Old Testament theology. In like manner, we bracket out all questions of ontology, which ask about the "really real." It may well be, in the end, that there is no historicity to Israel's faith claim, but that is not the position taken here. And it may well be that there is no "being" behind Israel's faith assertion, but that is not a claim made here. We have, however, few tools for recovering "what happened" and even fewer for recovering "what is," and therefore those issues must be held in abeyance, pending the credibility and persuasiveness of Israel's testimony, on which everything depends.[4]

Second, Brueggemann's view of Scripture as "testimony" leads him to describe the nature and function of the biblical canon along the lines of "testimony and trial." His use of this metaphor greatly shapes his un-

---

3. Brueggemann, *Theology of the Old Testament*, pp. 44-53.
4. Brueggemann, *Theology of the Old Testament*, p. 118.

148

derstanding of both text and reader. The Bible, according to Brueggemann, contains Israel's witness to the Lord's sovereignty, a testimony offered amid rival, competing claims about the nature of reality. In the
exilic literature this is particularly clear when, as a disestablished, exilic
community, Israel has no access to the vehicles of sanctioned legitimation and its only recourse is testimony.[5] That testimony is now in the
hands of present-day readers. As a consequence, readers stand in relation to the text something like a court jury called to decide the "truthfulness" of certain testimony. Because it is only the witness that "alleg-
edly had access to [the] actual event," the court is inherently dependent
on the testimony of the witness: "The court . . . has no access to the 'actual event' besides the testimony. It cannot go behind the testimony to
the event, but must take the testimony as the 'real portrayal.' Indeed, it
is futile for the court to speculate behind the testimony."[6] Functioning
as jurors who have not participated in the events to be adjudicated,
readers consider carefully the testimony of the witness and then render
a judgment about its truthfulness.

Brueggemann's creative use of the metaphor of testimony and trial
commends itself on several fronts, not least of which is that it is excep-
tionally appropriate to the postmodern era, where the former "agreed-
upon" metaphysics have passed and each community must "make its
case" before any and all who will listen. Taking the postmodern milieu
and biblical text equally seriously, Brueggemann perceives in the biblical narrative not simply the record of a particular religion but a claim
to an alternative reality, and he dares to set that reality amid all the
competing realities of the day.[7] Further, Brueggemann rightly directs
us to the witness of the biblical canon itself, those texts under and
around which we gather as a community of faith, reminding us that
whatever we may wonder or suspect about the historicity of events behind the text, its "speech is the reality to be studied."[8] Finally,
Brueggemann offers a compelling sense of the preacher as "the last in a
long line of witnesses" who, dependent on all the witnesses that have

5. Brueggemann, *Cadences of Home,* p. 45.

6. Brueggemann, *Theology of the Old Testament,* pp. 120-21.

7. In this regard, Brueggemann rightly perceives that where Lyotard claims an "end
to metanarratives," the situation is actually "one of conflict and competition between
deeply held narratives" (*Theology of the Old Testament,* p. 712).

8. Brueggemann, *Theology of the Old Testament,* p. 118.

come before, is now called to give voice to the Bible's own claims and in this way "hope to convince the court that this is a credible account of how the world is."[9]

Despite these clear strengths, however, I believe that Brueggemann's construal nonetheless makes it difficult to speak intelligibly of the Bible as God's dynamic Word. This becomes most clear as Brueggemann describes the function of the readers of Scripture, not simply to assess the Bible's truthfulness, but to *make* it truthful. As he writes,

> when the court makes a decision and agrees to accept some version of reality based on some testimony, the testimony is accepted as true — that is, it becomes true. In the decision of a court, the process of the verdict, the testimony is turned into reality. The defendant is pronounced to be acquitted or guilty. In the parlance of the court, the verdict is the establishment of a legal reality.

In such a scenario, there is no "Word of God" in any *external* or *extrinsic* sense. There are only words *about* God shaped and uttered by humans to be received by humans as true or false and, if true, deemed as "revelation." As Brueggemann continues,

> If we describe this process theologically — or, more specifically, in the practice of the Old Testament — we may say that testimony becomes revelation. That is, the testimony that Israel bears to the character of God is taken by the ecclesial community of the text as a reliable disclosure about the true character of God. Here we touch on the difficulty of the authority of Scripture, which has usually been articulated in the scholastic categories of inspiration and revelation. It is simpler and more helpful, I believe, to recognize that when utterance in the Bible is taken as truthful, human testimony is taken as revelation that discloses the true reality of God.[10]

The authority of the Word, then, resides entirely with the human community that utters, interprets, proclaims, and ultimately verifies its authenticity. Brueggemann's description, reminiscent at several points of George Lindbeck's postliberal understanding of "truth," rests

9. Brueggemann, *Cadences of Home*, p. 45.
10. Brueggemann, *Theology of the Old Testament*, p. 121.

on the conviction that the Bible cannot refer beyond its own semiotic universe and therefore can be validated only "from within."[11] Ultimately, there is no "really Real" beyond the testimony of Israel, as even God becomes *a product and consequence of Israel's testimony.*[12] In this sense, as he asserts, *"utterance is everything."*[13]

But whatever the merits of Brueggemann's position vis-à-vis postmodern, antifoundational categories of "truth" and "reference," one is pressed to question whether it accurately reflects either the biblical text's own presentation of itself or the way Christians have traditionally received it. My concern is not to determine whether Brueggemann is *right* in some absolute sense, but rather to ask whether he presents a description of the biblical texts that the church will recognize. I suspect that he does not for at least two reasons. First, and as even Lindbeck admits, it is doubtful that either the authors or significant interpreters of the Bible have ever viewed Christianity and its scriptural texts in anything other than ontologically referential terms.[14] In short, it is difficult, if not impossible, for Christian faith to dismiss Scripture's ability and intention to refer to some Reality beyond itself. As Brevard Childs contends, "It is basic to Christian theology to reckon with an extra-biblical reality, namely the resurrected Christ who evoked the New Testament witness."[15]

Second, I question both the legitimacy and fidelity of assuming that God's activity is entirely limited to the pages of Scripture. That is, while we may not have access to the "events" the Bible narrates, we do have access to the God to whom it witnesses, the God whom Israel and

11. On Brueggemann's affinity for Lindbeck, see *Theology of the Old Testament*, p. 574; and *Texts Under Negotiation* (Minneapolis: Fortress Press, 1993), p. ix.

12. *Cadences of Home*, p. 45; see also *Theology of the Old Testament*, p. 714.

13. *Theology of the Old Testament*, p. 122.

14. "Paul and Luther, at any rate, quite clearly believed that Christ's Lordship is objectively real no matter what the faith or unfaith of those who hear or say the words." George A. Lindbeck, *The Nature of Doctrine: Religion and Theology in a Postliberal Age* (Philadelphia: Westminster Press, 1984), p. 66.

15. Brevard Childs, *Biblical Theology of the Old and New Testaments* (Minneapolis: Fortress Press, 1993), p. 20. One might also add the Holy Spirit, who the church confesses inspires both Old and New Testaments, as another "extra-biblical reality." It should be noted, however, that Brueggemann believes that Childs has succumbed to the "temptation" to "lust for Being, for establishing ontological reference behind the text" (*Theology of the Old Testament*, p. 714).

the early church confessed stands behind those events. Childs again is helpful: "to see the Bible as a type of symbol system construing reality into which the reader is invited to enter does not, in my opinion, accord with the model of biblical proclamation, whether by the Old Testament prophets or the New Testament apostles, in which God's Word enters into our world to transform it."[16] Similarly, as Terrence Fretheim writes,

> The God of the Bible, according to its own witness, is actively engaged in the world outside Israel; this work has good effects and shapes Israel's own testimony. God's continuing activity in that extrabiblical story is of such a character as to bring a potentially critical word to bear on the Bible and its testimony regarding God (one thinks of patriarchy) and to enable its readers to hear more clearly where *the Bible itself* is being self-critical, where the Bible would say no to one or another element in its own testimony. Difficult issues of discernment and criteria are quickly at hand, but we cannot in the face of those difficulties retreat into the narrative world of the Bible, so that the text is thought to absorb every human story into its own.[17]

The risk of positing that Israel's — or the church's — utterance is not simply the supreme, but in fact the *only* reality, it seems to me, is that the "text" moves so forcibly to the foreground that the saving God to which the text refers all but disappears into the background.[18] In so doing Brueggemann erases the distinction between the Creator and the creature and ends up with, not *God's* Word, but only *words about* God.

We can locate the problem of Brueggemann's analysis, I believe, not so much in his understanding of *the text as witness*, but rather in his understanding of the nature of *witness* itself. This appears the case in at

16. Childs, *Biblical Theology*, p. 22.

17. Terence E. Fretheim, "Some Reflections on Brueggemann's God," in *God in the Fray: A Tribute to Walter Brueggemann*, ed. Tod Linafelt and Timothy K. Beal (Minneapolis: Fortress Press, 1998), p. 26.

18. What Ronald Thiemann wrote of George Lindbeck's intratextuality applies as well to Brueggemann, as Thiemann perceives that "the real danger that in much of Lindbeck's essay talk about 'text' stands in the place of talk about 'God.'" Ronald Thiemann, "Response to George Lindbeck," *Theology Today* 43 (1986): 378.

least four ways. First, Brueggemann takes what is a minor motif in Scripture — the legal use of "witness" — and develops it into a governing theme.[19] As we shall see below, there are other, more frequent, uses of "witness" throughout the Bible.

Second, at various points he fundamentally misunderstands the legal understanding of testimony and, indeed, the function of the court more generally. As both Bernhard Anderson and James Barr suggest, courts rarely depend so entirely on testimony that they may not inquire "behind it." Not only is there cross-examination and counter-testimony (as Brueggemann acknowledges to good effect), but also physical and historical *evidence* that supports, contradicts, or in some way explains and helps make sense of the testimony.[20] While physical evidence in and of itself is no more or less ambiguous than testimony, it seems imprudent to rule out any and all investigations "behind" the testimony, especially when (as I will argue later) such research can be put in service of hearing the testimony in question more fully. More importantly, however, Brueggemann conflates "legal reality" and "reality" itself.[21] While a court is convened to render judgment on disputed positions, its conclusions are hardly received, even by the court itself, as incontrovertible; hence, lawyers press for either conviction or acquittal (decisions that can be reexamined and overturned), not primarily for final determinations of guilt or innocence.[22]

Third, Brueggemann greatly inflates the role and importance of the readers, at least in relation to the self-understanding of the biblical witness. As Rolf Jacobson points out, while in Brueggemann's treatment the reading community stands as judge and jury of the validity of

19. See Hermann Strathmann, "μάρτυς," *Theological Dictionary of the New Testament,* vol. 4, ed. Gerhard Kittel, trans. Geoffrey W. Bromiley (Grand Rapids: Eerdmans, 1967), pp. 474-515.

20. Bernhard W. Anderson, *Contours of Old Testament Theology* (Minneapolis: Fortress Press, 1999), pp. 26-27; James Barr, *The Concept of Biblical Testimony: An Old Testament Perspective* (Minneapolis: Fortress Press, 1999), pp. 548-49.

21. Hence, Jacques Derrida discriminates between a deconstructible law that rests upon human convention *(droit)* and an "undeconstructible" justice that transcends such conventions. Derrida, "Force of Law: The 'Mystical Foundation of Authority,'" *Cardozo Law Review* 11, nos. 5-6 (1990): 919-1045, esp. 943-45.

22. It is precisely the court's inability to establish "reality" in so many cases — consider, for instance, the number of "wrongful convictions" overturned recently — that opponents of capital punishment argue warns strongly against imposing the death penalty.

the testimony, most often in the Old Testament, "when the trial metaphor is used, God is judge, prosecutor, and jury while humanity is the defendant."[23]

Fourth, and of greatest concern, is the degree to which Brueggemann's employment of "witness" as a legal term underplays its more prevalent religious use. Because Brueggemann relies at this point on the discussion of biblical testimony by Paul Ricoeur, it will be helpful to sketch briefly Ricoeur's contribution.[24] In an influential essay on "The Hermeneutics of Testimony," Ricoeur explores the "semantics" of testimony; that is, how "testimony" and "witness" function in everyday speech. He draws attention to two main uses of the word. First, there is what he calls a "quasi-empirical" meaning, where "witness" simply designates the action of testifying.[25] It is "quasi-empirical" because it is not perception itself, but rather the report of previous perception. This entails two implications: (1) The one who hears testimony is ineluctably dependent on the one who reports, and (2) testimony is at the service of judgment; it is offered, that is, to determine not simply what *happened*, but what it *means*.[26]

The second arena of semantic meaning Ricoeur describes as "quasi-juridical," for "testimony" is normally associated with the court.[27] Here Ricoeur outlines three implications. First, to speak of "testimony" is to imply some level of ambiguity (a situation of probability, not certainty) and some measure of contention between parties.[28] Second, it implies the question of justice (what is right and true) and the need to move toward judgment about the testimony (whether it is true or false).[29] Third, testimony is therefore always caught in the

23. Rolf Jacobson, review of *Theology of the Old Testament: Testimony, Dispute, Advocacy*, by Walter Brueggemann, *Koinonia* 11 (1999): 126.

24. Brueggemann acknowledges his debt to Ricoeur at several points. See *Theology of the Old Testament*, pp. 119-20; *Cadences of Home*, pp. 26, 59-61.

25. Paul Ricoeur, "The Hermeneutics of Testimony," in *Essays on Biblical Interpretation*, ed. Lewis S. Mudge (Philadelphia: Fortress Press, 1981), p. 123. His third category, the "problem of the witness," falls generally under his juridical concern (p. 129).

26. Ricoeur, "Testimony," p. 123. Hence, as Ricoeur indicates, simply being an "eyewitness" is not enough; one must have some sense of what light one's testimony sheds on the meaning of the events in question.

27. Ricoeur, "Testimony," p. 124. Not every report, that is, is considered "testimony."

28. Ricoeur, "Testimony," p. 125.

29. Ricoeur, "Testimony," p. 126.

"network of proof and persuasion"; it is part of a larger argument that seeks assent.[30] It is for this very reason — because it is inherently rhetorical — that the character (ethos) of the witness is involved. The quality of the testimony therefore necessarily involves the caliber of the witness, as the whole juridical system depends upon the witness's "good faith."[31]

Despite elucidating the value of these two uses, Ricoeur fails to name and describe explicitly an additional "semantic use" of testimony referring to religious conviction, one that we might describe as "quasi-religious." Not only is this the most dominant use of "witness" in the Old and New Testaments, but it also continues to function importantly in the church today.[32] Ricoeur does, in fact, explore what I have described as the "quasi-religious" dimension of testimony by comparing it to "confession," but he does not explicitly accord it the same "semantic" status as his earlier designations, and Brueggemann and others largely ignore this treatment.[33]

Interestingly, while Ricoeur distinguishes between "confession" and "testimony" — taking "confession" to relate primarily with the level of "meaning" or "significance" and "testimony" to a narrative history of events — he views them as inextricably dependent on each other.[34] For where testimony apart from a confession of meaning is mere report, confession apart from a narrative testimony quickly devolves into gnostic belief: "There is . . . no witness of the absolute who is not a witness of historic signs, no confessor of absolute meaning who

---

30. Ricoeur, "Testimony," p. 127.

31. Ricoeur, "Testimony," pp. 128-29.

32. See Strathmann, "μάρτυς," *TDNT* 4:474-515; and Mary McClintock Fulkerson, *Changing the Subject: Women's Discourses and Feminist Theology* (Minneapolis: Fortress Press, 1994), pp. 271-79.

33. As Brueggemann writes, "This notion of testimony has something in it of the religious 'testifying' of Baptists who tell in the congregation about the evidence for God in their lives. But I have reference to a different image, namely, a court of law before which Israel is to stand to give its testimony about the reality of Yahweh" (*Cadences of Home*, p. 45). Similarly, before commending a juridical reading of "witness," Thomas G. Long writes, "'witnessing' and 'giving a testimony' have often been associated with some of the more aggressive forms of evangelism. Homileticians have sniffed the odor of manipulation around these words and thus have stayed far away from them." *The Witness of Preaching* (Louisville: Westminster/John Knox Press, 1989), p. 43.

34. Ricoeur, "Testimony," p. 133.

is not a narrator of the acts of deliverance."[35] While noting that different gospels may emphasize one of these two over the other (Luke is more interested in testimony, John in confession), Ricoeur nevertheless asserts that both elements are always present and, because the gospels and so much of the Bible are essentially narrative, he describes the whole of Scripture as "testimony" built around a "confessional kernel." For this reason, Ricoeur then characteristically describes the dialectic between narration and confession that is held together by the fact that the biblical texts seek to make a case and validate their argument.[36]

In his eagerness to harvest the juridical content of "witness," Brueggemann tremendously underplays the religious significance of the term and its inherent similarity to "confession."[37] It is precisely through this relationship, however, that one might describe more satisfactorily a Christian understanding of the Bible as "the Word of God." For this reason, while wanting to retain the many positive elements of Brueggemann's suggestive proposal, I want also to advocate another view of Scripture, one that takes its dual status as the words of humans *and* the Word of God with equal seriousness.

The Bible as Confession

In seeking to reclaim a sense that the Bible is not merely words about God, but also somehow God's own dynamic Word, I want to return to the linguistic analyses of J. L. Austin and John R. Searle. By employing once again the language of "speech acts" and "performative utterances," I want to be clear that I do not seek to *prove* that the Bible is God's Word but rather only to *make sense* of typical, even common Christian descriptions of the Bible as the Word of God. In other words, in seeing how language "works" in everyday usage, we may learn better how the written words of Scripture also "work" and thereby explore how we might understand the Bible to function as the "living and active" Word of God today (Heb. 4:12).

35. Ricoeur, "Testimony," p. 134; see also p. 139.
36. Ricoeur, "Testimony," p. 142.
37. This is particularly the case in the use of "witness" in John, where, as Strathmann writes, "μαρτυρεῖν and ὁμολογεῖν merge into one another" (Strathmann, "μάρτυς," *TDNT* 4:498).

Recall that while Austin began his investigation by contrasting constative speech (which can be assessed as "true or false" independent of any human conventions) and performative speech (which depends upon human convention to act upon the hearer), by the end of his work he had entirely rejected this dichotomy, contending that all language is inherently performative. Such a view of the dynamism of speech coincides with the Bible's own sense of the potency of language. According to the Bible, language, and especially God's language, is not merely descriptive but causal (Jer. 1:1-10; Heb. 4:12-13). The Bible depicts a God who creates by speaking (Gen. 1:1–2:3) and redeems through the Word made flesh (John 1:1-18). According to Donald Evans, it is precisely Austin's sense of the "force" of language that helps it to "make the biblical conception" of God's potent language "less alien."[38]

For this reason, it is not difficult to see why several theologians have seized upon the work of Austin and his heirs to characterize the language within the biblical witness. In particular, writers have focused on the nature of the gospel as promise. As Evans points out, a "promise," as a commissive utterance, is the most transparently self-involving of speech acts and therefore conveys clearly God's commitment to us through the series of covenants to which the Bible witnesses.[39] Christopher Morse notes the way in which promissory speech mediates between speech about God and the reality of God. Following Luther, he observes that promises do not fit the typical sign-to-reality relationship of descriptive speech. Rather, promises are causal, bringing into being something that formerly did not exist. Further, they establish a relationship between the promisor and the promisee and not only imply the commitment of the promisor but also call for a response (trust) from the promisee.[40] The Bible, according to Morse, is essentially "promissory narration" that reveals God as promisor, locates those promises in the concrete narratives of the Bible, and calls for a "correlative" response of faith and trust that orients believers toward mission

38. Donald D. Evans, *The Logic of Self-Involvement: A Philosophical Study of Everyday English with Special Reference to the Christian Use of Language about God as Creator* (London: SCM Press, 1963), p. 164.

39. Evans, *The Logic of Self-Involvement*, p. 32.

40. Christopher Morse, *The Logic of Promise in Moltmann's Theology* (Philadelphia: Fortress Press, 1979), pp. 21-22, 72.

to and for the world.[41] Similarly, Ronald Thiemann seeks to overcome Christianity's penchant during the modern era for grounding its claim to "truth" on foundational presuppositions by shifting the question from whether Christian faith is "true" to whether it is "warranted."[42] He does so by describing faith as trust in God's promises and arguing that while complete validation of a promise comes only in its complete fulfillment, in the meantime the identity of the promisor matters; hence the importance of the gospel as "narrated promise."[43]

Two observations are in order at this point. First, promise is certainly not the only performative utterance ascribed to God, but is confessed by Christians to be paradigmatic, and both halves of this assertion are important. As Evans indicates, God's Word is not only commissive (promissory) but also directive (commanding and sending) and declarative (judging and forgiving, commissioning and naming), and all of these call for a response from humans.[44] But whereas God is regularly "active" in and through all these kinds of speech, the Christian gospel, because it lives between Christ's cross and resurrection and Christ's triumphant return, is inherently promissory, living between the promise made and its final and complete fulfillment (1 Cor. 15).

Second, and perhaps more importantly for my purposes, the theologians employing speech-act theory pay insufficient attention to the means by which the ostensibly human words of the Bible (and preaching) may also simultaneously function as God's dynamic Word. Morse is most helpful in describing the nature and function of promissory speech:

> the human proclamation of God's promise is neither a human belief-utterance nor a human report of divine promise. It is the medium in which God's own act of promising may intelligibly be said to occur. Whether "God" indeed does so act can only be proven in

41. Morse, *The Logic of Promise*, pp. 75-81.

42. Ronald Thiemann, *Revelation and Theology: The Gospel as Narrated Promise* (Notre Dame: University of Notre Dame Press, 1985), pp. 71-91.

43. Thiemann, *Revelation and Theology*, pp. 93-94.

44. Evans actually uses Austin's terminology, "exercitive" and "verdictive," but for the sake of consistency I have supplied Searle's terms. See *The Logic of Self-Involvement*, p. 158.

forthcoming events. But is not such the case with any promise? One must take another at the other's word.

Hence, according to Morse, the need for faith, as faith

> is present whenever the proclamation of the gospel is heard as God's first-person, present indicative promise to us. The self-involvement which is evidenced in proclamation insofar as it becomes for faith a commissive speech-act is never dependent upon or equatable with the involvement or lack of involvement of any human speaker.[45]

Here and throughout his treatment of Moltmann's theology, Morse seems content to state that God has adopted the linguistic medium of promise and therefore that the Bible and preaching, because they make promises, are God's Word. Several questions persist in the face of such a construction. How do the specific promises of the Bible (and preaching), as opposed to all other promises, function to convey God's Word? Further, do all promises, even biblical promises, convey God's Word? For instance, are the promises to destroy Israel's enemies as pertinent as God's promise to bless all the world through Israel? If not, how do we discriminate between them? And what of the other types of speech acts in the Bible? Are these also God's Word? Finally, at times Morse seems to collapse illocutionary and perlocutionary acts, as the self-involvement of the speaker (the biblical author or preacher) is unimportant while the correlative response of the hearer (faith) seems critical in speaking of the promise as God's Word.

For his part, Thiemann speaks briefly of the complex act of "double agency," whereby one person speaks for another. Taking the example of absolution from Christian liturgy, Thiemann illustrates, "Though the speaker in the liturgical act is the presiding minister, the speaker who is committed to action is *God*." Such instances of double agency, Thiemann continues, are part and parcel of everyday communication.

> Consider the following examples: A sister calls to her brother, "Mom says, 'it's time for dinner!'"; a town crier reads a royal decree in the public square; a minister reads a Presidential proclamation from the

---

45. Morse, *The Logic of Promise*, p. 77.

pulpit on Thanksgiving morning. In every case one speaker speaks on behalf of another agent and acts the agent's intention to "call," "decree," or "proclaim." All that is required for intelligibility is that the context and/or content of the address make clear the situation of double agency.[46]

Because the Bible openly purports to speak for God, according to Thiemann, it does; in short, Thiemann seems to think that double agency ensures that the Bible speaks for God. But lots of people purport to speak for others and for God. My mother may not, in fact, have called us to dinner, even though my sister says so because she wants to sit in the chair I occupy. Somewhat similarly, do all the voices of Scripture — which can be said to employ double agency in a similar fashion — speak God's Word equally? Further, and more importantly, how do the promises *in* the narrative address the reader of the narrative directly? That is, one might read a lot of narratives with promises, even promises attributed to God, and not perceive them as direct address but, instead, as report, hearsay, even fiction. Thiemann speaks of the "openness" of Matthew's gospel as an invitation to the reader to enter into the narrative world, but surely Matthew's work is no more "open" than any good work of literature.[47] In short, I do not think Thiemann successfully addresses Bultmann's charge that such a Jesus — this time taken as a narrated character rather than a historical figure — "does not make any direct demand on us, nor does he condemn us for any deed we have committed against him. . . . For actually he is only seen making demands on others and pronouncing judgment on others. . . . I have done him no wrong and he has nothing to forgive me."[48]

While appreciating the contributions of Morse and Thiemann, I want to move beyond their use of linguistic analysis to describe how discrete speech acts within the Bible operate and employ speech-act theory to illumine how the Bible as a whole may function as God's

46. Thiemann, *Revelation and Theology*, p. 106. While speaking of the liturgy, Thiemann makes clear that he intends his illustration to explain both liturgical and biblical speech (p. 105).

47. Thiemann, *Revelation and Theology*, p. 143.

48. Rudolf Bultmann, "On the Question of Christology," in *Faith and Understanding*, ed. Robert W. Funk, trans. Louise Pettibone Smith (Philadelphia: Fortress Press, 1987 [1969]), pp. 126, 127, 128.

Word. In seeking to do so, I want to borrow John Searle's distinction between "fictional" and "serious" discourse.[49] Searle examines two excerpts of written discourse, one from an article written by Eileen Shanahan and printed in the *New York Times,* another from an Iris Murdoch novel. Searle first notes that while each contains discrete and recognizable illocutionary acts, we react to them differently. The reason, he suggests, is that beneath the obvious or surface level of illocutionary utterance exists two distinct sets of linguistic conventions.

Shanahan's article is essentially assertive; it purports to correspond to reality and therefore exists by adhering to what Searle describes as the "vertical" conventions of assertion. These include (1) the speaker commits him or herself to the truth of the statement; (2) the speaker must be in a position to give some reason for the truth of the statement; (3) the statement must not be obviously true to both speaker and hearer; and (4) the speaker believes that the statement is true. As Searle writes, if Shanahan "fails to meet the conditions specified by the rules, we will say that what she said is false or mistaken or wrong, or that she didn't have enough evidence for what she said, or that it was pointless because we all knew it anyhow, or that she was lying because she didn't really believe it."[50] Murdoch's novel, in contrast, involves an intentional and explicit act of pretense and adheres to what Searle describes as a horizontal set of conventions that suspends the rules of "assertive" speech and therefore disavows any notion of exact correspondence to extra-literary, or external, reality.[51] For this reason, while each text involves performative utterances on a surface level, we experience them differently, essentially suspending, or at least reacting differently to, the force of the illocutionary acts when we recognize that someone is "pretending."

Before applying Searle's distinctions to the biblical texts, I must modify it in response to Stanley Fish's objection to Searle's treatment. In short, while Fish agrees that readers are regularly aware of whether

---

49. John R. Searle, *Expression and Meaning: Studies in the Theory of Speech Acts* (London: Cambridge University Press, 1979), p. 60. For J. L. Austin's brief, but originating, treatment, see *How to Do Things with Words,* 2nd ed., ed. J. O. Urmson and Maria Sbisà (Cambridge, Mass.: Harvard University Press, 1975), p. 22. In making this move, Searle moves closer to Bakhtin's focus on speech genres.

50. Searle, *Expression and Meaning,* p. 62.

51. Searle, *Expression and Meaning,* pp. 64-65.

they are invited to take a text "seriously" or not (and thereby uphold or suspend specific literary expectations), he fears that in linking serious discourse to its correspondence to reality, or "brute facts," Searle undercuts his entire program. Ultimately, as Fish convincingly demonstrates, a distinction between texts that in almost no way seek to refer to reality and texts that in almost every way seek to do just that becomes useless, as the former does not exist. That is, all fictional accounts draw to one degree or another upon our experience of the "real world." Hence, Searle's distinction between serious and fictional literature does not hold.[52] In response, Fish proposes that what we encounter in "non-fictional" or "serious" texts is what he describes as "standard stories" in which we act, rather than which we tell, and those stories set the terms for determining what counts as "brute facts" and the testing of "truth" in the first place. In this sense, all of the world is storied, but while we recognize that we are listening to some discrete stories (we call them fictions), we are generally not aware that we also live within another, standard story that sets the terms for our ability to experience and assess all the other discrete stories we hear. Thus, the difference between Shanahan's *New York Times* article and Murdoch's novel is that while the former seeks self-consciously to align itself with — that is, correspond to — the standard story in which it exists, the latter does not.[53]

Putting the matter this way, it would appear that when reading texts (including the Bible), we must adopt either Searle's foundationally guaranteed correspondence-theory of language, as the church has for most of its history but which is becoming increasingly difficult to maintain, or Fish's nonfoundationalist view of language that is only self-referential, as does Brueggemann in response to this crisis. But here I think both Searle and Fish overstate the matter. For as far as the illocutionary force of a text is concerned, the issue is not, finally, whether it "actually" corresponds to reality, but rather that it *asserts* and *believes* that it does.[54] Here we must return to a critical, postfoundational distinction: the fact that there is no reality available to us

52. Stanley Fish, "How to Do Things with Austin and Searle," in *Is There a Text in This Class? The Authority of Interpretive Communities* (Cambridge, Mass.: Harvard University Press, 1980), pp. 235-38.

53. Fish, "How to Do Things with Austin and Searle," pp. 239-44.

54. As Fish also notes. See "How to Do Things with Austin and Searle," p. 239.

that is not mediated by discourse does not mean that there is no such reality.[55] Ultimately, we must remain essentially agnostic on questions of final reality. For this reason, either claiming to be able to describe reality accurately or asserting that there is no reality to be described apart from a sociosymbolic construction is to assert too much. While Fish is thus correct in saying that all reality is storied and that there are several stories claming accurately to depict an external reality, he is incorrect in assuming that this means there is no external reality to be described. In fact, even this description *is an assertion about the nature of reality.* To return to themes articulated in Chapter Two, there simply is no way to avoid making penultimate claims about the nature of reality; the task is to refuse to remove those claims from scrutiny, critique, and even refutation.

From this vantage point, I want to contend that the biblical accounts are, at least on an illocutionary level, more like Shanahan's *New York Times* article than Murdoch's novel. This may, of course, not be accurate in terms of either their *literary genre* or *method of composition,* but it is accurate in terms of the conventions to which the biblical authors adhere and the illocutionary forces they seek to exert. In short, the authors conform to the four rules of "assertive" discourse previously discussed and do not, in any way, seek to suspend these rules.

While each of the four rules has important implications, I want to focus on those pertaining to the fourth, namely that the author believes in the truth of what he or she is writing. This suggests that the intention of the writer is important. This does not assume that we can necessarily determine the full intention of the author, but that we can at least detect which set of conventions, vertical or horizontal, to which he or she intends to adhere. Or, perhaps more accurately, the intention we ascribe to the author or speaker greatly determines how we read/hear the discourse in question and thus affects our response to it.

Here, however, a few cautionary notes are in order. First, I do not mean to imply that just because the biblical authors believed in what they wrote that makes it true. If we have good reason to believe they are wrong, we will undoubtedly read them differently, just as we read Aristotle's *Physics* differently than Einstein's work, largely suspending the

---

55. See Fulkerson, *Changing the Subject,* pp. 372-73. See also Hilary Putnam, *Reason, Truth, and History* (Cambridge: Cambridge University Press, 1997 [1981]), esp. pp. 49-74.

illocutionary forces of the former.[56] Rather, it simply implies that, lacking "proof" that they are certainly wrong, their belief facilitates our experience of the illocutionary force of their writing. Second, this does not mean that we are not moved by fiction, or that fiction cannot reveal to us something that is true. Rather, it implies that we *respond* very differently to assertive, serious, or non-fictional discourse and fictional discourse and therefore speak of the "truth" of these two discourses in utterly distinct fashions.

At this point, I want to recall my sense that the biblical witness is primarily a collection of confessions, of testimony, of claims and assertions that purport to speak of truth and reality both accurately and with integrity. I want now to add that the Bible addresses us today as God's dynamic Word largely because this is the case. If accepted, this assertion addresses, I believe, the concerns I raised about the proposals of Thiemann, Morse, and Brueggemann. I can group these responses in five categories. The first deals with the ability of Scripture to address us. In distinction to Thiemann, I contend that the narrative quality of much of the biblical witness, while significant, becomes secondary to its character as confessional, assertive, or serious discourse. (In fact, this recognition helps to reclaim the many portions of Scripture that are not narrative and place them on equal footing with the narrative parts.) That is, we are not so much drawn into the narrative world of the Bible as the Bible (in its narrative and non-narrative sections) addresses us in our worlds by making assertions to which we are called to respond.

The second area of concern regards the importance of the self-involvement of the writer. On the one hand, I want to affirm with Morse that God is the ultimate promisor and therefore that it is God's faithfulness, rather than the writer's, that guarantees the promise. On the other hand, I want also to contend that God works through the writer's self-involvement so as to address and affect us through the illocutionary force of that confession. This is, of course, already a statement of faith, a confession, made from within the "storied universe" of the Bible. But it nevertheless helps to describe how the Bible may function as God's Word, not merely as words about God, by asserting that

---

56. This phenomenon also explains, in part, the different "effect" (or lack thereof) of the apocryphal gospels on most Christians in comparison with the canonical gospels.

in electing the human medium of language, God has made even God's Word to some extent dependent on the human vehicle employed. This is not to collapse the distinction between God's Word and human words, but rather, as Thiemann writes, to affirm that "once God has claimed a piece of creaturely reality as his own and bound himself to it, then we are warranted in accepting the God-forged link between the human and divine."[57]

Recalling the "rules" or "conventions" of serious discourse enables us to address a third concern, that of the ability to assess whether all biblical texts are equally God's Word. Two of the four conditions are most relevant at this point. First, if we accept that the biblical authors believe what they are confessing, the illocutionary forces of their words are more likely to affect us (rule #4). Second, we must also believe that they are not mistaken about their belief (rule #1). Thus, even if we grant their sincerity, we may doubt their veracity in particular texts and in this way assess to what degree individual passages of Scripture are fully God's Word. This may seem to place the interpreter above the text, but if one accepts that the Bible is God's Word, one inevitably enters into such discernment on the basis of other texts.[58]

The fourth issue we need to address is the thorny question of how we can reasonably speak of the Bible as, not just words about God, but God's own Word. Both Thiemann and Nicholas Wolterstorff assert that the phenomenon of "double agency" best accomplishes this goal. Thiemann, as we saw, contends that double agency is simply a matter of clearly indicating that one speaks on behalf of another. Wolterstorff, by comparison, insists that the biblical authors not only assert that they speak for God but that one can rationally establish that they have been divinely authorized to do so by God.[59] The trouble with each pro-

---

57. Thiemann, *Revelation and Theology,* p. 95.

58. I will give this issue much greater attention below.

59. "Suppose the apostles were commissioned by God through Jesus Christ to be witnesses and representatives (deputies) of Jesus. Suppose that what emerged from their carrying out this commission was a body of apostolic teaching which incorporated what Jesus taught them and what they remembered of the goings-on surrounding Jesus, shaped under the guidance of the Spirit. And suppose that the New Testament books are all either apostolic writings, or formulations of the apostolic teaching composed by close associates of one or another apostle. Then it would be correct to construe each book as a medium of divine discourse. And an eminently plausible construal of the pro-

posal, however, is the difficult, if not impossible, challenge of verifying such claims, as far too many people purport to speak for God to make the mere assertion of it so. If, however, we ultimately can accept that the Bible is somehow God's Word only by faith, as both Thiemann and Wolterstorff acknowledge, then their emphasis on "double agency" might be better employed. For rather than use double agency to explain how the Bible *is* God's Word, we might use it instead to describe how the Bible *functions as* God's Word, by working within the "vertical conventions" of serious or, perhaps better, assertive discourse that allow the illocutionary utterances of the text to affect us. That is, in purporting to speak for God, the biblical authors force us to contend with, and respond to, their claims to the degree that we do not discount their witness as wrong or intentionally deceptive.

But is this not a similar position to that posed by Brueggemann, that the hearers determine whether the testimony is true and therefore revelation? This question brings us to my fifth and final concern, that of reference. What distinguishes my proposal from Brueggemann's is the assertion that the biblical authors are confessing or, to borrow from Searle, that they are engaging in assertive discourse and therefore self-consciously intend that their writing corresponds to reality and that they are, in fact, invested in and committed to that correspondence. The biblical texts, therefore, are inherently and unabashedly referential, and construing them predominantly in narrative (or what Searle describes as "horizontal") terms (as Brueggemann, Thiemann, and Frei do) is to misunderstand their fundamental nature and, in terms of speech-act theory, to commit a grave category error. Again, the issue is not whether we can determine whether they actually *do* correspond to some extra-textual reality, but rather that they *intend to*. In this way, the attention is shifted away from the reception of the text by the readers (as in Brueggemann) and back toward the text that unabashedly claims to witness to the truth (as in classic Christian interpretation).

The utility of speech-act theory, once again, is not in determining

<hr>

cess whereby these books found their way into a single canonical text, would be that by way of that process of canonization, God was authorizing these books as together constituting a single volume of divine discourse." Nicholas Wolterstorff, *Divine Discourse: Philosophical Reflections on the Claim That God Speaks* (London: Cambridge University Press, 1995), p. 295. On "double agency" in general, see pp. 37-57.

that the Bible is true and therefore that it is the Word of God, but rather in elucidating how it might function as such. I am contending that it is because the biblical texts purport to speak for God that, if we believe them, we accept that they do and, even if we do not believe their claims, we can at least admit that they still might speak for God, however unlikely that seems to us. In either case, we have introduced the distinct possibility that the words are not merely words *about* God but also, perhaps, God's own Word. This neither explains why some believe and some do not (the mystery of election), nor proves the Bible's truthfulness in an absolute sense, whether or not it is *really* God's Word (the question of inspiration). As we must with all confessions and promises that are verified ultimately only by their fulfillment, we will have to wait and see whether the Bible is God's Word. In the meantime, through its assertive confession the Bible proclaims to us the promises and declarations of the God we know in Jesus Christ and, as Morse and Thiemann point out, the self-involving language of confessions and commissives alike points to a promisor, a guarantor, a speaker. In this way, we are drawn through the text into a relationship with the living God who continues to speak to us through God's dynamic Word.

The Text's Confession — Confessing the Text

On the basis of the above study, in this section I want to move beyond merely asserting that the text is best understood as confession and testimony to describing the difference this assertion makes for reading the texts with the intention of preaching those texts. In particular, I want to suggest three significant consequences for the way we approach the biblical texts as Christians and as preachers. Each deserves careful attention and exploration:

1. Our exegetical study should be directed toward discerning the distinct confession of faith of the text in question.
2. We recognize that we come to Scripture with our own confessions that simultaneously enable and limit our ability to make sense of the variety of confessions within the text.
3. As with all confessional speech, the biblical text seeks a response and, for preachers, that response is the sermon.

1. Our exegetical study should be directed toward discerning the distinct confession of faith of the text in question.

Viewing the biblical canon as a collection of confessions leads to a radical reorientation for biblical studies. Most biblical scholarship during modernity was aimed at peering through the text as one would a window, seeking by historical-critical means to reconstruct the actual events that prompted the writing in the first place.[60] But if we regard Scripture primarily as testimony, our focus changes. As Brueggemann rightly contends, Israel's — and the early church's — confession of faith, its testimony, is "the reality to be studied." While this acknowledgment puts a premium on those methods, like literary and rhetorical studies, that refuse to disassociate the content and form of passages, it does not at all rule out the many varieties of historical-critical biblical study. Rather, it suggests that all exegetical methods are best employed to enable us to discern and hear more clearly the distinct testimonies and confessions of faith being offered by the text in question.[61]

Further, by pursuing the discrete testimony or confession of the text we alert ourselves to the lively, dynamic character of the Bible and, potentially, of our biblical study. Because testimony and confession are performative discourse, they *do* something to the hearer, eliciting a reaction and seeking some kind of response to their claims. It will therefore greatly aid our exegetical study if we keep in mind that *the biblical*

60. According to John H. P. Reumann, the image originates with Murray Krieger, *A Window to Criticism* (Princeton: Princeton University Press, 1964), pp. 3-4 and passim. For examples of its use in biblical studies, Reumann directs us to Norman R. Petersen, *Literary Criticism for New Testament Critics* (Philadelphia: Fortress Press, 1978) and R. Alan Culpepper, *Anatomy of the Fourth Gospel: A Study in Literary Design* (Philadelphia: Fortress Press, 1983), pp. 3-5. See Reumann, "After Historical Criticism, What? Trends in Biblical Interpretation and Ecumenical, Interfaith Dialogues," *Journal of Ecumenical Studies* 29 (1992): 59 n. 15.

61. As Raymond E. Brown writes in his *The Death of the Messiah* (New York: Doubleday, 1994), "the primary concern of a commentary is making sense of what the biblical writers have given us, not in reconstructing preGospel traditions or in detecting history" (p. 22). Brown's work, and my own, proceed on the belief that one can at many points detect with some confidence the original "sense" of the text and in this respect recognize the "intention" of the biblical authors. For a defense of that position, see Brown, pp. 6-9; see also Thomas G. Long, *Preaching and the Literary Forms of the Bible* (Philadelphia: Fortress Press, 1989), pp. 13-29.

text is not neutral. Rather, it seeks assent, confirmation, judgment, and validation about the confession of faith it makes about the nature of reality, of the world, of our situation, and most especially about the God it confesses.

In order to illumine "what is at stake" for the biblical authors, we may profitably turn to two revealing passages in the New Testament. The first is the "introduction" to the Gospel according to Luke, the only formal literary introduction among the four gospel accounts:

> Many have undertaken to draw up an account of the things that have been fulfilled among us, just as they were handed down to us by those who from the first were eyewitnesses and servants of the word. Therefore, since I myself have carefully investigated everything from the beginning, it seemed good also to me to write an orderly account for you, most excellent Theophilus, so that you may know the certainty of the things you have been taught (1:1-4, NIV).

This highly stylized passage, intentionally patterned after the form of ancient biography, is striking on several counts.[62] It reveals that Luke was most likely not himself an eyewitness but dependent on other testimony and suggests that Luke's is not the only account available. Significantly, it also implies that the literary and rhetorical goal of Luke's "orderly account" (καθεξῆς) is to provide "certainty," "confidence," or "assurance" (ἀσφάλειαν) of those "things" or "words" (λόγων) of which Theophilus has been instructed.[63]

We see here several things that confirm our discussion thus far. First, Luke's account is offered as "testimony" and therefore provides a literary and rhetorical link between the reader and earlier events that must be either accepted or rejected by the reader. Second, as there are other accounts available, we detect a purposefulness to Luke's writing that urges us to give close attention to the form of the Third Evangelist's "orderly account" if we are to perceive its content aright. Third, Luke writes in order to confirm the reliability, certainty, even truth (NRSV) of the instruction the reader has already received. Luke writes, that is, for reasons that go well beyond mere description.

62. See Charles H. Talbert, *Reading Luke: A Literary and Theological Commentary on the Third Gospel* (New York: Crossroad, 1982), pp. 7-11.
63. See Karl Ludwig Schmidt, "ἀσφάλεια," *TDNT* 1:506.

The same is true of the Fourth Evangelist, as becomes clear in the formal conclusion to the Gospel according to John:

> Now Jesus did many other signs in the presence of the disciples, which are not written in this book. But these are written so that you may come to believe that Jesus is the Messiah, the Son of God, and that through believing you may have life in his name (20:30-31).

Once again, there is evidence of a clear and calculated intentionality. According to John, "Jesus did *many other things . . . that are not written. But these are written so that you may come to believe.*" The emphasis, of course, is not on everything else Jesus said and did — as if to draw attention to Jesus' other signs — but rather on what is written here and its evangelical purpose.[64] Thus, as Gail O'Day notes, the passage not only communicates clear christological and soteriological concerns, but it links these to the actual form of the gospel (what was chosen):

> The Fourth Evangelist does not say, "These things were *done* in order that you may believe." He says, "these things *are written* in order that you may believe." The locus of revelation does not lie in the myriad of signs and deeds done by Jesus that are not recorded in the text, even if they were done in the presence of his disciples. . . . Rather, the locus of revelation lies *in* the written narrative of those things to which the reader of the Gospel is given access.[65]

Like Luke, John also writes with a purpose and through his intentionally and carefully composed confession seeks to elicit a response of faith from the reader.[66]

The point, once again, is that the biblical witness is not neutral. It seeks our faith and desires our commitment. To borrow a metallurgical example, the text is less like lead or iron, waiting for us to mine and fashion it, than it is like uranium, pulsing and radiating and shaping whatever comes near. As a consequence, preachers may find their

---

64. See Raymond E. Brown, *The Gospel According to John (I–XII)* (New York: Doubleday, 1966), pp. 1057-58.

65. Gail O'Day, *Revelation in the Fourth Gospel: Narrative Mode and Theological Claim* (Philadelphia: Fortress Press, 1986), p. 94.

66. See Rudolf Bultmann, *The Gospel of John*, trans. G. R. Beasley-Murray, R. W. N. Hoare, and J. K. Riches (Philadelphia: Westminster Press, 1971), pp. 698-99.

exegetical study both more fruitful and more lively by asking some of the following questions:

- What is this text trying to convince me/us of?[67]
- What does this passage assert about the human condition and about God?
- How does this text seek to lay hold of me/us? That is, what literary and rhetorical devices does it employ in order to provoke me/us to faith? How do its structure and form make clear its confessional claims?
- What do I/we know of the text's original setting and the history of its composition that helps to make sense of the claims it is making?
- What do I/we feel actually happening to me as I/we read and study and pray about this passage? What is the text asking me/us to believe, to do, and to say?
- And finally, do I/we believe what the text is saying and accept what it is asking, so that I/we can tell and ask it of others?

This last question, of course, raises a host of issues. For it reminds us, again, that Scripture seeks not simply assent, but commitment; it drives not simply toward recognition, but judgment. As confession and testimony, that is, the biblical text seeks a response and therefore not only makes its case but provides the distance in which the reader can come to faith (or unbelief).[68] The challenge rests in ascertaining how the preacher reaches such conclusions. Should we not avoid "judging" Scripture? From what place do we render such a "verdict"? Keeping in mind that Scripture, as testimony, asks us for judgment of its validity, we turn to these questions next.

2. We recognize that we come to Scripture with our own confessions that simultaneously enable and limit our ability to make sense of the variety of confessions within the text.

---

67. Because I want to encourage group study of biblical passages as a helpful corrective to the individualistic interpretation of Scripture common to our culture (as will become more clear in the next section), I will suffer the awkwardness of the "I/we" "me/us" construction to emphasize this point.

68. On this aspect of John, in particular, see R. Alan Culpepper, *Anatomy of the Fourth Gospel*, pp. 145-48.

One of the watchwords of modernity is "objectivity," the goal of disinterested and "pure" observation, description, and evaluation.[69] This standard was prized by academicians of all fields, including biblical scholars.[70] By the outset of the twentieth century, this goal had been largely undermined. Not only was "objective study" nearly impossible to achieve — hence the force of Schweitzer's *The Quest of the Historical Jesus* — but it was also increasingly viewed as undesirable. Hence, in the opening sentence of his *Jesus and the Word*, for instance, Rudolf Bultmann contends that "the essence of history cannot be grasped by 'viewing' it, as we view our natural environment in order to orient ourselves in it. Our relationship to history is wholly different from our relationship to nature."[71] For this reason, one approaches study of the Bible — for whatever else it was to Bultmann, the Bible was also a historical document — not seeking to discern merely *what* actually happened but rather what a particular event *meant* and, more importantly, what it *still might mean* to us today.[72] As he writes, "the examination of history is no neutral orientation about objectively determined past events, but is motivated by the question how we ourselves, standing in the current of history, can succeed in comprehending our own existence, can gain clear insight into the contingencies and necessities of our own life purpose."[73]

69. Allan Megill traces this sense particularly to Kant's *Critique of Pure Reason*. See *Rethinking Objectivity*, ed. Allan Megill (Durham, N.C.: Duke University Press, 1994), pp. 2-5.

70. Hence, according to Schleiermacher, for instance, language is the medium through which one expresses one's thoughts, and hermeneutics is the science of reading texts via historical and psychological means so as to describe and understand as fully and objectively as possible the author's own intentions. See "Foundations: General Theory and the Art of Interpretation," in *The Hermeneutics Reader*, ed. Kurt Mueller-Vollmer (New York: Continuum, 1997), pp. 72-97, esp. 73-79.

71. Rudolf Bultmann, *Jesus and the Word*, trans. Louise Pettibone Smith and Erminie Huntress Lantero (New York: Charles Scribner's Sons, 1962 [1934]), p. 3.

72. Herein lies the significance of Bultmann's well-known appropriation of Martin Kähler's distinction between the "historical" *(historisch)* and the "historic" *(geschichtlich)*: although everything that happens is historical, only that which remains significant for the present is historic. Such a judgment, of course, is *always* a matter of interpretation and therefore implies a confession of faith. For while anyone can state the fact that "Jesus died," only the person of faith can proclaim with the Apostle that he died "for our sins" (1 Cor. 15:3).

73. Bultmann, *Jesus and the Word*, p. 10.

Far from reducing historical inquiry to mere subjectivity, however, Bultmann's sense of "involved" study makes possible an authentic dialogue between history as an external authority and those historians who take responsibility for their prior commitments, both personal and methodological. For this reason, he asserts that the confession of personal or vested interest cannot simply be admitted and laid aside but rather permeates — and must permeate! — the entire study. Only insofar as we come to the text with our questions, concerns, and expectations (which Bultmann also describes as "presuppositions" or "preunderstanding") can the text say anything of import to us or call those presuppositions into question.[74]

More recently, Thomas G. Long has argued that this is especially the case in preaching:

> While preachers are called to careful and faithful attention to the biblical texts, attending to them with all of the tools and skills at their disposal, they are freed from the paralyzing fears associated with *eisegesis*. The text must be listened to, lived with, encountered on its own ground; but a sterile, presuppositionless, methodological move from text to sermon is neither possible nor desirable.[75]

In order for the text to speak to us, we must also speak to it. As Long writes, "The boldest way to put this is that a certain kind of *eisegesis*, the kind that renders us completely present before the text and passionately concerned to hear a word that addresses our worlds, is not a sin to be avoided, but rather is an earnestly sought prerequisite to productive *exegesis*." In this way only, as he continues, does biblical study become a relational, eventful encounter between preacher and text:

---

74. Hence, Bultmann's wariness of the flight to methodological objectivity. As he writes, "There is an approach to history which seeks by its *method* to achieve objectivity; that is, it sees history only in a perspective determined by the particular epoch or school to which the student belongs. It succeeds, at its best, in escaping the subjectivity of the individual investigator, but still remains completely bound by the subjectivity of the method and is thus highly relative" (*Jesus and the Word*, p. 5). See also "Is Exegesis Without Presuppositions Possible?" in *Existence and Faith: Shorter Writings of Rudolf Bultmann*, trans. Schubert M. Ogden (Cleveland: World Publishing Company, 1960), pp. 289-96.

75. Thomas G. Long, "The Use of Scripture in Contemporary Preaching," *Interpretation* 44 (1990): 348.

Preachers do not draw pure biblical ideas from texts and then figure out what they might mean for today. In the act of interpretation, everything we know and experience about our present world and everything we know and experience about the ancient text come together in a volatile, exciting, and free ranging moment of imaginative encounter.[76]

Only by coming to the text with questions and expectations that arise from our communal, theological, and personal locations can the text, in fact, enter into critical dialogue with the interpreter. As Long elsewhere writes, "The text . . . may call [the preacher's] questions into question. The truth found there may resolve a problem, and then again it may deepen that problem."[77]

We come to the biblical text with questions and concerns, then, for at least three reasons. First, as confessional, assertive testimony, the text expects us to enter into dialogue with it and seeks some kind of "in kind" response, of faith or unbelief. Second, we can enter into such dialogue only by treating the text not merely as the object of our study but as a subject and, indeed, as drawing us into a relationship with its (ultimate) Author. In this way we enter into what Martin Buber termed an "I-thou," rather than "I-it" relationship. Third, only insofar as we admit and voice our presuppositions, can the text call them into question.

But there is still a fourth reason, as well, and that is to make sense of, and discern between, the varied confessions we find in Scripture. As Elisabeth Schüssler Fiorenza describes, the diversity of the perspectives, experiences, and theologies reflected in Scripture is not only enriching but also problematic:

> Insofar as Biblical texts reflect diverse experiences in ancient cultures, they are not just liberating texts, but they also codify the oppressive structures and mindsets of the cultures. As one author has put it, the Bible contains not just the "good news" but also some bad news. Or, in other words, the New Testament contains some texts that bring to the fore the Gospel and are given for "the sake of our salvation," whereas other texts express the religious-cultural systems

76. Long, "The Use of Scripture," p. 349.
77. Long, *Witness of Preaching,* p. 45.

of their times or seek to adapt the early Christian ethos to the societal norms of their times.[78]

As we have already seen, Walter Brueggemann similarly asserts that the entire textual process — its formation by the biblical authors and editors, its interpretation by exegetes and preachers, and its reception by present-day readers and hearers — is "always a mixture of faith and vested interest" and therefore advises preachers to employ simultaneously a hermeneutics of suspicion and one of retrieval.[79]

For all of these reasons, then, we must not — indeed, cannot! — come to the biblical canon as passive interpreters; rather we come as living, breathing, *confessing* Christians, filled by doubts and faith, suspicion and trust, questions and hopes, but most especially with expectations of the God we will find revealed in its pages.

In his textbook, *The Witness of Preaching,* Long also acknowledges the need to come to our biblical study with some clear and keen expectations, and he suggests we direct our attention to two particular sources that contribute to those expectations. Our pastoral circumstance is the first, and our theological heritage is the second. Preachers, Long writes, "must take the people [of their congregations] with them, since what will be heard there is a word for them."[80] This means that preaching is contextual from start to finish, a theme that Long touches on but is explored more fully by Leonora Tubbs Tisdale in her work, *Preaching as Local Theology and Folk Art.* According to Tisdale, preachers need to exegete their congregations as carefully as they do the biblical texts, not simply to better *translate* theology for their parishioners but rather so that they may become better architects of *local theology,* that is, "theology crafted for a very particular people in a particular time and place."[81] Before preachers can hear the confession of the biblical text, that is, they need to listen to and articu-

---

78. Elisabeth Schüssler Fiorenza, "Response," in *A New Look at Preaching,* ed. John Burke (Wilmington, Del.: Michael Glazier, 1983), p. 50.

79. Walter Brueggemann, "The Social Nature of the Biblical Text," in *Preaching as a Social Act: Theology and Practice,* ed. Arthur Van Seeters (Nashville: Abingdon Press, 1988), p. 131.

80. Long, *Witness of Preaching,* p. 55.

81. Leonora Tubbs Tisdale, *Preaching as Local Theology and Folk Art* (Minneapolis: Fortress Press, 1997), p. xii.

late the confessions — of faith and doubt, curiosity and estrangement, hope and pain — of their hearers.[82]

Long identifies the preacher's "theological heritage" as another source from which the questions, expectations, and confessions we take to the biblical canon arise, and he gives several reasons for its importance. First, traditions serve as the "memory" of the church:

> When the preacher goes to the text, new ground is not being broken. The church has been to this text before — many times — and a theological tradition is, in part, the church's memory of past encounters with this and other biblical texts. A theologically informed interpreter of scripture enters the text guided by a map drawn and refined by those who have come to this place before. Coming to a text from a theological tradition, the interpreter arrives not as a disoriented stranger but as a pilgrim returning to familiar land, recognizing old landmarks and thereby alert for new and previously unseen wonders.[83]

Further, theological traditions steer the preacher "away from the distortions of the gospel that can result when a single text is heard in isolation from all others. Since a theological tradition is a way of seeing the Christian faith whole, it provides a means for placing the word of one text into the larger pattern of the witness of the whole Bible."[84] While theological traditions, if left to harden into dogmatic truth, can impede hearing, when they are brought forth as living confessions into a critical dialogue with the text they prepare and enable the preacher to entertain a lively conversation with the text.

To these two sources that Long names, I would add two more. The first is the presence of the text in the church's liturgy, as the pattern of Christian worship offers an interpretive grid by which to read the whole canon.[85] What a text means on a given preaching occasion is de-

---

82. Tisdale not only offers a sophisticated rationale for exegeting one's congregation, but also offers a practical and insightful strategy for discerning and interacting with the theological and cultural presuppositions that shape the community (*Preaching as Local Theology*, pp. 56-90).

83. Long, *Witness of Preaching*, p. 53.

84. Long, *Witness of Preaching*, pp. 53-54.

85. See Gordon Lathrop, *Holy Things: A Liturgical Theology* (Minneapolis: Fortress Press, 1993), esp. pp. 15-32; Geoffrey Wainwright, *Doxology: The Praise of God in Worship, Doctrine, and Life* (New York: Oxford University Press, 1980), pp. 149-81; and James F. Kay,

termined in part by what else is happening around it: what other texts are being read, sacraments celebrated, festivals observed, prayers offered, and hymns sung. Most simply, what we hear in any given text depends in part on what the other voices in the larger liturgical chorus are singing. The second is the preacher's own experience with the texts. Each time we approach the biblical canon, we do so with some memory of previous encounters, with past experiences of reading, hearing, praying, interpreting, and preaching these texts. This personal memory orients us to the fresh conversation we expect to have with an "old friend" who nevertheless regularly surprises us, and sometimes upsets or disturbs us, in the course of our speaking and hearing.

Allowing these four sets of concerns — pastoral, theological, liturgical, and personal — to shape the confession(s) we bring to Scripture not only opens us to dialogue with the text but also gives us purchase on two distinct challenges that most exegetes face. I will describe the first as the "methodological mayhem" of the postmodern world. Long aptly describes our condition. "Once upon a time," he writes, "any preacher who wished to take up the challenge of responsible biblical preaching could at least be clear about the task." With the unraveling of the preeminence of the historical-critical method in biblical studies, Long continues, such is no longer the case:

> Nowadays, however, things are not so plain and simple for the biblical preacher. . . . [T]he alleged neutrality of historical-criticism has been unmasked as itself biased, the product of a set of ideological assumptions about the nature of meaning. . . . Not only that, rival methods of interpretation — feminist, liberationist, and post-modernist, just to name a few — have risen on the hermeneutical skyline. We have moved in textual interpretation from village simplicity to urban complexity, and the consensus regarding interpretational method has broken down.

In an article exploring the "breakdown" Long describes, biblical scholar John Reumann compares different exegetical methodologies

---

"The *Lex Orandi* in Recent Protestant Theology," in *Ecumenical Theology in Worship, Doctrine, and Life: Essays Presented to Geoffrey Wainwright on His Sixtieth Birthday,* ed. David S. Cunningham, Ralph Del Colle, and Lucas Lamadrid (New York: Oxford University Press, 1999), pp. 11-23.

on the basis of where in the history of a text's composition, interpretation, and use each method locates meaning. I have borrowed and adapted his chart on page 179.[86]

What becomes almost immediately apparent in Reumann's chart of the "significant moments of meaning" for a text is the degree to which each methodology is rival to all the others when it comes to assessing where "meaning" resides. To put it another way, each methodology harbors hermeneutical aspirations, demanding that the text be read in such and such a way to yield predictable results. The only recourse, in such a situation, is to "equalize" all exegetical methods by fashioning some criterion derived from the material content of the canon itself, some sense of what is most important or definitive, and then employing that standard by which to read all of Scripture.[87] That criterion can only be, of course, a matter of confession. For this reason, I advocate reclaiming "content" or "material criticism" as a viable — indeed, necessary — option for biblical interpretation in a postmodern context, while simultaneously demanding that such a criteria as confessions of faith be admitted and thereby not exempted from conversation, critique, development, and even reversal.[88]

While such criticism on the basis of the subject matter always involves certain risks — preeminently, to impose artificially on the text some sense of unity or order that it would otherwise resist[89] — if we are candid about our practices, we will probably admit that we already, al-

86. Reumann, "After Historical Criticism, What?" p. 78.

87. "Justification by grace through faith" served as just this kind of hermeneutic for many of the Reformers. "God's preferential option for the poor," "liberation," and "equality" may serve the same function to liberation and/or feminist theologians today. Schüssler Fiorenza similarly calls for fashioning a hermeneutical key by which to read all of Scripture and cites Augustine and Thomas Aquinas as models of doing just this ("Response," p. 51).

88. For a recent discussion of the merits and risks of what is sometimes called *Sachkritik,* see the recent collection of essays in *Jesus Christus als die Mitte der Schrift: Studien zur Hermeneutik des Evangeliums,* ed. Christof Landmesser, Hans Joachim Eckstein, and Hermann Lichtenberger (Berlin: Walter de Gruyter, 1997).

89. Heinz Werner Neudorfer, for instance, charges that *Sachkritik* introduces as many problems into exegesis as it resolves, especially with regard to "harmonizing" distinct passages, and that it is therefore "not necessary." See his "Ist Sachkritik nötig? Anmerkungen zu einem Thema der biblischen Hermeneutik am Beispiel des Jakobusbriefs," *Kerygma und Dogma* 43 (1997): 279-302.

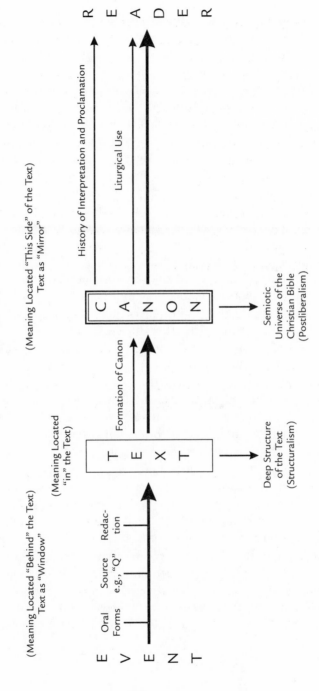

The Significant Moment(s) of Meaning in the Text

(Meaning Located "Behind" the Text)
Text as "Window"

(Meaning Located "in" the Text)

(Meaning Located "This Side" of the Text)
Text as "Mirror"

READER

History of Interpretation and Proclamation

Liturgical Use

CANON

Semiotic Universe of the Christian Bible (Postliberalism)

Formation of Canon

TEXT

Deep Structure of the Text (Structuralism)

Redaction

Source e.g., "Q"

Oral Forms

EVENT

beit often unconsciously, employ such a "confessional" lens. That is, I suspect that if we tracked the preaching career of a company of capable pastors we would discover that most return to particular passages, not simply as the stated texts, but rather as the texts-of-reference that are used hermeneutically to make sense of the whole canon. By confessing from the outset one's hermeneutical criterion, one at least attains a level of accountability that invites critical discussion. Further, and as we saw in the third chapter, confession as summary of the gospel has regularly served the church as a hermeneutical key by which to interpret all of Scripture and can perhaps be profitably employed in this fashion again. Finally, because this criterion is derived from lively encounter with the text, it is never fully refined and never above being critically, even fundamentally called into question by one's continuing relationship and conversation with the biblical canon and the community that gathers around it.

I have already suggested the second benefit yielded by admitting and naming our "confessional commitments" in approaching Scripture by noting that many preachers (and exegetes) employ "texts-of-reference" in working with other difficult, obscure, or oppressive passages of the canon. Recognizing, again, that the biblical texts are written by context-bound, limited, and sinful humans calls us to exercise critical discernment in interpreting Scripture. As Long writes, "Some New Testament passages, for example, refer to the Jews in ways that could lead to a harsh anti-Semitism, were these texts not seen in the brighter light of the whole life of Christian faith, with its affirmation of the God who keeps promises and who, as Paul wrote, has by no means rejected Israel."[90] One could make similar statements about the biblical text's portrayal of women, stance on slavery, sanctioning of violence, views on human sexuality, or a host of other issues.

Far from being unfaithful, such critical reconsideration of the text, according to Brueggemann, is warranted in part by the number of passages in the Bible that serve to call into question God's presence and trustworthiness. Brueggemann calls such passages "counter-testimony" and suggests that they serve both as example and invitation for believers to "cross-examine" their texts. In fact, Brueggemann maintains, "core testimony and cross-examination belong to each

90. Long, *Witness of Preaching*, p. 54.

other and for each other in an ongoing exchange."[91] To choose either testimony or cross-examination, faith or suspicion, is, according to Brueggemann, "not only to cheat the testimonial corpus, but to misunderstand the dialectical, resilient, disputatious quality that is definitional" of biblical faith.[92] In fact, it is precisely because the biblical text itself has provided the heart of our confession, our hermeneutical criterion, that we can, with Brueggemann, approach the canon in trust (a hermeneutics of retrieval), even as we wield that criterion to elucidate, question, and sometimes critique its witness (a hermeneutics of suspicion).

Asking and answering the following questions can clarify the hermeneutical "lens" by which we all read and preach the Scriptures and thereby make that lens both more useful and more accountable.

- In several years' worth of sermons, what themes and passages appear repeatedly? Or, and especially if new to preaching, if I/we were to choose the five passages I/we deem most important, most worthy of teaching someone new to the faith, what would they be?
- What passages seem to me/us to reveal God's will for, and intentions toward, humanity most clearly?
- What passages am I/are we drawn to in times of distress, celebration, loneliness, or devotion?
- In recent reading and preaching, what texts have most thrilled or inspired me/us, and what passages did I/we find most difficult or painful to work with? (And how did I/we deal with the difficult ones?)

In addition, preachers can continue to test, refine, and challenge their "confessions" by reaching for the commentaries of scholars *not* from their socio-economic or cultural group and by inviting group study of the appointed pericopes.[93] As Justo L. González and Catherine G. González point out, such strategies help us to overcome what they describe as a "Lone Ranger" approach to biblical study and call

91. Brueggemann, *Theology of the Old Testament*, p. 317.
92. Brueggemann, *Theology of the Old Testament*, p. 400.
93. See, for instance, Ernesto Cardenal, *The Gospel in Solentiname*, 4 vols. (Maryknoll, N.Y.: Orbis Books, 1976-1982).

our own presuppositions into question.[94] Again, asking and answering several questions can be helpful in keeping one's confession account-able, especially when encountering interpretations that diverge from one's own.

- What is it about this reading that troubles me/us? What concerns does it evoke and why?
- Conversely, what does this interpretation reveal to me/us that my/our method may have overlooked or underestimated? What limita-tions does this highlight in my/our hermeneutical lens?
- What would it take for me/us to "see the text this way" and change my/our reading? Or, under what circumstances might I/we con-sider this reading appropriate?

Throughout, it is important to recognize that we come to Scrip-ture with a sense of what to expect from Scripture that is shaped by our communal, theological, and experiential commitments, and these ex-pectations allow us to enter into a lively conversation with Scripture that not only gives shape to, refines, and sometimes calls into question those very expectations, but also invites the biblical canon to speak to us anew a word of life that deserves and, indeed, demands to be pro-claimed.

3. As with all confessional speech, the biblical text seeks a response and, for preachers, that response is the sermon.

I want to draw on three sources in order to explore my contention that the biblical texts demand a response from their readers and that when those readers are preachers that response takes shape most ap-propriately in the sermon.

First, I want to recall my earlier contention that the biblical text is performative; that is, it not only *says* something to those who listen but also *does* something to those who read or hear it. Namely, as confession and testimony, the biblical text elicits a response of belief or unbelief, of trust or mistrust, of confirmation or dissent in relation to its asser-

---

94. Justo L. González and Catherine G. González, *The Liberating Pulpit* (Nashville: Abingdon Press, 1994), pp. 47-65 (and 66-95). See also Schüssler Fiorenza, "Response," pp. 52-55.

tions about reality and the nature and presence of the God it confesses. I want now to suggest that the confession of Scripture realizes its intent only insofar it leads to a confession "in kind," either of belief or unbelief but one that represents the reader's ultimate convictions about the witness of the text. That is, Scripture expects a response that does not merely report on, but responds to, its own witness.

This is a critical distinction to make when it comes to preaching, as those preachers who only talk "about" the gospel in their sermons fundamentally misunderstand the character of the biblical witness. Gerhard Forde distinguishes between proclaiming (or "doing") the gospel versus "talking about" the gospel by describing the former as primary speech and the latter as secondary. Preaching, Forde contends, should always be primary discourse that exhibits and demands in response particular kinds of speech:

> As primary discourse, proclamation ideally is present-tense, first-to-second person unconditional promise authorized by what occurs in Jesus Christ according to the Scriptures.
> . . . The only appropriate response to such primary discourse is likewise primary: confession, praise, prayer, and worship. Proclamation as primary discourse demands an answer in like discourse be it positive or negative: "I repent, I believe" or "I don't, I won't. I can't."[95]

Rudolf Bultmann similarly emphasizes the lively, even "provocative" nature of the gospel, writing that,

> the word of proclamation is no mere report about historical incidents: It is no teaching about external matter which could simply be regarded as true without any transforming of the hearer's own existence. For the word is *kerygma,* personal address, demand, and promise; it is the very act of divine grace. Hence its acceptance — faith — is obedience, acknowledgment, confession.[96]

---

95. Forde, *Theology Is for Proclamation* (Minneapolis: Fortress Press, 1990), p. 2. On the present-tense character of performative speech, see J. L. Austin, "Performative Utterances," in *Philosophical Papers,* 2nd ed., ed. J. O. Urmson and G. J. Warnock (Oxford: Clarendon Press, 1970), p. 242.

96. Bultmann, *TNT,* 1:319. For a discussion of Bultmann's sense of the gospel as "direct address" *(Anrede),* see James F. Kay, *Christus Praesens: A Reconsideration of Rudolf Bultmann's Christology* (Grand Rapids: Eerdmans, 1994), pp. 45-49, 111-17.

Similarly, in his *Homiletics,* Karl Barth describes the sermon as inherently "responsive" in terms not dissimilar to those of Bultmann: "No sermon can be anything other than an act of response to the call," he writes. "What happens here does not happen according to a plan or on the basis of an idea. Here something is heeded. We have heard the Word of God and we answer."[97] Ultimately, it is preeminently because the Word of God demands a response that we preach.

Second, I want also to return to Paul Ricoeur's dialectic of understanding *(verstehen)* and explanation *(erklären).* Whereas Romanticist interpreters clearly distinguished between the two — one first "understands" the meaning of the text before one explains, or applies, it to the current situation — Ricoeur suggests that the relationship between them is not strictly linear but rather dialectical, as one's initial understanding of any text is subjected to dialogical critique through one's attempt at explanation.[98] This, in turn, leads to greater understanding, and so forth, a dialectic that Ricoeur describes as the ongoing act of interpretation.[99]

Ricoeur's work has two major implications for my own at this point. First, understanding and explanation are not two easily divisible elements of interpretation but rather are interpenetrating and co-dependent: understanding moves toward explanation as its actualization and explanation moves toward greater understanding.[100] Second, the "meaning" of the text is no longer located exclusively in the history of the text's composition — e.g., the intention of the author, the original setting of its composition, the circumstances of its receivers — but rather is in front of the text, in the act of the interpretation itself as the interpreter, the text (and this, I would argue, at times includes one's educated guesses about the intentions of the author), and those to whom the text is "explained" together create the meaning of the text and in so

97. Karl Barth, *Homiletics,* trans. Geoffrey W. Bromiley and Donald E. Daniels (Louisville: Westminster/John Knox Press, 1991), p. 65.

98. Paul Ricoeur, *Interpretation Theory: Discourse on the Surplus of Meaning* (Fort Worth: Texas Christian University Press, 1976), pp. 75-79. Ricoeur describes the process of critique — distinguishing on a variety of bases between the "fitness" of an interpretation — validation. Validation, in turn, leads to another level of understanding, approaching comprehension, that will inevitably be risked again in public discourse and explanation toward validation (pp. 80-88).

99. Ricoeur, *Interpretation Theory,* p. 86.

100. Ricoeur, *Interpretation Theory,* p. 86.

doing realize the text's own intention by bringing its confession once more to expression.[101] This coincides with our earlier discussion of Ricoeur's dialectic of participation and distanciation leading to appropriation.[102] The goal of interpretation, according to Ricoeur, is comprehension as appropriation, the making of one's own what was once foreign.[103] Successful interpretation, then, is appropriation that "yields something like an event, an event of discourse, which is an event in the present moment."[104] With regard to preaching, Ricoeur's sense that interpretation yields an event implies that one's encounter with the text is not then *applied* to the congregation but rather, to the degree that the text is appropriated, it is *given living expression* — and in this sense reaches its climax and fulfills its purpose — in the moment of proclamation.[105]

101. "The sense of the text is not behind the text, but in front of it. It is not something hidden, but something disclosed. What has to be understood is not the initial situation of discourse, but what points toward a possible world, thanks to the nonostensive reference of the text. Understanding has less than ever to do with the author and his situation. It seeks to grasp the world-propositions opened up by the reference of the text" (*Interpretation Theory*, p. 87).

102. Recall, again, that for Ricoeur "distanciation" is not primarily a negative element to be overcome but a factor that dislodges meaning from standing "behind" or "in" the text and moves out front, into the interaction between the text and its interpreter (*Interpretation Theory*, p. 89).

103. Distinguishing between the Romanticist sense that interpretation was understanding/appropriating the original "genius" of the author and his own convictions, Ricoeur writes, "What has to be appropriated is the meaning of the text itself, conceived in a dynamic way as the direction of thought opened up by the text. In other words, what has to be appropriated is nothing other than the power of disclosing a world that constitutes the reference of the text" (*Interpretation Theory*, p. 92).

104. Ricoeur, *Interpretation Theory*, p. 92.

105. Nancy Lammers Gross has demonstrated that most contemporary homileticians employ a two-part process roughly equivalent to the Romanticist distinction between understanding and explanation. That is, one first interprets the text to discern its meaning or discover an experience of the gospel, then one explains that meaning or re-creates that experience. In either case, the actual idea or event is lodged firmly in or behind the text. Gross argues instead that, following Ricoeur, preachers see in their sermons the culmination and actualization of their interpretive work, as the text does not "mean" apart from its appropriation and, homiletically, its articulation in the gathered assembly. See her "A Re-examination of Recent Homiletical Theories in Light of the Hermeneutical Theory of Paul Ricoeur," Ph.D. dissertation, Princeton Theological Seminary, 1992, pp. 114-25, 189-223. See also her book *If You Cannot Preach Like Paul . . .* (Grand Rapids: Eerdmans, 2002), pp. 75-87, 125-27.

Third, I want to recall our earlier discussion of the use of "confession" in the New Testament to point out not only that "confession" is a word offered in response to external circumstances, but also the degree to which confession brings to expression the Christian's own identity and nature in response to the proclaimed word. As Paul wrote, emphasizing the interpenetrating nature of faith and confession, "But just as we have the same spirit of faith that is in accordance with scripture — 'I believed, and so I spoke' — we also believe, and so we speak" (2 Cor. 4:13). Luther's confession at Worms offers an example of the degree to which confession is tied to the believer's very sense of self: "My conscience is captive to the Word of God. Here I stand. *I can do no other. So help me God. Amen.*"[106] Luther's statement indicates that, as compelling as the external circumstances may have been, his confession is also driven by internal necessity. Thus, as Luther writes, it is not simply that the Emperor's questioning demands from him a response, but also, as he writes, that his conscience *is captive to the Word of God*. Therefore, he — the man, Martin Luther, a believer whose conscience is bound to and by God's Word — cannot do otherwise; it would be unthinkable, a betrayal of his very being.

Confession, then, is both the appropriate response one makes to the biblical witness but also the means by which one claims one's identity and ongoing life as a believer. James O'Donnell describes the degree to which this is true of Augustine's best-known work, his *Confessions*. Describing the situation that prompted Augustine to confess, O'Donnell writes,

> Augustine was . . . deeply troubled by the implications of his new office [as Bishop].
> Who was he to stand in such a place of eminence, with so many people depending on him? He was still a sinner, but somehow he was

---

106. See Roland Bainton's *Here I Stand: A Life of Martin Luther* (New York: Abingdon-Cokesbury Press, 1950), pp. 181-86. While the historicity of this scene is debated, Luther makes a similar confession at the outset of his Smalcald Articles, writing, "I have decided to publish these articles so that, if I should die before a council meets . . . , those who live after me may have my testimony and confession . . . to show where I have stood until now and where, by God's grace, I will continue to stand." *The Book of Concord: The Confessions of the Evangelical Lutheran Church,* trans. and ed. Theodore G. Tappert (Philadelphia: Fortress Press, 1959), p. 289.

also the conduit of divine grace bringing redemption to other sin-
ners. Now a preacher, he needed to be preached to himself, but there
was no one to do that. He had to stand alone before the people of
Hippo each week and proclaim God's word. How could the expectations of these people not drive him to despair?

Two literary answers came out of this personal crisis. The first
was perfectly theological, detached, and serious: Christian Doctrine. . . . How do I preach, he asked himself. Christian Doctrine was
the answer. But it was an incomplete answer, in more ways than one.
At about this time he turned instead to writing the *Confessions*.[107]

For this reason, as O'Donnell continues, "The *Confessions* are not to be
read merely as a look back at Augustine's spiritual development; rather
the text itself is an essential state in that development, and a work
aware both of what had already passed into history and of what lay
ahead."[108] As Augustine's work illustrates, confession is part and parcel
of the believer's *being-in-the-world*, and not to confess one's deepest convictions is therefore not really, or at least not fully, to *be*.

The preacher, then, is called to confess, by the text, by the world,
and by the preacher's own sense of self; and that confession takes shape
most clearly in the sermon offered to the gathered assembly of Christian believers awaiting the Word of faith.

From Canon to Community

Perhaps the greatest concern of preachers is to move with integrity and
confidence from their study of the biblical text to their actual writing
and preaching of the sermon, so as to offer a faithful confession to the
congregation gathered at worship. Having given significant attention
to how understanding the biblical canon as inherently confessional il-
lumines our conversational engagement with the text, it is now time to
consider how we render our own, responsive confession verbally in the
sermon. We turn next, that is, to consider *how* the sermon can embody
the living confession of faith of the text that comes through the
preacher to the community of faith.

107. James J. O'Donnell, *Augustine* (Boston: Twayne, 1985), p. 81.
108. O'Donnell, *Augustine*, p. 82.

CHAPTER 6

Confession and Community

Having considered in the previous chapter our encounter and conversation with the biblical texts, we move in this one to consider how we give shape to the confession of faith that arises from that encounter so as to offer it to the congregation to spark, nurture, focus, and direct their ongoing conversation of faith. It will be important not to see this stage as somehow disconnected from what has come before. As we have already seen, the confession offered to the community is not the application of previous biblical study but rather its culmination, for only by confessing do we realize the intention of the texts themselves. In this light, I want to suggest that there are four related stages in moving from the biblical text through the sermon to the community of faith.

We may characterize each stage by its chief activity. The first deals with *approaching* the text on behalf of the congregation. The second describes our *listening* for the text's distinct confession of faith. The third concerns *discerning* what that confession may mean in light of the rest of the canon, the community's context, and one's hermeneutical experience and expectations. The fourth involves *articulating* that new confession for the community so as to actualize the text and offer it to the community to be appropriated through the power of the Holy Spirit. It is important to realize, at this point, that each step of this process is itself an act of interpretation, of decision, of confession.

Because, as preachers, we approach the text not simply on our own behalf, but also on behalf of the congregation, we must always attend closely to the circumstances, needs, and questions of our parishioners. This involves not only a pastoral commitment to our people but also a keen sense of intuition. Even granting these qualities, one must still interpret what we see in our parish and in the lives of our people, and these choices — correct or mistaken — will inevitably shape our approach to the text.

On the level of listening for the confession of the text, even one minimally acquainted with biblical scholarship is aware of the range of possible interpretations on any given passage, whether seemingly innocuous or controversial. That is, the "obvious" meaning of the text is rarely, if ever, obvious. For every reading of a text there are other, often quite distinct, possible readings. One inevitably chooses between readings; and that choice, while undoubtedly supported by numerous scholarly and personal "good reasons," cannot be proved and therefore is ultimately a matter of confession.

Similarly — perhaps even more clearly — one also must determine what this "confessed confession" of the text has to say to the contemporary community in light of several factors. The meaning of the text in relation to the community and preacher is, again, not obvious; it is a process of discernment and interpretation. On any given Sunday, different pastors preach vastly different sermons on the same texts. Even when several preachers attend to the same set of hearers — in, for instance, a preaching class or workshop — each preacher "reads" the meeting between text and community differently and therefore preaches a different sermon. On this level too, then, we make decisions among a variety of possibilities and "confess" those choices, as they surely could have been otherwise.

Finally, the preacher chooses among a variety of rhetorical elements — including, among other things, the form and language of the sermon — by which to embody the confession she wishes to make to and for the gathered community. Once again, these choices are in no way self-evident, but reflect decisions the preacher makes about the community, the context, and the confession she wants to voice. Given the range of options available, and the consequent decisions required of the preacher, the final form of the sermon is also a matter of interpretation. The sermon could have been otherwise; the preacher chose to do it this way, and in choosing confesses.

The whole process, then, is fraught with interpretation, with choices and decisions, with confession. The movement of the confession, as I have said, arises from an encounter with the text and moves *through* the sermon to be actualized in the life of the community that appropriates that message for itself, as the chart below depicts:

From Text *Through* Sermon

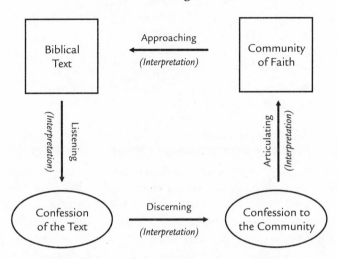

At each stage, these choices, these confessions, matter. While this may seem obvious in the first three stages — where the preacher seeks to read the congregation, to determine what the text is saying, and to discern what the preacher wants to say in response — it is not always so apparent in the fourth, the question of *how* to say it. In fact, in their effort to witness to the truth of the gospel, Christian preachers have often assumed that rhetorical concerns — that is, the particular form and language of the sermon — are entirely secondary to the content of the sermon.[1] While this has been most readily apparent in those preachers who eschew formal rhetoric altogether, even those who, like Augustine, have embraced the study and use of rhetorical categories often assume that rhetoric serves as a neutral vehicle, a mere container in which to place the gospel message.[2]

1. See Thomas G. Long, "And How Shall They Hear? The Listener in Contemporary Preaching," in *Listening to the Word: Studies in Honor of Fred Craddock,* ed. Gail R. O'Day and Thomas G. Long (Nashville: Abingdon Press, 1993), pp. 174-79; and André Resner Jr., *Preacher and Cross: Person and Message in Theology and Rhetoric* (Grand Rapids: Eerdmans, 1999), pp. 58-65.

2. See Resner, *Preacher and Cross,* pp. 46-47.

Given our earlier observation that biblical form and content cannot be cleanly divided, however, I am hesitant to assume anything different when it comes to the sermon. In fact, I would contend that the decisions we make about the form and language we use — that is, our rhetorical choices — are not simply matters of *how* we say something, but actually shape *what* we say in the first place.[3] According to H. Grady Davis, form renders thought: "An unformed thought, a thought not yet turned to shape, is only a vague impression, sensed but not grasped, an airy nothing, until given a local habitation and a name."[4] Similarly, as Thomas G. Long suggests,

> Instead of thinking of sermon form and content as separate realities, it is far more accurate to speak of the form *of* the content. A sermon's form, although often largely unperceived by the hearers, provides shape and energy to the sermon and thus becomes itself a vital force in how a sermon makes meaning. . . . If a sermon is structured in a manipulative, deceptive, or incoherent manner, then, regardless of what else is said in the sermon, manipulation, deception, or incoherence is spoken too. On the other hand, if the form of the sermon is clear, lively, and respectful of the listeners, then clarity, life, and dignity become a part of the sermon's word to the hearers.[5]

Whatever else they may be, then, form, language, and other rhetorical concerns are decidedly *not* neutral.

For this reason, in this final chapter I want to explore some of the rhetorical dimensions of confessional preaching by returning to the interrelated elements of confession as (1) grounding hearers in a narrative, communal identity while simultaneously (2) providing the critical space in which they can be encountered by the proclaimed word and appropriate the faith and identity offered through the work of the Holy Spirit.

3. Rhetoric includes, of course, more than language and form, but it is to these particular "rhetorical concerns" that I wish to attend. For a fuller treatment of rhetoric as it relates to Christian theology, see George A. Kennedy, *Classical Rhetoric and Its Christian and Secular Tradition from Ancient to Modern Times* (Chapel Hill: University of North Carolina Press, 1984); and David S. Cunningham, *Faithful Persuasion: In Aid of a Rhetoric of Christian Theology* (Notre Dame: University of Notre Dame Press, 1990).

4. H. Grady Davis, *Design for Preaching* (Philadelphia: Fortress Press, 1958), p. 2.

5. Thomas G. Long, *The Witness of Preaching* (Louisville: Westminster/John Knox Press, 1989), p. 93.

The point of the chapter, let me be clear, is not to explore fully the relationship between rhetoric and homiletics; rather its more modest aim is to discern some guidance in making rhetorical decisions based on my conviction that preaching is preeminently an act of confessing Jesus Christ. By paying close attention, once again, to the distinct dynamics of Christian confession, I hope to offer concrete guidance in preparing sermons as responses to the confession of the biblical text now offered to the gathered community.

To accomplish this goal, I will first propose a "confessional rhetoric" that faithfully reflects Christian confession as I have described it, and then I will address more specific questions of the form and language of a sermon. The purpose, throughout, is to give some thought and direction to how our preaching may confess Jesus Christ.

A Rhetoric of Confession

To invoke the name "rhetoric" in homiletics is inevitably to wade into a long and often contentious discussion. It's not much of an exaggeration to say that there have been, for the most part, two predominant attitudes about rhetoric: "those fer it, and those agin' it."[6] On one side of the equation, homileticians from Augustine to Fred Craddock suggest that rhetoric is either neutral or inevitable: if neutral, they contend, then the truth deserves as eloquent expression as the false; if inevitable, then by learning the art of rhetoric preachers can proclaim the gospel more effectively. On the other side, from Tertullian, Jerome, and other Latin "fathers" to Karl Barth and his heirs, those opposed to rhetoric charge that either it is incompatible with the gospel or it makes the gospel dependent on human capability.[7]

According to André Resner, the differences between these two positions arise from their distinct emphasis upon opposite ends of the pole between human and divine activity. While each side demonstrates some significant strengths, according to Resner each ultimately takes its po-

6. See, for instance, the contrasting articles by Lucy Lind Hogan, "Rethinking Persuasion: Developing an Incarnational Theology of Preaching," and Richard Lischer, "Why I Am Not Persuasive," both in *Homiletic* 24, no. 2 (Winter 1999): 1-12, 13-16.

7. See Resner, *Preacher and Cross,* esp. chapter 2, "*ēthos* in the Homiletical Tradition," pp. 39-82; and Kennedy, *Classical Rhetoric and Its Christian and Secular Tradition,* pp. 120-60.

sition to such an extreme that it risks heresy. Those who embrace rhetoric grant the importance of the human element and as a consequence take their hearers far more seriously. These gains are offset, however, to the degree that such "rhetoricians" leave so little room for God that the burden of salvation seems to rest on the frail shoulders of humanity (whether preacher or hearer), thereby approaching the brink of a kind of "homiletical Donatism." Conversely, those who denounce rhetoric emphasize the sovereign freedom and power of God's Word and therefore avoid making faith and salvation human "works" dependent on the person of the preacher or rhetorical devices. At the same time, however, such "theologians" dismiss the "human" element of God's act of accommodation to such an extent that they risk making the import of the gospel frightfully remote to their hearers and ultimately verge on "homiletical Docetism."[8]

Resner points out that the problem he observes in homiletics is representative of the larger problematic of practical theology itself, in that practical theology inevitably emerges from the nexus of theological and secular disciplines. Each of the competing positions he outlines in homiletics, from his point of view, has resolved this tension only by resorting to interdisciplinary reductionism, subsuming the categories of one of the disciplines entirely within those of the other.[9] Thus, the "rhetoricians" largely "assume" the gospel, treating it simply as the "message" to be communicated in a larger rhetorical-communicative strategy. In this way, they leave no room for Christian theology to articulate its voice and thereby make the gospel nearly indistinguishable from any other "message." Similarly, the "theologians" naïvely seek to avoid any and all rhetorical strategies, assuming a nearly unmediated gospel. In this way their rhetorical strategies and anthropological presuppositions cannot even be discussed, let alone called into question, because they are denied from the outset.

In distinction to either of the positions just examined, I agree with Resner that as Christian preachers we cannot artificially divide between rhetoric and theology, and therefore that we would do well to seek to describe a rhetoric that arises from, and is accountable to, an under-

8. Resner, *Preacher and Cross*, pp. 58-82. See also *The Witness of Preaching*, pp. 24-41, where Long distinguishes between the "herald," "pastor," and "storyteller."

9. Resner, *Preacher and Cross*, p. 137.

standing of the gospel rooted in the cross and resurrection of Jesus Christ.[10] As James F. Kay writes,

> The cross does not mean we forsake the language of human beings or of our culture for that of the angels. The word of the cross always retains a human form. Nevertheless, what the crucified Christ reveals is that no creaturely form has in itself the power to render the identity or the reality of the new creation. Moreover, the rupture between the old and the new, revealed in and caused by God's apocalyptic deconstruction of *kata-sarka* norms for the word, means that rhetoric (and poetics) cannot be unquestionably baptized for Christian use in some version of "pulpit eloquence" or "sacred rhetoric" or "communication theory." Rather, the word of the cross overturns reigning rhetorical strategies, "taking them captive" (2 Cor. 10:5) in the service of its message.[11]

At a minimum, this means that we need to attend to both the rhetorical and theological sides of the equation with equal seriousness or, to return to a governing motif of this work, to keep them in "critical conversation" with each other.

I have already contended at some length that Christian confession suggests an approach to communication that involves (1) offering hearers a narrative, communal identity that suggests patterns for making meaning of the world (participation) while simultaneously (2) providing the critical space (distanciation) in which they can be encountered by the claims made by that identity and through the work of the Holy Spirit enter into that identity for themselves (appropriation). To explore in greater detail the rhetorical implications of this proposal, I turn, first, to several works in Christian theology and homiletics that help outline the theological "marks" of a Christian understanding of rhetoric and then, second, to a recent proposal from communication studies that resonates with this understanding at several points.

---

10. Resner, *Preacher and Cross*, pp. 138-41.

11. James F. Kay, "The Word of the Cross at the Turn of the Ages," *Interpretation* 53 (1999): 48.

The "Reverse" Rhetoric of Cross and Resurrection

To speak of "confessing Jesus Christ" implies, or perhaps only assumes, a particular understanding of "Christ." In order both to make that assumption more explicit and to discern the demands such a confession makes upon rhetoric, I will consider several theological and homiletical works that bear on my subject, turning first to André Resner's recent *Preacher and Cross: Person and Message in Theology and Rhetoric.*[12]

After surveying classical rhetoric's treatment of *ēthos* in his first chapter, and homiletical theory's relationship to the same in his second, Resner discerns an impasse between two positions as we discussed above, a standoff that he summarizes as follows:

> Some, operating with rhetorical principles as primary, have followed Aristotle to draw the conclusion that the person of the preacher, as with any orator, is perhaps the most important factor in the persuasion of the hearers. Others, operating with theological assumptions as primary, have argued that since preaching is nothing less than God's word for which God alone is responsible and which God alone makes efficacious, then any talk of the human person making the word "more efficacious" is idolatrous.[13]

In response, Resner turns in his third chapter to the Apostle Paul, and especially Paul's defense of his person and authority (his *ēthos*) in his correspondence with the church in Corinth. Where numerous scholars have read Paul's remarks as a radical break with, and even denigration of, classical patterns of rhetoric, Resner perceives that Paul does not so much dismiss classical rhetoric's understanding of *ēthos* as he does invert it. For where classical rhetoric conceives of *ēthos* as the speaker's ability to assess the audience's expectations of what makes a good speaker and "act accordingly," Paul refuses to accommodate himself to the Corinthians' expectations and, in fact, attempts to reframe their sensibilities altogether in light of the cross of Jesus Christ.[14]

---

12. While Resner's main interest lies in the rhetorical category of *ēthos*, or the person of the preacher, his study provides a pattern for thinking about the relationship between rhetoric and theology that will prove helpful at several points.

13. Resner, *Preacher and Cross*, p. 134.

14. Resner, *Preacher and Cross*, pp. 105-6.

According to Resner, the central *ēthos* issue shifts for Paul from the trustworthiness of the preacher to the trustworthiness of God. The God "who justifies the ungodly" and "did not spare his own Son" is the one who guarantees the trustworthiness of the message. Precisely because the preacher is one of the "ungodly" in need of justification, the preacher must refuse to ground the validity of the message in his or her own moral qualities. In such a situation, Paul as a Christian preacher can be faithful to his calling only insofar as he describes his own plight as a sinner, his own need for mercy, his own unworthiness of forgiveness, and his own status as a beneficiary of God's grace.[15]

While Paul's decision to adopt an *ēthos* of "self-effacement" appears foolish in terms of classical standards of rhetoric, it is grounded in the *logos* of the crucified Christ, a "logic" that offers a whole "new framework for understanding and discernment in community and world."[16] From Paul's perspective, Jesus' cross and resurrection challenge all human understandings of God and human community as inherently distorted by sin, a condition he describes as understanding *kata sarka* ("according to the flesh"). In its place, Paul articulates a vision of life *kata pneuma* ("according to the spirit") which, this side of the eschaton, Christians perceive only *kata stauron* ("according to the cross").[17] That is, while the cross creates a crisis for this world — really, announces its end — it does not remove the Christian to the world to come. Rather, it announces God's new world and places the believer at the juncture where the two worlds meet.[18] Thus, as Resner writes, "The new way of knowing afforded by the cross necessitates a new way of being in the world which is destined to conflict with old-age ways of knowing, such as the ways that people adjudicate authenticity and credibility."[19]

15. Resner, *Preacher and Cross*, pp. 106-10.

16. Resner, *Preacher and Cross*, p. 110 n. 69.

17. Here, see J. Louis Martyn's seminal article, "Epistemology at the Turn of the Ages," in *Theological Issues in the Letters of Paul* (Nashville: Abingdon Press, 1997), pp. 89-110. Martyn's article was originally published as "Epistemology at the Turn of the Ages: 2 Corinthians 5:16," in *Christian History and Interpretation: Essays Presented to John Knox*, ed. W. R. Farmer, C. F. D. Moule, and R. R. Niebuhr (Cambridge: Cambridge University Press, 1967), pp. 269-87.

18. As Martyn writes, "The cross is the epistemological crisis for the simple reason that while it is in one sense followed by the resurrection, it is not replaced by the resurrection" ("Epistemology," p. 109).

19. Resner, *Preacher and Cross*, p. 115.

Paul's "reverse *ēthos*" solves the dilemma Resner originally posed. Because Paul locates the trustworthiness of the message, not with the preacher, but with God, Paul avoids the "homiletical Donatism" of those who uncritically embrace rhetoric.[20] Simultaneously, however, Paul accepts that the preacher's *ēthos* — inverted so that the preacher is the example of a sinner that God has saved and a weak vessel through which God deigns to work — nevertheless embodies the gospel proclaimed to the community. In this way, Paul likewise avoids the "homiletical Docetism" of those who dismiss rhetoric.[21] Thus, the preacher proclaims Christ's cross by embodying it and, in so doing, does not reject rhetoric but inverts its categories, viewing and assessing them through a cruciform lens.

Daniel Patte, in his book *Preaching Paul*, applies a similar pattern to the whole of Christian proclamation. According to Patte, Paul's chief interest is not simply in *preaching* the gospel but in *transmitting* it, that is, in *communicating faith so that hearers can make it their own*.[22] As Patte explains, while preaching is a necessary, even essential element for such transmission, apart from manifestations of God's power and presence transmission will not occur. Because the gospel is essentially the *promise* that God has intervened in Christ — and continues to intervene! — for the salvation of the world, preaching is validated insofar as hearers perceive by faith signs of *fulfillment*, or manifestations of God's continued activity in the world for the good of the world. The trouble is, however, that like the Corinthian believers, we do not know where to look for manifestations of God's power and, in fact, most often look to all the wrong places.

For Paul, God's intervention in Christ sets a type of all of God's manifestations, past, present, and future. Hence, Paul looks for God's manifestations in Christ-like situations; situations, that is, that bear resemblance to *both* Christ's cross and resurrection.[23] This creates a crisis for those who hear the gospel. For while they seek God in the places God "ought" to be according to the wisdom of the world (most often in places of strength or glory; i.e., *kata sarka*), God constantly shows up

---

20. Resner, *Preacher and Cross*, pp. 106-10.
21. Resner, *Preacher and Cross*, pp. 118-28.
22. Daniel Patte, *Preaching Paul* (Philadelphia: Fortress Press, 1984), p. 14.
23. Patte, *Preaching Paul*, pp. 33-38.

just where we least expect God to be (places of weakness and broken-ness; i.e., *kata stauron*).[24] Only by "counting as loss" our former conceptions of divine manifestation can we perceive signs of the fulfillment of the promise and therefore come to faith, to a living trust and confidence in the message that God continues to work for the good of the world in Christ.[25]

Resner's study offers an acute example of this. While the Corinthians desire to receive the promise of God's forgiveness of their sin, they look for the fulfillment of that promise through the distorted lens of the categories of classical rhetoric; fulfillment, in such terms, means that the message should come in the form of eloquence and worldly wisdom. Confronted by Paul's "weakness," the Corinthians are offended and reject the messenger and, consequently, the message as fulfilled-promise. Hence, Paul's great concern is not primarily that he be accepted by the Corinthians but rather that they do not reject evidence of God's fulfillment of the promise and therefore also reject the gospel promise itself.[26] Given that living and knowing *kata sarka* is implacably opposed to living and knowing *kata stauron*, we can appreciate better not only why the Corinthians resisted Paul's message but also why Paul himself describes the transition between one age to the other as the move from death to life (Rom. 6:1-11).

Taken together, Resner and Patte suggest that in order to "confess Christ" one must first perceive God's work in Christ as most clearly revealed in Christ's cross and resurrection and, therefore, that the rhetorical means by which we seek to proclaim and embody the gospel message must likewise conform to this cruciform pattern. Recent developments in feminist approaches to rhetoric and communication theory suggest movement in just such a direction, and it is to one of these works that I now turn.

---

24. Luther's declaration in the Heidelberg Disputation comes immediately to mind: "It does [a person] no good to recognize God in his glory and majesty unless he recognizes him in the humility and shame of the cross." "The Heidelberg Disputation, 1518," *LW*, 31:52-53.

25. Patte, *Preaching Paul*, pp. 38-49.

26. Resner, *Preacher and Cross*, pp. 129-31; Patte, *Preaching Paul*, pp. 35-36.

An Invitational Rhetoric

In their article, "Beyond Persuasion: A Proposal for an Invitational Rhetoric," Sonja K. Foss and Cindy L. Griffin provide some of the resources by which we might construct a "rhetoric of confession" by eschewing the persistent and dominant role that "persuasion" occupies in most rhetorical theory.[27] Describing persuasion as "the conscious effort to change others," Foss and Griffin trace such a motive to the inherently patriarchal bias of much rhetorical theory.[28] Charging that such an attitude stands in contradiction to the traditional feminist values of equality, immanent value, and self-determination, they seek to offer a feminist alternative of an "invitational rhetoric."

As they describe it, "Invitational rhetoric constitutes an invitation to the audience to enter the rhetor's world and see it as the rhetor does."[29] To accomplish this goal, the rhetor consistently values the perspectives of the hearers, even if they differ markedly from the rhetor's own. Through such interaction, both speaker and hearer come to greater understanding and, more importantly, have created a relationship of mutual regard and reciprocity with each other. While change may occur through such an exchange, it is a by-product, rather than the purpose, of the interaction.[30]

The two main components of such a rhetoric, what Foss and Griffin name "communicative options" or "rhetorical forms," are (1) offering perspectives and (2) creating external conditions of safety, value, and freedom. While the perspective of the speaker plays a role in traditional rhetoric, it functions differently in an invitational one:

> Individual perspectives are articulated in invitational rhetoric as carefully, completely, and passionately as possible to give them full

27. Sonja K. Foss and Cindy L. Griffin, "Beyond Persuasion: A Proposal for an Invitational Rhetoric," *Communication Monographs* 62 (1995): 2.

28. "The traditional conception of rhetoric, in summary, is characterized by efforts to change others and thus to gain control over them, self-worth derived from and measured by the power exerted over others, and a devaluation of the life worlds of others. This is a rhetoric of patriarchy, reflecting its values of change, competition, and domination" ("Beyond Persuasion," pp. 3-4).

29. Foss and Griffin, "Beyond Persuasion," p. 5.

30. Foss and Griffin, "Beyond Persuasion," pp. 5-6.

expression and to invite their careful consideration by the participants in the interaction. This articulation occurs not through persuasive argument but through offering — the giving of expression to a perspective without advocating its support or seeking its acceptance.[31]

By offering, rather than imposing, their perspectives, speakers expressly value the "otherness" of their hearers by allowing for the possible validity of other perspectives, perspectives that may challenge and even transform their own. In this way, speakers *risk* their perspective as a "tentative proposal" in the public exchange rather than *force* it upon the audience. Sometimes, especially when this offering is met by suspicion or hostility, such offering involves what the authors describe as "re-sourcement," a rejection of the terms of the antagonist and a complete reframing of the engagement. Re-sourcing therefore involves both (1) disengaging from the antagonistic or dominant scheme *and* (2) proposing an entirely alternate pattern or worldview for understanding the issues at hand. In this sense, the speaker invites the hearer not simply to entertain another perspective but to enter an alternative world that suggests different terms of interaction, different values, even a different vocabulary.[32]

Creating external conditions of safety, value, and freedom is the second component of an invitational rhetoric.[33] Hearers feel safe when the speaker "makes no attempts to hurt, degrade, or belittle audience members or their beliefs, and audience members do not fear rebuttal of or retribution for their most fundamental beliefs." Such a climate allows hearers to preserve their sense of order intact and therefore, trusting the speaker, they are more likely to entertain the speaker's perspective. Speakers create a sense of value by acknowledging "that audience members have intrinsic or immanent worth" by regarding them as individuals and refusing to define them through their speech. Freedom, the third condition necessary in order to promote the possibility of mutual understanding, comes when hearers perceive that they will not

31. Foss and Griffin, "Beyond Persuasion," p. 7.

32. Foss and Griffin, "Beyond Persuasion," pp. 9-10.

33. While these two components, or forms, can be employed independently, Foss and Griffin suggest that for mutual understanding to occur they need to be offered in tandem ("Beyond Persuasion," p. 10).

be coerced into adopting a viewpoint but rather retain "the power to choose or decide" about the perspective the speaker offers. This is manifested particularly clearly by the speaker's explicit commitment to the hearer regardless of the outcome of the exchange. As Foss and Griffin write, "Should the audience choose not to accept the vision articulated by the rhetor, the connection between the rhetor and the audience remains intact."[34]

Foss and Griffin's invitational rhetoric evinces several affinities with the notion of a cruciform "confession" that I have culled from the New Testament and Christian theology. First, in their desire to eschew persuasion they echo my contention that confession is primarily responsive rather than persuasive. It may very well be that one cannot communicate without attempting to persuade; be that as it may, the issue in ὁμολογεῖν, it will be recalled, is less about the *end* of such activity and more about the *impetus* for its undertaking. Confessing arises most usually in response to (1) the word of faith proclaimed and (2) the external circumstances (be they a service of baptism, a question put to the speaker, or a situation of doubt, duress, or need) that call for confession. In this sense, confession is most concerned for its *fidelity* to the word prompting it and for its *attentiveness* to the situation occasioning it. For this reason, I affirm the sentiments of Foss and Griffin and similarly want to suggest an alternative to the common assumption that "persuasion" is the primary goal of rhetoric and, therefore, also of preaching. This is not to say that good preaching (or, for that matter, bad preaching) may not in fact be persuasive, or even to deny that preachers hope their words are believed, counted as trustworthy, and to that extent are persuasive. Rather, it is to assert that persuasion is not the central goal of preaching and cannot be allowed to supplant the inherently responsive character of confessional preaching.

Second, Foss and Griffin's description of offering perspectives appears akin to my own desire to confess Jesus Christ so as to offer a narrative, communal identity in which believers discover a distinctively Christian pattern for making meaning (participation).[35] While I have

<hr>

34. Foss and Griffin, "Beyond Persuasion," pp. 11-12.

35. See, again, Brian Gerrish's chapter on "The Confession of Faith," in *Saving and Secular Faith: An Invitation to Systematic Theology* (Minneapolis: Augsburg Press, 1999), pp. 49-66.

already suggested that Christian confession is somewhat different from either Rose's, or Foss and Griffin's, "tentative proposal," confession's willingness to live apart from certitude makes the distinction one of degree, not of category. Further, and as Foss and Griffin point out, offering perspectives involves more than the giving of opinions; it is an "inventive" and "creative" way for passionately proposing an entirely new "frame of reference." Interestingly, they contend that it proves especially effective for "marginalized groups to use in their efforts to transform systems of domination and oppression."[36] As Foss and Griffin describe,

> Although invitational rhetoric is not designed to create a specific change, such as the transformation of systems of oppression into ones that value and nurture individuals, it may produce such an outcome. Invitational rhetoric may resist an oppressive system simply because it models an alternative to the system by being "itself an Other way of thinking/speaking."[37]

Given that a view of the world *kata stauron* will always be in conflict with the reigning worldview, their strategy for creative re-sourcement may prove particularly helpful to Christian preachers. For this reason, and perhaps not surprisingly, when Walter Brueggemann describes preaching as testimony, he employs a number of kindred phrases to those of Foss and Griffin. Acknowledging that preaching is a matter of advocating an "odd truth" that is in "deep tension with the dominant, commonly accepted givens" of the world, Brueggemann writes,

> Rhetoric among the decentered not only has a different intention, that is, to propose a countertruth that subverts but also *a different style or mode of articulation*. It is not excessively solemn or rationalistic or final or given with too much sobriety. Rather, it is an utterance that is playful, open, teasing, inviting, and capable of voicing the kind of unsure tentativeness and ambiguity that exiles must always entertain, if they are to maintain freedom of imagination outside of the hegemony. Such utterances do not yield flat certitudes that can be everywhere counted upon. Rather they yield generative possibili-

36. Foss and Griffin, "Beyond Persuasion," p. 16.
37. Foss and Griffin, "Beyond Persuasion," pp. 16-17.

ties of something that is not known or available until this moment of utterance.[38]

Third, in Foss and Griffin's description of the need to create an environment of safety, value, and freedom in which hearers can order their world, I find a remarkably clear restatement of my own interest in preserving the critical distance of the hearer (distanciation). By creating this kind of environment, Foss and Griffin's rhetor maintains the integrity of her position without risking the relationship between rhetor and audience.[39] Similarly, I have suggested that confession is inherently self-validating and therefore the preacher need neither rely on the hearer for confirmation nor, consequently, put the hearer under any pressure to produce a particular response.

Finally, Foss and Griffin's desire through their rhetoric to invite the "audience to enter the rhetor's world and see it as the rhetor does" bears a distinct affinity to my own sense that the goal of preaching is for hearers to appropriate (rather than merely give assent to) the Christian identity and pattern of meaning offered. That affinity can be strengthened by noting two things related to their description of the rhetoric they propose as "invitational." First, and as they admit, one's acceptance of an alternative worldview does not always feel like a matter of "choice"; in fact, and as we observed at the end of Chapter Four, we are sometimes drawn to distinct positions against our conscious will.[40] Second, "invitation" itself, according to speech-act theory, is not completely benign or innocuous, as it is a directive, demanding some kind of volitional choice from the hearer. Nevertheless, I do appreciate their intention to offer an alternative, noncoercive rhetoric to the classical one. For all these reasons, Foss and Griffin offer some concrete resources for constructing a rhetoric of confession.

38. Walter Brueggemann, *Cadences of Home: Preaching Among Exiles* (Louisville: Westminster/John Knox Press, 1997), p. 57.

39. Foss and Griffin, "Beyond Persuasion," p. 12.

40. Foss and Griffin, "Beyond Persuasion," pp. 14-15. Recall, also, that for Thomas Kuhn adopting a new paradigm is always to some degree against one's will; hence his use of the word "conversion." See Kuhn, *The Structure of Scientific Revolutions,* 2nd ed. (Chicago: University of Chicago Press, 1970), pp. 198-204.

A *"Kenotic" Rhetoric*

Our study in Chapter Three contended that God's decisive activity in Jesus Christ and, in particular, in his cross and resurrection, stands at the very center of the Christian confession. Similarly, Resner and Patte argue that preaching, in order to be *Christian* preaching, must also be shaped and formed entirely by the cross and resurrection of Jesus Christ. In short, because there can be no separation between form and content — that is, no formulation of a message apart from the distinct shape and means for its communication — the "how" as well as the "what" of our preaching must conform itself to the pattern of the cross and resurrection of Jesus Christ. It is on this basis that I want to contend that confession is a helpful, and perhaps at this time crucial, way of conceiving of preaching not simply because it is (1) suitable to our postmodern context and (2) represents a pattern found in the New Testament and therefore is distinctively Christian, but also (3) because *it faithfully model's God's own act of self-disclosure in the cross and resurrection of Jesus Christ.* Confession, as a summary of the Christian tradition, witnesses to the cross and resurrection by its *content.* Further, confession, as the articulation of that tradition (1) in response to the need of the world and (2) in a way that does not coerce appropriation of that tradition, witnesses to the cross and resurrection also by the *pattern of its activity.*

For this reason, and following Resner and Patte, I want to propose an inverse rhetoric of Christian confession by which we can think more clearly and faithfully about the nature of our sermons as acts of confessing Christ. This means, most importantly, challenging the dominant perspective that rhetoric and preaching are first and foremost about "persuading" hearers to accept what we earnestly believe.[41] For in the cross of Jesus Christ we find that God's most eloquent Word is spoken, not principally to persuade us of something, but in response to our desperate need. The cross and resurrection do, in fact, offer an entirely new framework in which to view ourselves, others, the world, God, and our relationships to all of these, but even — and perhaps especially — the cross confronts us as an inherently ambiguous event that itself demands interpretation. It does not absorb us, but rather con-

---

41. For opinions to the contrary, see Lucy Lind Hogan and Robert Reid, *Connecting with the Congregation: Rhetoric and the Art of Preaching* (Nashville: Abingdon Press, 1999).

fronts us with an alternative reality that makes a claim upon us and unfailingly prompts, but does not coerce, some kind of response.[42]

Such a homiletic is, then, simultaneously bold and tentative, both assertive and vulnerable. In describing Christ's assuming our human nature and condescending to take on our lot and our life, even to the point of dying on the cross, theologians have sometimes employed the Greek word *kenosis,* which means "emptying." In the hymn quoted by the Apostle Paul, Christ "though he was in the form of God, did not consider equality with God something to be exploited, but emptied himself (ἑαυτὸν ἐκένωσεν), taking the form of a slave, being born in human likeness, and humbled himself to death, even death on the cross" (Phil. 2:6-8). Given that the cross — a moment of supreme weakness according to the standards of the world — reveals God's power, Paul is not surprised that the message of the cross appears similarly weak, even "foolish" (1 Cor. 1:18-25). As a follower of Jesus Christ, Paul empties himself and willingly appears weak, even foolish to his hearers so as to proclaim the cross faithfully (1 Cor. 2:1-5; 9:19-23; 2 Cor. 6:3-10).

Similarly, by refusing to contend that preaching is inherently the "strong" word of persuasion and by adopting instead "weaker" words like "confessing" and "witnessing" to describe the goal of faithful preaching, I seek to describe a similarly kenotic rhetoric, one that proclaims Christ by following his lead through the darkness of Good Friday to the dawn of the new day at Easter. In short, preachers of the cross must be prepared to empty themselves and risk the rejection of the "weak" word of the gospel in terms of both the content and form of their confession.

In proposing Paul Ricoeur's dialectic of participation and distanciation toward appropriation as a means by which to conceive of the dynamics of confession, and by drawing upon the invitational rhetoric of Sonja Foss and Cindy Griffin as a vehicle by which to execute the same, I am less interested in constructing an "appropriate" homiletic for our postmodern context than I am in elucidating and illustrating a homiletic governed by the pattern of God's manifestation made

---

42. This shift from understanding the goal of rhetoric from "persuasion" to "understanding" and "cooperation" also reflects more recent treatments of rhetoric. See, for instance, Kenneth Burke, *A Rhetoric of Motives* (Berkeley: University of California Press, 1950), and *Language as Symbolic Action* (Berkeley: University of California Press, 1966).

most clear in the cross and resurrection of Jesus Christ. The narrative, communal identity I seek to offer is none other than that of being followers of the crucified and risen Lord rendered in the New Testament. Similarly, in my call to preserve the critical distance of our hearers that they may appropriate, rather than merely assent or adhere to, that identity, I seek to echo the "incarnational" stance of vulnerability of the one "who . . . emptied himself" (Phil. 2:7). From my point of view — that is, from my confession of faith — Ricoeur, Foss, Griffin, and others present creative analogues or, maybe better, to borrow from Barth, "secular parables" of God's own form of communication through Christ.

God's speaking to us through Jesus Christ has already emerged as a distinct concern of this project and has governed the content of the confession we seek to proclaim and our understanding of the nature of the biblical texts from which that confession is drawn. It is time, now, to think about the concrete implications of God's "most eloquent Word" to us in Jesus Christ for the shape of our preaching. That is, I want to explore the question of how we give shape, and thereby call into existence, the confession we have received from our conversation with the biblical canon so that we might articulate it with, to, and for the community and offer it for their appropriation to spark and nurture their ongoing conversation of faith. For this reason, I turn now to consider the form and language of our preaching.

Form as Movement

As Cornelius Plantinga observes, the "hottest issues" in homiletics these days "center on sermon design."[43] This has been increasingly the case ever since 1958 when, in his *Design for Preaching*, H. Grady Davis invited preachers to imagine that "a sermon should be like a tree."[44] By supplanting the dominant construction image of "building," "assembling," or "putting together" a sermon with a more organic image of a growing tree, Davis shifted attention away from the sermon's content

43. Cornelius Plantinga, Jr., "Dancing the Edge of Mystery," *Books and Culture*, September/October 1999, p. 17.
44. H. Grady Davis, *Design for Preaching*, p. 15.

to its form or, to borrow the phrase of Long, the *form of its content.*[45] Since then, books emphasizing the form, structure, or plot of the sermon have flourished, offering preachers a variety of forms with which to enflesh their confession.[46] My intent in this chapter is not to sort through this vast literature but rather to offer one observation and follow a few of its implications: *the form of the sermon should embody its essential movement.*

This is not an original observation. As early as 1971, Fred Craddock drew attention to the definitive place a sermon's movement held in its entire composition, seeking to displace the traditional deductive movement from universal principles to particular application with its reverse, an inductive movement from the particular to the universal.[47] Since then, Eugene Lowry, Robin Meyers, and others have pointed to the movement of the sermon as the determining element expressing the preacher's interaction with the text as it emerges on the pages of the sermon. What I seek to accomplish in this section, then, is not so much to *make the point* about the centrality of the sermon's movement to its composition, as I want to describe the necessary movement inherent in a sermon that seeks to confess Jesus Christ and then offer several observations that may help preachers lend shape to their sermon in relation to the distinct confession they seek to offer.

The clue to the movement of confession comes from recalling that preaching "according to the cross" of Jesus Christ, because it creates a crisis for the world, inevitably meets resistance. As André Resner pointed out, viewing life from the vantage point of the cross demands a new orientation toward all of life, including preaching, and therefore brings one into opposition with the norms and expectations of the

45. Long, *The Witness of Preaching*, p. 93; see also Eugene Lowry, *The Sermon: Dancing the Edge of Mystery* (Nashville: Abingdon Press, 1997), p. 12.

46. For instructional surveys of the literature on forms, see Fred Craddock, *Preaching* (Nashville: Abingdon Press, 1985), pp. 170-93; Long, *The Witness of Preaching*, pp. 92-132; Henry Mitchell, *Celebration and Experience in Preaching* (Nashville: Abingdon Press, 1990), pp. 37-60. For samples of sermons written in different forms, see Thomas G. Long and Cornelius Plantinga, Jr., *A Chorus of Witnesses: Model Sermons for Today's Preacher* (Grand Rapids: Eerdmans, 1994), esp. pp. 163-233; and Ronald J. Allen, ed., *Patterns of Preaching: A Sermon Sampler* (St. Louis: Chalice Press, 1998).

47. Fred Craddock, *As One without Authority,* 3rd ed. (Nashville: Abingdon Press, 1983 [1971]).

governing order.[48] As James F. Kay writes, "the word of the cross effects the same death to the construals and patterns of the old age and the resultant awakening to those of the new as the original cross-event itself."[49] In short, the very presence of the "new order" calls into question the terms of the old.[50] To borrow the language of Griffin and Foss, preachers of the gospel live in an inherently hostile environment and therefore must employ a strategy of re-sourcement, a disengagement from the dominant framework so as to offer an alternative vocabulary, perspective, and world.[51]

At this point one might wonder whether "disengagement" and "offering" are strong enough terms to describe the radical break from the patterns of this world that life "according to the cross" implies. In point of fact, however, Foss and Griffin's proposal depends upon a strong and clear indictment of the persuasive goal of classical rhetoric that stems from patriarchal desire for control and domination.[52] This is not at all to accuse Foss and Griffin of inconsistency, but rather to suggest that disengaging and offering often necessitate indicting, unmasking, and betraying the lie of the hegemonic forces of opposition. In this vein, I would suggest that as preachers we are similarly called to "expose," "name as idolatrous," and "tell the truth about" worldly realities that conflict with life *kata stauron,* just as Paul frankly "told the truth" about the infidelity of life *kata sarka* in his correspondence with the Corinthians (2 Cor. 6:11; 7:2-13).

By framing our discussion of the movement of the sermon in terms of "truth telling," we have ventured into the terrain of one

---

48. Resner, *Preacher and Cross,* p. 115.

49. Kay, "The Word of the Cross," p. 47.

50. See Gerhard Forde, "The Work of Christ," in *Christian Dogmatics,* vol. 2, ed. Carl E. Braaten and Robert W. Jenson (Philadelphia: Fortress Press, 1984), pp. 1-99.

51. Foss and Griffin, "Beyond Persuasion," p. 9.

52. Consider, for instance, the quotation employed by Foss and Griffin to describe the "pervasive" consequences of patriarchal domination: "We conquered trees and converted them into a house, taking pride in having accomplished a difficult task. We conquered rivers and streams and converted them into lakes, marveling in ourselves at the improvement we made on nature. We tramped with our conquering spaceboots on the fine ancient dust of the Moon and we sent our well-rehearsed statements of triumph back for a waiting world to hear." S. M. Gearhart, "The Womanization of Rhetoric," *Women's Studies International Quarterly* 2 (1979): 196; quoted in Griffin and Foss, "Beyond Persuasion," pp. 1-2.

homiletician who in recent years has also described the task of preaching, or at least part of that task, as "confession." In her 1992 book, *Preaching as Weeping, Confession, and Resistance: Radical Responses to Radical Evil,* Christine Smith makes "confession" the middle piece of a three-part sermonic movement that seeks to name and transform the evil in our midst.[53] First, according to Smith, preachers must weep, not simply to express sadness, but rather to give voice to the depths "of human experience that most of us have known." Weeping, therefore, is when preachers "engage their deepest passions, their highest values, their surest convictions" and "make them present and alive in moments of proclamation."[54]

In addition to passionate weeping, however, preachers must also confess. As with "weeping," Smith also envisions a different kind of "confessing" than the reader may immediately imagine. As she writes,

> But weeping is not enough. A world infected and diseased by radical evil also needs truth just as radical. Much of the Christian community has come to understand confession as speaking about the sinfulness of our lives and receiving God's forgiveness and grace. . . . How might confession change in the liturgical expressions of Christian communities if we understood it as profound truth telling? Confession is a time to speak truth about our lives and about the nature of our world.[55]

Preaching, according to Smith, is just this kind of "confession, a moment in the life of the Christian community where truth is spoken."[56] Such truth telling in turn fosters resilient hope, for "hope is not engendered by illusions or lies; hope is engendered by truth." Therefore, "in the act of preaching we strive to speak the truth about life in the perpetual belief and abiding hope that such truth, as devastatingly ugly and as frighteningly beautiful as it is, is precisely what we bring to be offered, blessed, and transformed by God in the sacred act of preaching."

From such weeping and confession flows resistance, which "is not

---

53. Christine M. Smith, *Preaching as Weeping, Confession, and Resistance: Radical Responses to Radical Evil* (Louisville: Westminster/John Knox Press, 1992).

54. Smith, *Weeping, Confession, and Resistance,* p. 4.

55. Smith, *Weeping, Confession, and Resistance,* p. 4.

56. Smith, *Weeping, Confession, and Resistance,* p. 4.

just our reaction to the evil we experience and participate in, but it is our stand against it. It is not an act of standing still and defending ourselves against the evil that surrounds us, but it is a movement into it, and through it, with speech and presence and action."[57] In this way, preaching moves from passionate honesty to a steadfast resistance that transforms both preacher and listeners:

> To suggest that preaching is resistance is to invite members of religious communities to oppose the occupying power of evil in our world and to place their lives in the stream of those who are working for change. When individuals and communities decide to be God's revelation in the world, their alliances and loyalties must shift; the coalitions they build will drastically change; and justice must be the criterion through which all their theology is forged.[58]

Taken together, this three-part movement leads to an entirely different mode of preaching, one that culminates in what Smith names "redemptive activity": "When this passion and truth and resistance stand in faithful opposition to the oppression and suffering of humanity and stand firmly rooted in a fidelity to life, this is redemptive activity; this is saving activity."[59]

In her provocative and passionate work, Smith redeems "confession" from standing as an archaic liturgical rite that centers on individual wrongdoing so as to reclaim it as the vehicle by which to speak a cathartic, even purging word of truth. While Smith's sense of truth comes inevitably as a word of judgment, as we are called to name the evils in our world without shrinking from their terror, it also echoes Jesus' own declaration that while he came to the world not to judge, but to save it, nevertheless the light reveals the judgment already levied against evil, as those who do evil flee from the light (John 3:17-21). Truth, according both to Smith and John's Jesus, announces judgment and in this way "makes you free" (John 8).

Smith is not alone in her insistence that preaching is about naming the realities of this world. In a slender, elegant work, Frederick Buechner also depicts preaching as unflinchingly *Telling the Truth*. But

57. Smith, *Weeping, Confession, and Resistance*, p. 5.

58. Smith, *Weeping, Confession, and Resistance*, p. 6.

59. Smith, *Weeping, Confession, and Resistance*, p. 6.

for Buechner such truth telling has two parts, which he describes as news both bad and good. The bad comes first:

> The Gospel is bad news before it is good news. It is the news that man is a sinner, to use the old word, that he is evil in the imagination of his heart, that when he looks in the mirror all in a lather what he sees is at least eight parts chicken, phony, slob. That is the tragedy.

But the bad news, according to Buechner, does not have the last word, as "it is also the news that he is loved anyway, cherished, forgiven, bleeding, to be sure, but also bled for. And that is the comedy." These two together — both bad news and good, tragedy and comedy — constitute what Buechner describes as the gospel as fairy tale, the promise that

> extraordinary things happen to [us] just as in fairy tales extraordinary things happen. Henry Ward Beecher cheats on his wife, his God, and himself, but manages to keep on bringing the Gospel to life for people anyway, maybe even for himself. Lear goes berserk on a heath but comes out of it for a few brief hours every inch a king. Zacchaeus climbs up a sycamore tree a crook and climbs down a saint. Paul sets out a hatchet man for the Pharisees and comes back a fool for Christ. It is impossible for anybody to leave behind the darkness of the world he carries on his back like a snail, but for God all things are possible. This is the fairy tale. All together they are the truth.[60]

From Buechner's point of view, then, it is not that Smith's sense of preaching as confession is wrong, but simply — and woefully — incomplete. The only news she asks preachers to tell is unrelentingly from the story of human activity: "Preaching is an act of public theological naming. It is an act of disclosing and articulating the truths about our present human existence. It is an act of bringing new reality into being, an act of creation." As Smith continues, it becomes clear that she believes that such naming of the human plight is enough, as preaching is not only an act of creation, but "it is also an act of redeeming and transforming reality, an act of shattering illusions and cracking open lim-

---

60. Frederick Buechner, *Telling the Truth: The Gospel as Tragedy, Comedy, and Fairy Tale* (New York: HarperCollins, 1977), pp. 7-8.

ited perspectives. It is nothing less than the interpretation of our present world and an invitation to build a profoundly different world."[61]

Remarkably, there is almost no mention of preaching as telling about God's intervention or announcing God's coming rule.[62] Smith, it appears, works with an entirely "realized" eschatology — she neither looks for nor announces God's intervention and seems to believe that passionately naming and resisting evil in our preaching is enough to overcome that evil and change the world. Such a view discloses not only her understanding of eschatology, but also her theological anthropology, as she describes a "deep, abiding belief that human beings are basically good" and a hope that "the human community is moving toward a day in which justice will prevail." These serve as assumptions that she does not want to give up, even as she confronts radical evil that questions (but does not ultimately contradict?) those foundational beliefs.

These themes surface also in her earlier work, *Weaving the Sermon: Preaching in a Feminist Perspective*. Here, too, the human activity of naming evil provides the foundation upon which to engage in the equally human activity of "salvation":

> Our experiences of pain and suffering and our empowered responses to that oppression becomes the context for salvific action. Salvation is not that which happens to us when we are "saved" from ourselves by a mediating savior; rather salvation is something we do with each other in community.[63]

Writing from her feminist position, Smith presents a compelling dimension of confession that resonates with my own to a certain degree. But in limiting her view of confession to exposing only the truth about the injustices we commit upon one another, she risks truncating the Christian tradition, which has always pointed not only to human sinfulness, but also to God's intervening and transforming mercy in the person of Jesus Christ. Apart from that witness, and the promise

---

61. Smith, *Weeping, Confession, and Resistance*, p. 2.

62. Indeed, "God" as an active agent is barely mentioned. God forgives the sins we confess (in the narrow understanding of confession she seeks to transcend) (p. 4) and God in some way blesses and transforms the preaching we offer (p. 5).

63. Christine M. Smith: *Weaving the Sermon: Preaching in a Feminist Perspective* (Louisville: Westminster/John Knox Press, 1989), p. 87.

that God is not yet finished with creation, preaching turns into the wan story of humanity's occasional resistance against, but far more frequent acquiescence to, radical evil. As Thomas G. Long writes, "there remains an aching loneliness" in Smith's approach to preaching: "There is no saving Word from the outside, and the community is, in the end, basically abandoned, left essentially to its own thoughts and emotions, finally able to talk meaningfully only to and about itself."[64] While such preaching may be termed "confession," it cannot properly be described as "confessing Jesus Christ."

Preaching as confession is unmistakably about telling the truth; but it is about telling both sides of the story. Re-sourcement, according to Griffin and Foss, is not only about disengaging, but also engaging, offering hearers another possibility, an alternative framework by which to understand life in God's world. Hence, confessional preaching has an inherently two-dimensional character, telling the story, as Paul Scott Wilson puts it, of both our "burden" and God's "burden." Our burden, according to Wilson, is all that is expected of us — from life, from God, from ourselves. Whether it appears at times bearable or, more frequently, unbearable, it is unmistakably ours. But authentic Christian preaching also speaks of God's taking on our burden, of making it God's own in Jesus Christ.[65]

The movement from perceiving the enormity of our burden to hearing that God has taken that burden upon God's own self is, in Buechner's terms, the move from bad news to good; according to Wilson, the movement from judgment to grace; and in Paul's terms, the movement from cross to resurrection and from death to life. Further, as Gustaf Wingren indicates, it is the narrative movement that dominates the whole of Scripture, for it tells the story of the conflict between God and all that opposes God and oppresses humanity, as well as tells the story of God's ultimate victory.[66] According to Wingren, this narrative tension and movement is recast several times. In the Old Testament, Adam and Eve are tempted by the serpent, and Israel is opposed first by Pharaoh and later by the surrounding nations (and their

64. Thomas G. Long, "And How Shall They Hear?" p. 185.
65. Paul Scott Wilson, *Imagination of the Heart: New Understandings in Preaching* (Nashville: Abingdon Press, 1988), p. 107.
66. Gustaf Wingren, *The Living Word: A Theological Study of Preaching and the Church* (Philadelphia: Muhlenberg Press, 1960), pp. 50-55.

gods); in the New Testament, Jesus is opposed by the demons and vanquishes the evil one through healing, exorcism, and ultimately through his death on the cross and vindication in the resurrection.[67] Despite its variations, however, from Genesis to Revelation the theme of God's conflict with, and triumph over, the forces of evil is one of the few unitary strands that holds all the books of the Bible together.[68]

Confession that is rooted in the biblical narrative, then, tells the truth both of the conflict of God with the forces of evil — and of our dual role as accomplices with, and victims of, oppression — and of God's victory over evil. While preaching must therefore embrace the harsh and somber truth telling advocated by Smith, it must also move to announce God's victory through Christ, the event in which all of God's other interventions in Israel's history find their consummation.[69] To put it another way, the two-dimensional character of confessional preaching becomes most obvious in the preaching of cross and resurrection, as in these pivotal events the entire drama of God's struggle to redeem humanity is not simply retold, but actually extended into the present moment.[70]

Putting matters this way, however, reminds us that we live between Christ's resurrection and our own; hence the need to continue telling the truth about our condition and God's response to it. God's victory, while decisive, is not yet fully realized.[71] For this reason, confessional preaching does not simply witness to the conflict and victory, but actually participates in it by announcing God's victory in Christ and God's coming reign and in this way provokes a response of faith in this God.

67. Wingren, *The Living Word,* pp. 42-46.

68. Wingren, *The Living Word,* pp. 55-58.

69. Wingren, *The Living Word,* p. 50.

70. See 1 Cor. 1:18-31. As Kay writes, "Ultimately, the truth of the cross, its logos, is conveyed or enacted not by the compelling power of Paul's word, but by the power of God at work in the cross and its word or message" ("The Word of the Cross," p. 49).

71. Oscar Cullmann's brilliant metaphor of living between D-Day and V-Day well captures the tension between the "already" of Christ's resurrection and the "not yet" of the redemption of all creation. After the Normandy invasion the victory of the Allies was assured; while subsequent battles remained for those who continued to fight until the official victory was declared and hostilities ceased, they at least knew that they fought for a "winning cause" and were encouraged by such hope. See Cullmann's *Christ and Time: The Primitive Christian Conception of Time and History* (Philadelphia: Westminster Press, 1964), pp. 139-43.

Confessional preaching, therefore, is inherently eschatological, and even apocalyptic, in that it prompts a confessional response that joins the believer to God's struggle and victory. As the Apostle Paul writes, "just as we have the same spirit of faith that is in accordance with scripture — 'I believed, and so I spoke' — we also believe, and so we speak, because we know that the one who raised the Lord Jesus will raise us also with Jesus, and will bring us with him into his presence" (2 Cor. 4:13-14).

Because confessional preaching implies not simply movement, but a consistent movement from the truth of our condition to the new truth of God's merciful response to our condition — a movement Foss and Griffin analogically describe as disengagement to creative response or, following Paul, the move from cross to resurrection — I want to suggest that the form we choose be employed to reflect this movement in the sermon. The sermon, therefore, seeks less to describe the journey of the preacher, let alone what a preacher "learned" from the text, than it does to witness to the dynamic movement from the "old" truth of our condition to the "new" truth of God's response to our condition encountered in the preacher's conversation with the text.

But while the movement from the "old" word of the world to the "new" word proclaimed in the cross and resurrection is consistent, and perhaps even to some degree predictable, it is not made by rote, but instead is shaped by the particular texts at hand and the context, circumstances, and needs of the congregation. For this reason, stressing that the sermon should move us from cross to resurrection helps us to perceive what the form *does,* but it does not decide for us *which* form to choose. There are a plethora of forms available, and in seeking to choose one that faithfully embodies and executes the confession we want to offer to the congregation, we may be aided by asking and answering these two questions:

1. What does the sermon seek to do to its hearers through its confession?
2. How does the intention of the preacher's confession relate to the confession of the text?

1. What does the sermon seek to do to its hearers through its confession?

Addressing this question is even more important than deciding what the sermon seeks to *say* to the hearers, as what the sermon does will largely determine what it says.[72] For example, the statement "The Lord is coming!" actually *means* different things when said as a word of comfort, of promise, or of warning. To put the matter this way is to ask what distinct illocutionary speech act the sermon seeks to perform.

Two notes are in order at this point. First, and to borrow again the insights of Mikhail Bakhtin and the language of John R. Searle, while preaching envisioned as the practice of confessing faith is always assertive in terms of its genre, it may nevertheless perform other speech acts in terms of its content. Recall Searle's distinction between serious and fictional literature. The difference determines the genre-specific force of the text — either I take the speech acts performed here seriously (as in a newspaper report, political speech, or sermon) or I "suspend" those forces and relate to them on a different level (as when reading a novel or watching a play). Thus, while every sermon is a confession in that it seeks to assert the truth of what it says and refuses to coerce the hearer into acquiescence, within that confession the sermon may perform any number of speech acts, just as the Bible is assertive in terms of its genre (it expects to be taken seriously) even as it does a number of things in terms of its content, commanding and promising, accusing and forgiving.

Second, when discerning what one wants to do through one's confession, it will be helpful to think not only in terms of Searle's broad categories, but also in terms of the nuances within them. For this reason, we may ask ourselves first and foremost whether by our confession we want to promise, to praise, to bless, to warn, to remind, to thank, to invite, to pray, to instruct, to name, to accuse, to forgive, and so forth. The sermon form, whatever else it may accomplish, should bring us to the point of executing the illocutionary intention in the sermon.

2. How does the intention of the preacher's confession relate to that of the text?

Because the Bible is central to confessional preaching, addressing this question often helps to specify the shape we may give to the movement of our confession. If, for instance, the confession of the sermon seeks largely to affirm the confession of the text, the text itself may offer the appropriate form. Hence, one may preach a sermon of praise on

---

72. For this reason, I would reverse Thomas G. Long's ordering of focus and function, inviting preachers to determine the sermon's function first. See Long, *The Witness of Preaching*, pp. 78-91.

a Psalm of praise, not only by affirming the Psalm's confession, but also by borrowing its form.[73]

Let's say, however, that upon reading Paul's affirmation that "God works for the good of all things for those who love him" (Rom. 8:28) the preacher wonders how this can possibly be true in light of the suffering she observes in the lives of her parishioners. Even if the preacher seeks ultimately to affirm Paul's assertion on the basis of her conversation with the text, in this case she will probably not seek simply to adopt Paul's boldly assertive form, but rather seek a form more suited to probing the confession of the text. Perhaps she will explore several common but unsatisfactory possibilities for affirming Paul's statement before coming to some sense of appropriation by sifting Paul's assertion through other biblical passages and her life experience. In this case, Craddock's sense of the "not this, nor this, nor this, but this" kind of form might suit.[74] Or, perhaps she believes Paul's assertion, but acknowledges her own objections and anticipates those of the congregation. As a consequence, she may decide to work through those objections toward some sense of resolution that results in a new understanding of the text. In this case, the preacher might be well served by Samuel Proctor's "dialectical" method.[75]

Similarly, one may wish to extend the confession of the text, broadening it to address contemporary concerns; or, conversely, one may want to call into question the confession of the text, usually on the basis of other texts. Each of these suggests yet other possibilities for working with established forms to reflect the confession of the sermon most clearly and faithfully. Sometimes, the preacher's own journey to her confession will suggest a form, as that journey may provide a clue as to how to confess to her hearers so that they may share in, and appropriate, the preacher's discovery.[76] Other times, the journey may not be nearly as important as the confession arrived at through study, in

73. See Thomas G. Long, *Preaching and the Literary Forms of the Bible* (Philadelphia: Fortress Press, 1989), pp. 43-126; and Wilder, *Early Christian Rhetoric* (Cambridge, Mass.: Harvard University Press, 1971), pp. 40-117.

74. See Craddock, *Preaching*, p. 174; see also Long, *The Witness of Preaching*, p. 128.

75. Samuel Proctor, *The Certain Sound of the Trumpet: Crafting a Sermon of Authority* (Valley Forge, Pa.: Judson Press, 1994).

76. This was one of the central insights behind Fred Craddock's *As One without Authority*. See esp. pp. 143-58.

which case the preacher's specific journey may contribute little to the form of her confession.

Finally, we should note that perceiving the degree to which the "new" word of the cross and resurrection inevitably calls into question and comes into conflict with the "old" word of the human condition enables us to appreciate the recent turn in homiletics to narrative sermonic forms. Conflict and its resolution are central to narrative; as a consequence, narrative offers a conducive vehicle to sermonic confession.[77] In this light, it is not surprising that preachers have seized upon plays, movies, books, and personal stories to help convey the confession they seek to make.[78] Preachers can also profitably harvest the work of biblical scholars who have demonstrated the literary power of the biblical narratives.[79] I have already stated in Chapter Four that insisting on starting always with either the biblical narrative or a story drawn from somewhere else is a mistake. The task is to set "our story" and the "biblical story" in conversation, that they may illumine each other, and different confessions will call for different starting places.[80] At the same time, it is important to recognize that preaching from the biblical narrative, and allowing that narrative to shape decisively the sermon, has several distinct advantages. At a minimum, it teaches hearers the Bible, grounds them in the narrative identity offered by the New Testament, and helps them to perceive the connection between God's work confessed in the texts and God's work in their lives. These benefits, and the fact that the biblical narratives are so ready at hand, commend preaching the biblical narratives highly. But the central task remains to relate the biblical narrative — including its non-narrative portions! — and our experience so that the hearer can perceive and ap-

77. See Aristotle, *Poetics,* trans. W. Hamilton Fyfe and W. Rhys Roberts (Cambridge, Mass.: Harvard University Press, 1932), pp. 39-45.

78. See, for example, *Journeys in Narrative Preaching,* ed. Wayne Bradley Robinson (New York: Pilgrim Press, 1990).

79. See, for instance, Robert Alter, *The Art of Biblical Narrative* (New York: Basic Books, 1981); and Mark Allan Powell, *What Is Narrative Criticism?* (Minneapolis: Fortress Press, 1990).

80. For several strategies for doing this, see Stephen Farris, *Preaching That Matters: The Bible and Our Lives* (Louisville: Westminster/John Knox Press, 1998), pp. 25-124; Campbell, *Preaching Jesus: New Directions for Homiletics in Hans Frei's Postliberal Theology* (Grand Rapids: Eerdmans, 1997), pp. 250-57; and Justo L. and Catherine G. González, *The Liberating Pulpit* (Nashville: Abingdon Press, 1994), pp. 96-119.

propriate a manifestation of God's power akin to that represented in the cross and resurrection of Jesus Christ. Thus, while narrative can be a very powerful element in sermons, especially when preaching on biblical narratives, it is neither the only element nor the singular form that preachers can draw upon.[81] In the end, the form of the sermon should (1) embody the confession the preacher drew from a lively encounter with the text so that (2) it executes its illocutionary intention in the lives of the hearers.

The Language of Confession

Sermonic form is one way in which we can attempt to enable our preaching clearly and faithfully to articulate the confession we derive from our conversation with the texts and now seek to offer to our congregations for their appropriation. Sermonic language is another.

Interestingly, by surveying the same literature in which we find an abundance of interest in sermonic form, we find nearly the opposite level of engagement with sermonic language. Most texts subsume considerations of language under headings designated as akin to either "writing for the ear" or "images and experience."[82] But language, perhaps even more than form, enables us to confess the faith so as not only to give voice to the classic tradition of the faith in a new setting, but also to do so in a way that grants the hearer the critical distance in which to appropriate that confession. For this reason, it does not surprise me that those homileticians who have most focused on the hearer's role in preaching have also devoted the greatest attention to language.

One such writer, Fred Craddock, suggests that good use of language makes illustrations nearly superfluous: that which has been evoked clearly and concretely needs no illustration.[83] He is right; the simple use of clear, evocative language can serve to engage the hearts and minds of hearers as well as any illustration and most narrative. But I want to go one step further: good use of language is also what embod-

81. See Farris, *Preaching That Matters,* pp. 22-24.

82. See, for example, Davis, *Design for Preaching,* pp. 268-94; or Long, *Witness of Preaching,* pp. 156-80. See also G. Robert Jacks, *Just Say the Word! Writing for the Ear* (Grand Rapids: Eerdmans, 1996).

83. Craddock, *Preaching,* p. 196.

ies our confessions in the preaching moment so as to offer the gathered community a narrative, communal identity while simultaneously preserving the critical distance in which they can consider and appropriate that identity.

Craddock also suggests that there are essentially two kinds of language: (1) that which primarily conveys information and (2) that which evokes feeling.[84] Here I disagree, remembering Austin's observation that all speech is ultimately performative, as even constative descriptions do something (namely, describe).[85] What I am interested in saying, instead, is that language in a confessional sermon primarily *does* two things: it offers to us a communal identity and/or creates the distance in which we can appropriate that identity. Notice that language does, not one *or* the other, but one *and/or* the other, as the same sentence, worded carefully, can simultaneously offer identity and preserve space within which to appropriate that identity. Notice, too, that my interest is not in certain words, but rather in our use of language; that is, in how we use words to achieve certain illocutionary ends. I want further to divide each of these two confessional categories once more, providing four kinds of language to discuss. I describe these four with the adjectives *ultimate, urgent, relational,* and *vulnerable.* The first two fall into the category primarily of offering identity; the second fall primarily into preserving space for the hearer to be encountered by, and appropriate, the claims of that identity.

Ultimate

The Christian gospel makes an ultimate claim: in the cross and resurrection of Jesus Christ God has acted decisively for the redemption of all

---

84. Craddock, *Preaching,* p. 196.

85. Austin, *How to Do Things with Words,* 2nd ed., ed. J. O. Urmson and Maria Sbisà (Cambridge, Mass.: Harvard University Press, 1975), pp. 133-47. Take Craddock's example of informational (Austin's constative) language, for instance: "At five-thirty this afternoon a twin-engine Cessna enroute from Louisville to Shreveport crashed into Laurel Mountain, killing all six people on board" (p. 196). Not only does this sentence do something — informs us of something (in this case not simply an event, but a tragedy), but it also arouses feelings such as alarm, compassion, and sorrow with words like "crashed" and "killing," not to mention "all six people."

humanity and the whole cosmos. Preaching that shies away from making such claims denies the gospel.[86] Ultimate statements can be made in a variety of ways, but in each case they move beyond mere report of an incident or emotion to announce its significance. Because the significance of an event is always an interpretation, that announcement is a confession of faith. Hence, were the Apostle Paul to state simply that "Christ died," he would be conveying the information of an event and its possible emotional impact just as anyone might. But Paul says more; he adds his interpretation of the significance of his death: "Christ died *for our sins.*" In this interpretation is his confession and in that confession his claim — in Jesus Christ God was doing something of decisive import; namely, God was reconciling the world unto God's own self.

Christian preaching that seeks to confess Jesus Christ needs similarly to interpret the biblical texts and current events and confess their significance. These can take a variety of forms and are often reminiscent of the early creedal and confessional elements we discerned in our earlier study: Jesus died for us; God loves us; Christ's death on the cross redeems the whole cosmos; Christ was raised; Jesus is Lord; for God so loved the world that he gave his only Son. In each case, there is a deliberate, decisive move beyond mere report to make a claim.[87] It is my contention that a Christian sermon not only needs such moments of declaration, of ultimate speech, but that the sermon's center of gravity is located in them, as in these moments the illocutionary intention of the sermonic confession is most clearly realized. That is, when you approach the heart or climax of your sermon, you are most likely to be speaking in ultimate language.

Consider, for example, the ringing series of ultimate affirmations with which Karl Barth concludes his sermon on Leviticus 26:12: "I will walk among you, and will be your God, and you shall be my people."

Is it not the most inconceivable and the most exalting message we have heard this evening that we are to be God's people? I am glad I did not invent it, and hence it is not my responsibility to defend it.

---

86. This is, perhaps, the greatest weakness of Lucy Rose's program. (See Cornelius Plantinga, "Dancing the Edge of Mystery," p. 19.)

87. In this sense we might say that Paul Ricoeur's "hermeneutics of testimony" demands a "homiletics of confession," as the narrated witness of the texts must be interpreted and its significance proclaimed anew.

My only task and privilege is to tell you that God himself said so and says so until this day. On his authority I may and I must say to you, "Yes, you shall be my people!" Let us hear this assurance as well as the two preceding ones as God's word. Let us take it to heart, let us take it home, and maybe ponder it a while before we fall asleep tonight. "I will walk among you! I will be your God! You shall be my people!"

I am at the end. I tried to explain this Bible passage as the word of God fulfilled in Jesus Christ. Read and heard, understood and believed in this light, this word radiates infinite power. It then not only says, "I will walk among you," but "I *walk* among you!" Not only "I will be your God," but "I *am* your God!" Not only "You shall be my people," but "You *are* my people!" Do you sense the power of the word? The power of him in whom it is fulfilled and becomes a present reality? Be it as it may, because this is the word of God fulfilled in Jesus Christ, you and I may be assured beyond disquiet or doubt that things stand exactly as I have tried to tell you today. Amen.[88]

Barth conveys the assertive, confessional nature of his sermon through his own admission of its miraculous, nearly inconceivable nature. Despite his own difficulty in comprehending God's Word of promise, however, Barth testifies to the truth of his message, grounds its authority in the God who speaks through the texts, and declares that God's promise has, in fact, already been fulfilled in Jesus Christ and so utters it as a present reality for his hearers.

In a sermon preached on Jesus' words to Thomas, "Have you believed because you have seen me? Blessed are they who have not seen and yet believe" (John 20:29), Fleming Rutledge similarly acknowledges the difficulty of believing the testimony of the resurrection. "Is there anyone here today who is wondering if the Resurrection could possibly be true?" she asks, before describing the sight of "faith" that Easter requires. Then, in language as clearly confessional, assertive, and ultimate as Barth, she declares,

This morning I have nothing to show you in the way of proofs — no legal arguments, no signs, no stigmata, no miraculous relics. Magical proofs have I none, but what I have I give you: what I have is no

---

88. Karl Barth, *Deliverance to the Captives* (New York: Harper & Row, 1961), pp. 65-66.

less than what the first apostles had, what the Christian church as had from the beginning — the gift of faith. The church was not built on seeing with eyes, but on the "bond of trust between those who live in the presence of Christ today and those who first carried the Easter message 2000 years ago."

And so this morning, through the words of this merely human witness, the risen Lord looks at you this very day — looks past Thomas and the other disciples through the walls of All Saints' Chapel and across eternity and says "Blessed are they who have not seen, and yet believe."

Alleluia! Amen.[89]

Urgent

Both Barth's and Rutledge's sermons illustrate that sermonic language that roots hearers in an identity is not only ultimate, it is also urgent. That is, it seeks a response from the hearer. Both preachers seek the hearer's participation through the use of questions: "Do you sense the power of this word?" "Is there anyone here today who is wondering if the Resurrection could possibly be true?" Both preachers also lend urgency to their ultimate assertions by addressing them directly to their hearers: "On his authority I may and I must say to you, . . ." "the risen Lord looks at you this very day. . . ." Such language, to borrow the terms of Austin and Searle, unabashedly seeks to do something to us. Further, according to Searle, we gain some sense of what they hope to achieve by the illocutionary force they exercise. Direct address, as an assertion, prompts a response of belief or unbelief, of trust or distrust, that the words spoken are true. Gerhard Forde illustrates the urgency of direct, or primary, speech by comparing it to the language of lovers: When someone confesses "I love you," only one *kind* of response will do, a confession of similar character: either "I love you, too," or "I don't love you," but certainly not, "That's interesting," "the poets have many interesting things to say about love," or, to echo Pilate, "What is love?"[90]

89. Fleming Rutledge, *The Bible and the New York Times* (Grand Rapids: Eerdmans, 1998), pp. 143-44.

90. Gerhard O. Forde, *Theology Is for Proclamation*, pp. 2-3. Forde's formulation bears a striking resemblance to that of Rudolf Bultmann; on the latter, see James F. Kay,

As we saw in the previous chapter, it is precisely by means of this kind of assertive, direct language that the Bible — and the preacher — bridge the historical and existential chasm between words written long ago and hearers listening for a Word from God today. In speaking forth the declarations and promises of God through their confessions, preachers become the vehicle by which God speaks (as declarations imply a declarer and promises imply a promisor) so that hearers encounter Christ's presence in the world today through the proclaimed Word.

Herein lies the force of Barbara Brown Taylor's sermon on John 10 and its description of Jesus as the "Good Shepherd." With clarity and precision, Taylor addresses God's promise and declaration directly to the hearers:

> Above all, understand that you belong here, as part of the flock. If you do not believe anything else, believe that — that whether you are here because you believe or because you want to believe, you are here because you belong to God's sheep just like the rest of us. And because we do, we hear his voice, and we follow him, and he gives us eternal life, and we shall never perish, and no one shall snatch us out of his hand. Believe it or not, here we are, and here we belong.[91]

This is also, without a doubt, the great strength of Paul Tillich's sermon, "You Are Accepted," on Romans 5:20, "where sin abounded, grace did much more abound" (KJV). For whatever concerns one may have about his willingness to "translate" the distinctive Christian speech of "grace" into the secular, even psychoanalytic terms of "acceptance," at the climax of the sermon there is little doubt in the hearers' mind that they who have been named and identified so poignantly are also being addressed by, and urged to respond to, the God to whom Tillich witnesses:

> Grace strikes us when we are in great pain and restlessness. It strikes us when we walk though the dark valley of a meaningless and empty life. It strikes us when we feel that our separation is deeper than

---

Christus Praesens: A Reconsideration of Rudolf Bultmann's Christology (Grand Rapids: Eerdmans, 1994), pp. 45-49, 111-17.

91. Barbara Brown Taylor, *The Preaching Life* (Cambridge, Mass.: Cowley Publications, 1993), pp. 145-46.

usual, because we have violated another life, a life which we loved, or from which we were estranged. It strikes us when our disgust for our own being, our indifference, our weakness, our hostility, and our lack of direction and composure have become intolerable to us. It strikes us when, year after year, the longed-for perfection of life does not appear, when the old compulsions reign with us as they have for decades, when despair destroys all joy and courage. Sometimes at that moment a wave of light breaks into our darkness, and it is as though a voice were saying: "You are accepted. *You are accepted,* accepted by that which is greater than you, and the name of which you do not know. Do not ask for the name now; perhaps you will find it later. Do not try to do anything now; perhaps later you will do much. Do not seek for anything; do not perform anything; do not intend anything. *Simply accept the fact that you are accepted!*"[92]

Relational

In moving from considering language that seeks to ground hearers in a narrative, communal identity (confession as *fides quae creditur*) to describing language that creates the space in which hearers can be encountered by, and appropriate, that confession and through the Holy Spirit come to faith (confession as *fides qua creditur*), we perceive immediately how closely these two types of speech may be related, even in the same utterances. Hence, both Taylor and Tillich not only address their hearers directly, but also identify with them and thereby create a relationship between preacher and hearers. Thus, after saying to her hearers, "understand that you belong here, as part of the flock," Taylor later comes back to this refrain, this time including herself: "Believe it or not, here we are, and here we belong." Moving in a reverse direction, Tillich describes the many ways in which "we" feel empty and lost, only then to announce to the hearer directly, "You are accepted."

Confessional language is inherently relational because assertive, direct address is itself relational; it lives, that is, not in the third-person language of description but in the first- and second-person language of

92. Paul Tillich, "You Are Accepted," in *The Shaking of the Foundations* (New York: Charles Scribner's Sons, 1953), pp. 161-62.

relationship, always seeking an "in kind" response. It is not a report, but rather, as William Willimon indicates, "promise and summons."[93]

Further, confessional language seeks to articulate the faith in a way that hearers can appropriate it themselves and live more fully into the community of faith.[94] In this sense, preaching does indeed seek to "build up the body" by creating the space in which hearers can imagine and come to believe that what the preacher is saying is not simply true, but true for them. One way to do this, as we have already seen, is to identify with the congregation by addressing them in the first-person plural, "wooing them with 'we's,'" as it were. This is especially important when the preacher is exposing the idolatries of the community (as in Tillich's sermon), so that the preacher not be exempt from the indictment, but it is also important when the preacher helps to solidify the identity of the community as the redeemed people of God (as in the closing lines of Taylor's sermon). In both cases, the hearer has not been isolated, but remains in the company of the preacher and therefore maintains a "safe space" in which to respond to the preacher's confession. Thus, even when a preacher announces God's law that puts to death the sinner, it nevertheless remains true that, as Paul writes, "all have fallen short," not simply the individual hearers (Rom. 3:23).

Preachers can also create a relationship between themselves and their hearers by posing questions and thereby inviting the participation of the hearers, as we saw in the sermons by Barth and Rutledge. Stephanie Kaper-Dale uses the same technique to good effect in a sermon on Miriam's song in Exodus 15:19-22. After describing the jubilation of the crossing of the Red Sea, Kaper-Dale directs the hearers to contemplate the wilderness to come: "After the moments of gazing in wonder out over the waters, didn't the Israelites turn and look out at what lay ahead of them? *It wasn't the promised land. It was the wilderness.*" Against this backdrop she turns to Miriam's defiant, confident song:

> I imagine the prophet Miriam with her eyes locked on that wilderness as she defiantly reached out her hand, still dusty from travel,

93. William H. Willimon, *Peculiar Speech: Preaching to the Baptized* (Grand Rapids: Eerdmans, 1992), p. 46.

94. See John McClure, *The Roundtable Pulpit: Where Leadership and Preaching Meet* (Nashville: Abingdon Press, 1995), pp. 73-95; and Robin R. Meyers, *With Ears to Hear: Preaching as Self-Persuasion* (Cleveland: Pilgrim Press, 1993), pp. 73-95.

and picked up her tambourine. It wasn't that she was unaware of the hardship of the wilderness — but rather that she knew a reality greater than anything that lay ahead of her. And so, surrounded by all of the women of Israel who were dancing with their tambourines in hand, Miriam lifted up her voice. Can you hear her?

That question — "Can you hear her?" — serves as the coda for the sermon, repeated several times, until finally it becomes not only an invitational question but also a word of gospel proclamation:

There is a song that is being sung. It is a song written in each of us by our very God. When we sing it, we praise God for the great things we have already seen in our lives and in all lives and in all creation. When we sing it, we can look bravely at the wilderness that lies ahead of us and around us, knowing that our God will take us to places greater than we have known. The song is being sung right now. And you are invited to sing.[95]

Vulnerable

To the degree that a confessional sermon is assertive, rather than coercive, and relational, rather than primarily directional, it is also vulnerable. To speak of preaching as vulnerable is to recognize that while the language of confession asserts a new reality, it does not claim to be able to prove it. This is not to imply that we do not think what we confess is true, but rather that we will not — indeed, must not — succumb to the temptation to prove its validity by some (hypothesized) external means. Vulnerable preaching, therefore, is simultaneously tentative *and* bold, tentative in that it is not offered with the pretense of proven finality but bold in that it is offered confidently and courageously despite the lack of definitive evidence.[96] We have seen this already in the sermons

95. Stephanie Kaper-Dale, "Miriam's Song," preached at Princeton Theological Seminary, February 21, 2000; used by permission of the preacher.

96. Lucy Rose has helpfully suggested that we raise up this dimension of the life of faith by speaking of preaching as "interpretations," "proposals," and "wagers." *Sharing the Word: Preaching in the Roundtable Church* (Louisville: Westminster/John Knox Press, 1997), p. 100.

of Barth and Rutledge, who confess the nearly in*credible* (in the etymological sense of the word) nature of the gospel, and then assert its truth
nonetheless.

One way to signal vulnerability is to allow room for questioning
and even rejection. Simply acknowledging self-consciously how one interprets the text can accomplish this. Kaper-Dale's "I *imagine* the
prophet Miriam . . ." admits that she does not possess the only interpretation and grants her hearer permission to imagine things another
way, thereby creating the space in which the hearer may also entertain
the preacher's suggestion and be encountered by the Word.

But one can be vulnerable in other ways, as well. For instance, the
preacher can share some element of personal struggle with the text or
in the shared life of the community. Homileticians have long debated
the appropriateness of self-disclosure in the pulpit, but to the degree
that the preacher's own experience embodies the confession of God's
activity in Christ, rather than spotlights the preacher's person or faith,
personal disclosure can be a powerful way by which to demonstrate a
vulnerability that grants hearers the critical distance in which to appropriate the faith confessed.[97]

Here we touch again on the question of the importance (or lack
thereof) of the preacher's belief, or self-involvement, in the message she
proclaims. Having now considered the nature of biblical confession
and discerned a confessional rhetoric, we are in a better position to say
that preaching as confession is not simply repeating the message of the
texts, but appropriating it and responding to it with one's own confession. Therefore, the self-involvement of the preacher matters. But, and
this is critical in light of our formulation of a *kenotic* rhetoric, the self-
involvement, belief, or even passion of the preacher is important neither because "passion is persuasive"[98] nor even because the assertive
character of the preacher's confession makes it easier for the hearer to
experience the illocutionary force of that confession. Rather, the
preacher's self-involvement matters because a *kenotic* rhetoric implies
that a preacher should model the passionate vulnerability and vulnera-

97. For guidance in the appropriate use of personal experience, see Richard L.
Thulin, *The "I" of the Sermon: Autobiography in the Sermon* (Minneapolis: Fortress Press,
1989); Carol M. Norén, *The Woman in the Pulpit* (Nashville: Abingdon Press, 1992), pp. 63-
87; and Resner, *Preacher and Cross*, pp. 157-75.

98. See Meyers, *With Ears to Hear*, p. 4.

ble passion of the Crucified One. That is, to confess Jesus Christ is to identify with him and his passionate commitment to God and the world "that God so loved." Therefore, a measure of self-disclosure that points to God's disclosure in Jesus Christ can help to render, not simply an effective, but a faithful embodiment of the gospel.

John Claypool does just this in a sermon juxtaposing the story of Abraham's binding of Isaac with the death of his daughter. After describing the similarity between Abraham's situation and his own, Claypool names the great disparity, that Abraham received his child back while he, the preacher, did not, and then against this backdrop offers his perspective to the congregation:

> But my situation is different. Here I am, left alone on that mountain, with my child and not a ram there on the altar, and the question is: how on earth do I get down and move back to the normalcy of life? I cannot learn from Abraham, lucky man that he is. I am left to grope through the darkness by myself, and to ask: "Where do I go from here? Is there a road out, and if so, which one?"
>
> Let me hasten to admit that I am really in no position to speak with any finality to such a question this morning, for I am still so much in shock, much at sea, very much broken, and by no means fully healed. What I have to share is of a highly provisional character, for as of now the light is very dim. However, if you will accept it as such, I do feel I have made a few discoveries in these last four weeks that may be of worth to some of you.

Claypool then traces several possibilities that he has explored and found to be false paths, before venturing that he has learned as never before that life is a precious gift, and echoes again through his vulnerability his invitation to the congregation to be transformed with him by God's redemptive Word:

> Now, having gone full circle, I come back to caution you not to look to me this morning as any authority on how to conquer grief. Rather, I need you to help me on down the way, and this is how: do not counsel me not to question, and do not attempt to give me any total answer. Neither one works for me. The greatest thing you can do is remind me that life is a gift — every last particle of it, and that the way to handle a gift is to be grateful. You can really help me if

you will never let me forget this fact, just as I hope maybe I may have helped this morning by reminding you of the same thing. As I see it now, there is only one way out of this darkness — the way of gratitude. Will you join me in trying to learn how to travel that way?[99]

As evidenced by Claypool's sermon, preaching that is vulnerable continues to expect a response from the listener but, because it seeks its validity in the integrity of its confession, it feels no pains to influence that response from the outset. In this regard, once again, persuasion according to the canons of classical rhetoric is not the primary goal of preaching. To allude to our earlier illustration, can one be persuaded to love? Confessional preaching knows that the response it seeks can be provoked, evoked, or prompted, but not persuaded or coerced, for to do so would invalidate the response.

Both-And

Because a confession articulates the essential Christian tradition in response to present context, circumstances, and need in a way that both (1) offers hearers a communal identity and simultaneously (2) preserves the space in which they may be encountered by and appropriate that identity for themselves, a confessional sermon involves language reflective of both of these intentions. At the same time, because the preacher seeks to embody the distinct confession that emerged from her conversation with the text, the sermon will generally lean in one way or another. That is, while a single sermon may both assert *and* question, or promise *and* invite, it will also allow one of these intentions to shape it most fully in consonance with the illocutionary aim of the confession animating the sermon, and that choice greatly influences one's use of language.

99. John Claypool, "Life Is a Gift," in *A Chorus of Witnesses: Model Sermons for Today's Preachers*, ed. Thomas G. Long and Cornelius Plantinga, Jr. (Grand Rapids: Eerdmans, 1994), pp. 123, 130.

Preaching as Confession

In this chapter I have argued that preaching that seeks to "confess Jesus Christ" is shaped *entirely* by God's self-disclosure in the cross and resurrection of Jesus Christ. That is, not only do the cross and resurrection supply the *content* of our preaching, but they also provide a *pattern* for our preaching, making demands upon the rhetorical devices we employ so as to confess Jesus Christ to the worshiping congregation.

In order to illustrate these convictions at work, in the concluding section of this project I offer two "confessional" sermons. While I do not hold them up as ideal models, I do offer them to other preachers as my own "good faith" efforts at confessing Jesus Christ in a postmodern world.

CONCLUSION

Confessions of the Faith

This project began by asserting that, whatever challenges the postmodern turn presents to those who seek to proclaim the gospel of Jesus Christ, it also provides a distinct opportunity. It concludes by reaffirming that position, claiming that there exists before us an unprecedented opportunity to clarify the nature and import of our preaching, as, robbed of the modernist foundations to which the church too eagerly clung, we now live and preach, as it were, *by faith alone.*

What postmodern thought lends to Christian theology, ultimately, is a clarification of its essential nature. Christian claims can rest upon *no* ultimate foundation, not even that of nonfoundationalism; rather, Christianity exists solely by confession, the conviction and assertion of truth apart from any appeal to some rational criterion. But while a "confessional" understanding of Christian faith and theology may certainly gain something from postmodernism, it also has something to contribute by calling us to refuse postmodernist nihilism and silence by speaking forth our deepest convictions.

Ultimately, if postmodernism presses us to confess the faith, then preaching takes on tremendous significance. It becomes, in fact, the way to speak into — and in this way only to reap — the postmodern whirlwind. Hence, I seek in this project to reclaim the Christian practice of confession as the most apt way of understanding preaching in our postmodern context. Because confession is the assertion of faith's deepest convictions, prompts the conversation of the faithful, and functions as both (1) a summary of the "essential" Christian tradition and (2) the articulation and actualization of that tradition in response to the proclaimed Word and the immediate circumstances of our hearers and world, it offers a unique way to re-envision preaching that is both faithful to the Christian tradition and responsive to our present context.

At this point, however, let me again be clear: confession is not the *only* thing we have as proclaimers of the Word. Certainly there is both room and need for instruction, exhortation, and even inculturation in our sermons. At the same time, I want also to assert that confession is in a very real way *everything* we have, in that every other element of preaching stems from the primary confession of faith, "Jesus Christ is Lord." As Luther once responded to Erasmus's contention that pious Christians should avoid assertions in matters "uncertain," one "must delight in assertions or he will be no Christian. And by assertion . . . I mean a constant adhering, affirming, confessing, maintaining, and an invincible persevering. . . ." To dissent from confessing those things that one cannot prove, Luther contends, "would be nothing but a denial of all religion and piety. . . ."[1] Such, I believe, is also the fate of the preacher in the midst of the postmodern whirlwind. It is both my hope and my conviction that we will yet emerge from this maelstrom grateful for its purifying winds.

I offer the following sermons, then, as my own efforts at confessing Jesus Christ and in this way reaping the postmodern whirlwind. These sermons were all preached in a mid-sized, suburban parish committed to social outreach. Because they were preached in the context of worship services using the Revised Common Lectionary, I have provided the central text of the sermon and the Sunday of the church's liturgical season.

---

1. *The Bondage of the Will* (1525), *LW,* 33:20-21. See also Kathryn A. Kleinhaus, "Why Now? The Relevance of Luther in a Post-modern Age," *Currents in Theology and Mission* 24, no. 6 (December 1997): 488-95.

19th Sunday after Pentecost, Series A; Matthew 21:33-43

"Now when the owner of the vineyard comes, what will he do to those tenants?"

Jesus has just told one of the darkest parables of Matthew's Gospel. It is the story of lawless, ruthless tenant farmers who not only refuse to pay the owner of the land for their use of it, but beat those who come to collect payment and then murder the owner's own son. Jesus' telling of the parable ends in a question: "when the owner of the vineyard comes, what will he do to those tenants?" But his question is more than just a question. It is an indictment, an accusation, an invitation to pronounce judgment.

The verdict in this case, of course, is obvious. Then, even more than now, to be placed in charge of another's land is to be given a sacred trust. To have these thankless tenants refuse to hand over the fruits of the vineyard is bad enough. To watch them beat the lawful representatives of the landlord time and time again is even worse. But to listen to the tale of them killing the rightful heir out of their greed and insolence is simply too much. And so without hesitation, the gathered crowd of Pharisees and elders rallies to the call for condemnation and responds with one voice, "He will put those wretches to a miserable death, and lease the vineyard to other tenants who will give him the produce at the harvest."

What a shock it must have been, then, to have Jesus turn to them and say in a stone-cold voice, "Therefore I tell you, the kingdom of God will be taken away from you and given to a people that produces the fruits of the kingdom." No doubt one could hear a pin drop in the silence that fell over the crowd. The Pharisees, you see, were nobody's fools; they realized in a painful flash of insight that Jesus was talking about them.

Matthew records that Jesus' word of judgment infuriated those Pharisees, and who can blame them? They were, after all, serious, God-fearing, devout Jews, those most committed to preserving and reforming their religion in the midst of Roman occupation. I mean, they took their faith so seriously that they attempted to obey the whole law, to make their whole lives reflect their devotion to their God. In short, they were intelligent, well-educated, and deeply committed to their faith, not unlike a lot of the people here I know and care for.

And so Jesus' pronouncement comes as a shock and an offense, as they have been duped by him into accusing themselves. Desperate to acquit themselves and escape indictment, the Pharisees are moved first to fear, then to hate, and finally to treachery and murder, living out the details of this dark parable.

Now here we must be both careful and serious. For one of the great failures of the church is that for centuries this parable has been read as a clear and unequivocal word of condemnation of the Jews and validation of the church as the "new Israel." So much tragedy has come — particularly in the twentieth century — from such a reading.

But to read it in this fashion is not only to perpetuate such a tragedy, but to miss the deeper implications of Jesus' words. For when Jesus tells a parable so similar to the "song of the vineyard" in the fifth chapter of Isaiah that we heard as today's first reading, he deliberately taps into a tradition of the biblical witness that highlights the rebellion, the fallenness, the desperation, not of individuals or select groups, but of an entire people. Jesus' parable is similar in that it also depicts the violent rebellion of people who ignore God's authority, who fail as stewards, and who seek their own ends above all else. And so unless we hear Jesus' parable also directed at us — at us who consume 80 percent of the world's produce while two-thirds of the world goes hungry — we do not, I think, hear it aright. For Jesus speaks to all those who hoard the resources God has entrusted to us as tenants and stewards.

And so we must hear in the question at the end of Jesus' parable a far more personal — and therefore troubling — question: "What will God do to you who are unfaithful?" And with this question, Jesus silences all of our excuses about mortgages or IRAs or college savings or whatever, and we are left silent, sullen, and no less guilty than the Pharisees in today's reading.

Now, before going any further I have to say that there are two things that confuse me about this parable. The first is the stupidity of the tenants. Quite frankly, I'm not shocked that they would resort to violence, even murder, to secure their ill-gotten gains; I read about that every day in the paper. No, what confuses me is their absolute stupidity. I mean, how can they believe they will receive the vineyard by killing the rightful heir, the very one with the authority to forgive and restore them?

Do they not know that they are sowing the seeds of their own destruction?

But maybe I shouldn't be so surprised. I mean, how often do we attempt to comfort or establish ourselves at the expense of our fellow humans beings, those very ones who can comfort us? How often do we seek to secure our future to the detriment of our planet, our vineyard, that which God has given to sustain us? We, too, I suppose, regularly sow the seeds of our own destruction.

But that's just the first thing that puzzles me; there is a second as well. And that is the stupidity of the landlord. For perhaps the only one crazier than those miserable tenants is that foolish landlord. I mean, my word, he should have gone to court or sent hired guns to collect his due from the beginning. But no, instead he sends messengers, and when they are beaten . . . he sends some more. And when they are mistreated also . . . he then sends his own son! And here's what defies all common sense and good judgment, for after having messenger after messenger returned beaten, why in the world would he send his son, his only son, into such danger?

There can be only one answer: that landlord is desperate, crazy desperate to restore relationship with those who have offended him. That is, that landlord loves these miserable tenants, not simply more then they love him, but even more than they could possibly love themselves. And so out of sheer desperation and love, this landlord sends his only son to bear a message of forgiveness and hope.

And so now — only now — can we dare address Jesus' question: What will God do to us who are unfaithful? What will one such as this do when confronted by our hoarding, insecurity, and sin? Scripture has but one answer: "For God so loved the world that he gave his only begotten Son, so that everyone who believes in him may not perish but may have eternal life" (John 3:16).

In the end, you see, this parable really isn't about wicked tenants; it's not about the Pharisees; it's not even about us. Instead, it's about this landlord, a landlord who hopes against hope that when they — no, when *we* — see the son being sent we will recognize the intention of the father and come to our senses. They don't; all too often we don't. Yet the sending of the son remains the strong affirmation of a landlord — *no, of a God!* — who will not give up on God's people.

Far from revealing only our desperation, you see, Jesus' parable reveals the desperation of God, the desperation of God *for you,* the desperation of God which can only be likened to the desperation of a loving parent who will do or try anything to achieve reconciliation with an estranged child. For in the end the question isn't "What will God do?" but "What has God done?" And what God has done is plain: God has sent Jesus Christ, God's only begotten and beloved Son, into the world to forgive, redeem, and restore us, so that we might be sent out as witnesses to this redemption.

But there's another question, too, that we dare not overlook. And that is, what will we do? What will we do, that is, now that we know God's love and mercy firsthand? Look, let's be honest, you and I have been blessed materially beyond what almost any people of any time and place have known. We enjoy riches that most of the world can only imagine and, in fact, will die imagining. And so what will we do?

Will we hoard these blessings, or share them? Will we embrace those in need, or shun them? Will we reach beyond the comfortable confines of our suburban homes and parish or retreat inside of them? Will we, finally, reach out to the Christ we perceive in our neighbor in need or seek some other god in the fragile security of our wealth and possessions?

Don't get me wrong — I'm not saying our eternal salvation hangs in the balance. God — this crazy, foolish, desperate God so much more loving of us than we are even of ourselves — this God has already seen to that. So I'm not saying it's a matter of our souls, but rather of the quality and character of our lives as Christians. For now we know ourselves to be those whom God loves unabashedly and shamelessly; we know ourselves to be those for whom God would — and did — risk everything; we know ourselves to be those for whom God sent God's only Son. And knowing this, we who have been healed can offer healing; we who have been reconciled can be instruments of reconciliation; we who have been so greatly blessed can bless others; and we who have been forgiven can forgive. Thanks be to God. Amen.

17th Sunday after Pentecost, Series A; Jonah 3:10–4:11

Jack doesn't know anything about Jonah yet, and I wish I could keep it that way!

As I watched our soon-to-be-two-year-old son Jack march off to his two-hour, twice-a-week preschool experience at our own Woodchuck Hollow this past week, it occurred to me how blissfully undiscriminating he is. Oh, sure, put him around other kids his age and he'll start either protecting his toys or coveting theirs. But by and large, he simply accepts the people he meets, unafraid. He doesn't know enough yet, you see, to distinguish between rich and poor, black and white. He couldn't care less whether you're male or female, gay or straight, a liberal or conservative. He just doesn't know any better. And so there is, as yet, no sense of social status, no pecking order in Jack's world.

But that's not the case with Jonah, the prophet we heard about in today's first reading. Jonah, you see, is keenly aware of the differences between one person or nation and the next, and his world is simply dominated by those distinctions. For Jonah is prophet to King Jeroboam, a man, who, while he was accused of great religious infidelity, was nonetheless a military success, greatly extending Israel's territory. And so Jonah knows he has, if not a good king, at least a powerful one, and so he keeps close track of who's in and out, who's up and down at the court and abroad.

In short, Jonah not only has a pecking order, but lives it, and at its very bottom is Nineveh, Israel's great rival and enemy. And this helps to put the passage just read into context.

Now, you probably know this tale; most of us grew up hearing about Jonah and the whale. But let me refresh your memory and bring matters up to the point we've just heard about.

One day the Lord commands Jonah to rise and go and preach to wicked Nineveh that they might turn to the Lord and be spared. Well, about the last thing patriotic Jonah wants is for Nineveh to be spared, and so he rises and goes, alright, about 180 degrees in the opposite direction, hopping a ship toward Tarshish, a city in southern Spain. Well, a storm comes up, engulfing Jonah's ship. Realizing that this storm is his fault, Jonah urges his shipmates to throw him overboard, and, after trying everything else they could think of, the sailors reluctantly do just that. The storm immediately abates, as Jonah, ever the poor swimmer, sinks like a stone toward the bottom of the sea.

But God sends a whale to swallow Jonah whole and save him from death. And after three days in the belly of the whale, Jonah is spewed up on a beach not far — you guessed it! — from Nineveh. And this time, when God commands him to rise and go and preach to wicked Nineveh, he does, walking through this bustling metropolis crying out a single line: "Forty days hence and Nineveh will be no more." And while Jonah must've appeared to them something like the half-crazed street-preacher declaring the end of the world we might meet in Manhattan, the people of Nineveh — from the poorest commoner right up to the king himself — heed Jonah's call and repent.

And this is where we pick up in today's reading. For upon seeing what the people did, God decides to relent and spare Nineveh, that great rival and enemy of Israel. And Jonah is furious. "I knew it," he whines to God as he climbs a hill outside the city. "I knew you were a gracious and merciful God, slow to anger and abounding in steadfast love. I knew you'd spare them. I just knew it!"

And there it is, you see, the reason I don't much want Jack to get to know Jonah: I want him to remain unbiased, undiscriminating, unafraid.

It's a futile effort of course; I know that. I mean, look around. What edition of the *New York Times* isn't filled with bad news stemming from humanity's penchant to judge others on the basis of our differences. And so one man shoots up a daycare center because the kids there are the wrong religion, while another torches a church because its worshipers are the wrong color. Soldiers in one part of the world slaughter their own citizens because of their ethnic background, while others beat those of a different political ideology. And on and on it goes. For differences simply dominate our world — from the homes we buy and the schools we attend even to the places where we worship. For as Martin Luther King Jr. once observed, the most segregated hour of the American week is Sundays from ten to eleven in the morning.

And so deep down, whatever my feelings for my son, I know that he too, in time, will come to know Jonah firsthand; he'll realize, that is, that people are different, and that those differences somehow matter in this world. And no matter how hard he tries, knowing that will influence his decisions and lead him to treat people differently. He will learn that, just as I did; just as you all did too.

But there's another reason I don't want Jack to get to know Jonah, too. And that is that I don't want him to die. For Jonah, you see, dies, there, right there, on that hill outside the city. He dies when he realizes that he's out of control. He dies when he sees the God of Abraham, Isaac, and Jacob — the God, after all, of Israel! — have compassion for Israel's mortal foe. He dies when all his schemes, all his distinctions and scorekeeping, all his pecking orders vanish in the moment of God's mercy. There, most surely, Jonah the great prophet of the even greater King Jeroboam dies.

And so do we. For we also have learned to define ourselves according to our differences; we also have learned, that is, to know who we are in relation to who we're not. For no matter how much we talk as Lutherans of being freely justified, of being equally recipients of God's unmerited grace, yet, truth be told, there's still a part of us that, just like the laborers in Jesus' parable, thinks we deserve God's grace, even if just a little; a part of us that wants to believe that somehow we're doing God a favor by being Christians and showing up here on Sundays; a part of us that, whatever our rampant insecurities, can still name those against whom we measure ourselves. And so when we see and hear that God accepts everyone — *everyone*, even those we refuse to accept — then we who so regularly and relentlessly define ourselves according to our differences perish.

For what Jonah discovers on that hill outside of Nineveh is that God makes no distinction among those God loves, not between Israel or Nineveh, not between man or woman, Black or White, North or South, gay or straight, rich or poor, Serb, Albanian, or American. No, this God makes no distinction about those God cares for, adores, cherishes, and longs for. Every time, in fact, that you try to draw a line between who's "in" and who's "out," you can be sure to find this God on the other side. For this God — Jonah's God, *our* God — is indeed unpredictably gracious and wildly merciful, so terribly slow to anger and ever abounding in steadfast love.

Does that surprise you? Strangely, it doesn't surprise Jonah. That's why he ran away in the first place. Often, however, it seems to surprise us, sometimes even upsetting us. And maybe that's because behind all our score keeping and finger pointing, behind all our categorizing and discriminating, rests our own deep-seated insecurity that, in the end, no matter what we've done, we won't measure up; no matter how much we've made, we won't be loved; no matter what we try, eventually all our worst fears about ourselves will be confirmed and we'll be found unworthy, undeserving, unlovable.

But here it is, you see. What we discover on that hill outside of *Jerusalem* is that Jonah's God, Jesus' God, *our* God, is a God who makes no distinction about those God cares for, adores, cherishes, longs for, and even dies for, and that includes *all* people, *even you and me.*

That's why we've committed to building a home through Habitat for Humanity, you see. That's why we work at the Trenton Area Soup Kitchen, collect clothes for the Kosovo refugees, and support homeless children through our Cherry Tree Club. That's why we reach out beyond the comfortable borders of our little church at all. Not because we want to help, which of course we do. Not because it's a good thing to do, which of course it is. Not even because it pleases God, which of course it does. But, rather, we reach out to others because God has first reached out to us. And, in fact, in reaching out to others we discover that *there are no others* but only those — all of us! — for whom Christ died. And so in reaching out to the "other" we meet ourselves, and know that we are all one in Christ and his love for us.

And so while I don't much want Jack to get to know Jonah, I do so very much hope and pray that he gets to know Jonah's God and thereby also comes to know how much he is loved. And so also, I hope, will you. Amen.

Bibliography

Adam, A. K. M. *What Is Postmodern Biblical Criticism?* Minneapolis: Fortress Press, 1995.

Allen, Diogenes. *Christian Belief in a Postmodern World: The Full Wealth of Conviction.* Louisville: Westminster/John Knox Press, 1989.

—————. *Philosophy for Understanding Theology.* Atlanta: John Knox, 1985.

Allen, Ronald J., Barbara Shires Blaisdell, and Scott Black Johnston. *Theology for Preaching: Authority, Truth, and Knowledge of God in a Postmodern Ethos.* Nashville: Abingdon Press, 1997.

Allen, Ronald J., ed. *Patterns of Preaching: A Sermon Sampler.* St. Louis: Chalice Press, 1998.

Alter, Robert. *The Art of Biblical Narrative.* New York: Basic Books, 1981.

Andersen, Hans. *Hans Andersen's Fairy Tales.* Translated by Valdemar Paulsen. Chicago: Rand McNally, 1916.

Anderson, Bernhard W. *Contours of Old Testament Theology.* Minneapolis: Fortress Press, 1999.

Aristotle. *Poetics.* Translated by W. Hamilton Fyfe and W. Rhys Roberts. Cambridge, Mass.: Harvard University Press, 1932.

Attridge, Harold W. *The Epistle to the Hebrews.* Edited by Helmut Koester. Philadelphia: Fortress Press, 1989.

Auerbach, Erich. *Mimesis: The Representation of Reality in Western Literature.* Translated by Willard R. Trask. Princeton: Princeton University Press, 1953; Princeton Paperback Edition, 1974.

Augustine. *On the Predestination of the Saints.* Translated by R. E. Wallis. *Basic Writings of Saint Augustine,* vol. 1. Edited by Whitney J. Oates. New York: Random House, 1948.

Aune, Bruce. *Knowledge, Mind and Nature.* New York: Random House, 1967.

Austin, J. L. *How to Do Things with Words.* 2nd ed. Edited by J. O. Urmson and Maria Sbisà. Cambridge, Mass.: Harvard University Press, 1975.

———. "Performative Utterances." In *Philosophical Papers,* 2nd ed., edited by J. O. Urmson and G. J. Warnock, pp. 233-52. Oxford: Clarendon Press, 1970.

Bainton, Roland. *Here I Stand: A Life of Martin Luther.* New York: Abingdon-Cokesbury Press, 1950.

Bakhtin, Mikhail M. "Discourse in the Novel." In *The Dialogic Imagination: Four Essays,* edited by Michael Holquist, pp. 259-422. Austin: University of Texas Press, 1981.

———. "The Problem of Speech Genres." In *Speech Genres and Other Late Essays,* translated by Vern W. McGee, edited by Caryl Emerson and Michael Holquist, pp. 60-102. Austin: University of Texas Press, 1986.

Barnett, Victoria. *For the Soul of the People: Protestant Protest Against Hitler.* New York: Oxford University Press, 1992.

Barr, James. *The Concept of Biblical Testimony: An Old Testament Perspective.* Minneapolis: Fortress Press, 1999.

Barrett, C. K. *The Epistle to the Romans.* New York: Harper & Row, 1957.

———. *The Gospel According to St. John.* 2nd ed. Philadelphia: Westminster Press, 1978.

Barth, Karl. *Credo: A Presentation of the Chief Problems of Dogmatics with Reference to the Apostles' Creed.* Translated by J. Strathearn McNab. London: Hodder and Stoughton, 1936.

———. *Deliverance to the Captives.* New York: Harper & Row, 1961.

———. *Dogmatics in Outline.* New York: Harper & Row, 1959.

———. *Homiletics.* Translated by Geoffrey W. Bromiley and Donald E. Daniels. Louisville: Westminster/John Knox Press, 1991.

Bauer, Walter, William F. Arndt, F. Wilbur Gingrich, and Frederick W. Danker. *A Greek-English Lexicon of the New Testament.* Chicago: University of Chicago Press, 1979 (1957).

Becker, Ernest. *The Birth and Death of Meaning.* New York: Free Press, 1962.

Berger, Peter L., and Thomas Luckmann. *The Social Construction of Reality: A Treatise in the Sociology of Knowledge.* New York: Doubleday, 1966.

Bernstein, Richard J. *Beyond Objectivism and Relativism.* Philadelphia: University of Pennsylvania Press, 1983.

Best, Steven, and Douglas Kellner. *Postmodern Theory: Critical Investigations.* New York: Guilford Press, 1991.

————. *The Postmodern Turn.* New York: Guilford Press, 1997.

Betz, Hans Dieter. *2 Corinthians 8 and 9: A Commentary on Two Administrative Letters of the Apostle Paul.* Edited by George W. MacRae. Philadelphia: Fortress Press, 1985.

Bordo, Susan R. *The Flight to Objectivity: Essays on Cartesianism and Culture.* Albany: State University of New York Press, 1987.

Bornkamm, Günther. "Das Bekenntnis im Hebraerbrief." *Theologische Blätter* 21 (1942): 58.

————. "'Ομολογέω', zur Geschichte eines politischen Begriffes." *Hermes, Zeitschrift für classische Philologie* 71 (1936): 377-93.

Brown, Raymond E. *The Death of the Messiah.* New York: Doubleday, 1994.

————. *The Gospel According to John (I–XII).* New York: Doubleday, 1966.

Brueggemann, Walter. *Cadences of Home: Preaching Among Exiles.* Louisville: Westminster/John Knox Press, 1997.

————. "The Social Nature of the Biblical Text." In *Preaching as a Social Act: Theology and Practice,* edited by Arthur Van Seeters, pp. 127-65. Nashville: Abingdon Press, 1988.

————. *Texts Under Negotiation.* Minneapolis: Fortress Press, 1993.

————. *Theology of the Old Testament: Testimony, Dispute, Advocacy.* Minneapolis: Fortress Press, 1997.

Buchanan, George Wesley. *To the Hebrews: Translation, Comment, and Conclusions.* New York: Doubleday, 1972.

Buechner, Frederick. *Telling the Truth: The Gospel as Tragedy, Comedy, and Fairy Tale.* New York: HarperCollins, 1977.

Bultmann, Rudolf. *The Gospel of John.* Translated by G. R. Beasley-Murray, R. W. N. Hoare, and J. K. Riches. Philadelphia: Westminster Press, 1971.

————. "Is Exegesis Without Presuppositions Possible?" In *Existence and Faith: Shorter Writings of Rudolf Bultmann,* translated by Schubert M. Ogden. Cleveland: World Publishing Company, 1960.

————. *Jesus and the Word.* Translated by Louise Pettibone Smith and Erminie Huntress Lantero. New York: Charles Scribner's Sons, 1962 (1934).

————. "New Testament and Mythology: The Problem of Demythologizing the New Testament Proclamation [1941]." In *New Testament and Mythology and Other Basic Writings,* edited and translated by Schubert M. Ogden. Philadelphia: Fortress Press, 1984.

———. "On the Question of Christology." In *Faith and Understanding,* edited with an introduction by Robert W. Funk, translated by Louise Pettibone Smith. Philadelphia: Fortress Press, 1987 (1969).

———. "The Primitive Christian and the Historical Jesus." In *The Historical Jesus and the Kerygmatic Christ: Essays on the New Quest of the Historical Jesus,* edited and translated by Carl E. Braaten and Roy A. Harrisville, pp. 15-42. New York: Abingdon Press, 1964.

———. Review of *Les premières confessions de foi chrétiennes,* by Oscar Cullmann. *Theologische Literaturzeitung* 74 (1949): 40-42.

———. *The Second Letter to the Corinthians.* Edited by Erich Dinkler. Translated by Roy A. Harrisville. Minneapolis: Augsburg Press, 1985.

———. *Theology of the New Testament.* 2 vols. Translated by Kendrick Grobel. New York: Charles Scribner's Sons, 1951, 1955.

———. "πιστεύω κτλ." In *Theological Dictionary of the New Testament,* vol. 6, edited by Gerhard Kittel and Gerhard Friedrich, translated by Geoffrey W. Bromiley, pp. 174-226. Grand Rapids: Eerdmans, 1968.

Burke, Kenneth. *Language as Symbolic Action.* Berkeley: University of California Press, 1966.

———. *A Rhetoric of Motives.* Berkeley: University of California Press, 1950.

Campbell, Charles. *Preaching Jesus: New Directions for Homiletics in Hans Frei's Postliberal Theology.* Grand Rapids: Eerdmans, 1997.

Campenhausen, Hans Freiherr von. "Das Bekenntnis im Urchristentum." *Zeitschrift für die Neutestamentliche Wissenschaft* 63 (1972): 210-53.

Cardenal, Ernesto. *The Gospel in Solentiname.* 4 vols. Maryknoll, N.Y.: Orbis Books, 1976-1982.

Childers, Jana. *Performing the Word: Preaching as Theatre.* Nashville: Abingdon Press, 1998.

Childs, Brevard. *Biblical Theology of the Old and New Testaments.* Minneapolis: Fortress Press, 1993.

Claypool, John. "Life Is a Gift." In *A Chorus of Witnesses: Model Sermons for Today's Preachers,* edited by Thomas G. Long and Cornelius Plantinga, Jr., pp. 120-30. Grand Rapids: Eerdmans, 1994.

Cochrane, Arthur C. *The Church's Confession Under Hitler.* Pittsburgh: Pickwick Press, 1976 (1962).

Copenhaver, Martin B. "Formed and Reformed." *The Christian Century* 115 (1998): 933, 937-40.

Craddock, Fred. *As One without Authority*. 3rd ed. Nashville: Abingdon Press, 1983 (1971).

————. *Preaching*. Nashville: Abingdon Press, 1985.

Cranfield, C. E. B. *A Critical and Exegetical Commentary on the Epistle to the Romans*. 2 vols. Edinburgh: T. & T. Clark, 1975-1979.

Cullmann, Oscar. *Christ and Time: The Primitive Christian Conception of Time and History*. Philadelphia: Westminster Press, 1964.

————. *The Earliest Christian Confessions*. Translated by J. K. S. Reid. London: Lutterworth Press, 1949.

Culpepper, R. Alan. *Anatomy of the Fourth Gospel: A Study in Literary Design*. Philadelphia: Fortress Press, 1983.

Cunningham, David S. *Faithful Persuasion: In Aid of a Rhetoric of Christian Theology*. Notre Dame: University of Notre Dame Press, 1990.

Danto, Arthur C. "Philosophy as/and/of Literature." In *Post-Analytic Philosophy*, edited by John Rajchman and Cornel West, pp. 63-83. New York: Columbia University Press, 1985.

Davis, H. Grady. *Design for Preaching*. Philadelphia: Fortress Press, 1958.

Derrida, Jacques. "Force of Law: The 'Mystical Foundation of Authority.'" *Cardozo Law Review* 11, nos. 5-6 (1990): 919-1045.

————. *Margins of Philosophy*. Translated by Alan Bass. Chicago: University of Chicago Press, 1982.

————. *Of Grammatology*. Translated by Gayatri Chakravorty Spivak. Baltimore: Johns Hopkins University Press, 1977.

————. *Writing and Difference*. Translated and with an introduction and additional note by Alan Bass. Chicago: University of Chicago Press, 1978.

Dibelius, Martin, and Hans Conzelmann. *The Pastoral Epistles*. Translated by Philip Buttolph and Adela Yarbro. Edited by Helmut Koester. Philadelphia: Fortress Press, 1972.

Dodd, C. H. *The Apostolic Preaching and Its Development*. New York: Harper & Brothers, 1962.

Ellison, Ralph. *Invisible Man*. New York: Random House, 1952.

Evans, Donald D. *The Logic of Self-Involvement: A Philosophical Study of Everyday English with Special Reference to the Christian Use of Language about God as Creator*. London: SCM Press, 1963.

Farley, Edward. *Ecclesial Reflection*. Philadelphia: Fortress Press, 1982.

————. *Theologia: The Fragmentation and Unity of Theological Education*. Philadelphia: Fortress Press, 1983.

Farley, Wendy. *Eros for the Other: Retaining Truth in a Pluralistic World.* University Park: Pennsylvania State University Press, 1996.

Farris, Stephen. *Preaching That Matters: The Bible and Our Lives.* Louisville: Westminster/John Knox Press, 1998.

Fiorenza, Elisabeth Schüssler. "Response." In *A New Look at Preaching,* edited by John Burke. Wilmington, Del.: Michael Glazier, 1983.

Fiorenza, Francis Schüssler. "The Crisis of Scriptural Authority." *Interpretation* 44 (1990): 353-68.

Fish, Stanley. *Doing What Comes Naturally: Change, Rhetoric, and the Practice of Theory in Literary and Legal Studies.* Durham, N.C.: Duke University Press, 1989.

————. "How to Do Things with Austin and Searle." In *Is There a Text in This Class? The Authority of Interpretive Communities.* Cambridge, Mass.: Harvard University Press, 1980.

Fisher, Walter. *Human Communication as Narration: Toward a Philosophy of Reason, Value, and Action.* Columbia: University of South Carolina Press, 1987.

Fitzmyer, Joseph. *Romans.* New York: Doubleday, 1993.

Forde, Gerhard O. *Theology Is for Proclamation.* Minneapolis: Fortress Press, 1990.

————. "The Work of Christ." In *Christian Dogmatics,* vol. 2, edited by Carl E. Braaten and Robert W. Jenson, pp. 1-99. Philadelphia: Fortress Press, 1984.

Foss, Sonja K., and Cindy L. Griffin. "Beyond Persuasion: A Proposal for an Invitational Rhetoric." *Communication Monographs* 62 (1995): 1-18.

Foucault, Michel. *The Foucault Reader.* Edited by Paul Rabinow. New York: Pantheon Books, 1984.

————. *Michel Foucault: Politics, Philosophy, Culture.* Edited by Lawrence Kritzman. New York: Routledge, 1988.

————. *Power/Knowledge: Selected Interviews and Other Writings, 1972-1977.* Edited by Colin Gordon. New York: Pantheon Books, 1977.

Fowler, Robert M. *Let the Reader Understand: Reader-Response Criticism and the Gospel of Mark.* Minneapolis: Fortress Press, 1991.

Frei, Hans. *The Eclipse of Biblical Narrative: A Study in Eighteenth and Nineteenth Century Hermeneutics.* New Haven: Yale University Press, 1974.

————. *The Identity of Jesus Christ: The Hermeneutical Bases of Dogmatic Theology.* Philadelphia: Fortress Press, 1975.

————. "The 'Literal Reading' of the Biblical Narrative: Does It Stretch or Will It Break?" In *The Bible and the Narrative Tradition,* edited by Frank McConnell. New York: Oxford University Press, 1986.

———. "Theology and the Interpretation of Narrative: Some Hermeneutical Considerations." In *Theology and Narrative: Selected Essays,* edited by George Hunsinger and William C. Placher. New York: Oxford University Press, 1993.

———. *Types of Christian Theology.* Edited by George Hunsinger and William C. Placher. New Haven: Yale University Press, 1992.

Fretheim, Terence E. "Some Reflections on Brueggemann's God." In *God in the Fray: A Tribute to Walter Brueggemann,* edited by Tod Linafelt and Timothy K. Beal. Minneapolis: Fortress Press, 1998.

Fretheim, Terence E., and Karlfried Froehlich. *The Bible as Word of God in a Postmodern Age.* Minneapolis: Fortress Press, 1998.

Friedrich, Karl J., editor and translator. *The Philosophy of Kant.* New York: Modern Library, 1949.

Froehlich, Karlfried. *Biblical Interpretation in the Early Church.* Philadelphia: Fortress Press, 1984.

Fulkerson, Mary McClintock. *Changing the Subject: Women's Discourses and Feminist Theology.* Minneapolis: Fortress Press, 1994.

Gearhart, S. M. "The Womanization of Rhetoric." *Women's Studies International Quarterly* 2 (1979): 195-201. Cited in Sonja K. Foss and Cindy L. Griffin, "Beyond Persuasion: A Proposal for an Invitational Rhetoric," *Communication Monographs* 62 (1995): 1-2.

Gerrish, B. A. *Saving and Secular Faith: An Invitation to Systematic Theology.* Minneapolis: Augsburg Press, 1999.

González, Justo L., and Catherine G. González. *The Liberating Pulpit.* Nashville: Abingdon Press, 1994.

Grenz, Stanley J. *A Primer on Postmodernism.* Grand Rapids: Eerdmans, 1996.

Gross, Nancy Lammers. "A Re-examination of Recent Homiletical Theories in Light of the Hermeneutical Theory of Paul Ricoeur." Ph.D. dissertation. Princeton Theological Seminary, 1992.

———. *If You Cannot Preach Like Paul . . .* Grand Rapids: Eerdmans, 2002.

Habermas, Jürgen. *Moral Consciousness and Communicative Action.* Translated by C. Lenhardt and S. Nicholsen. Cambridge, Mass.: MIT Press, 1990.

———. *The Theory of Communicative Action,* vol. 1: *Reason and the Rational-*

ization of Society. Translated by Thomas McCarthy. Boston: Beacon Press, 1984.

————. *The Theory of Communicative Action*, vol. 2: *Lifeworld and System: A Critique of Functionalist Reason*. Translated by Thomas McCarthy. Boston: Beacon Press, 1987.

Haenchen, Ernst. *John 2: A Commentary on the Gospel of John Chapters 7–21*. Translated by Robert W. Funk. Philadelphia: Fortress Press, 1984.

Hall, Douglas John. *Confessing the Faith*, vol. 3 of *Christian Theology in a North American Context*. Minneapolis: Fortress Press, 1996.

Haraway, Donna J. *Simians, Cyborgs, and Women: The Reinvention of Nature*. New York: Routledge, 1991.

Harvey, David. *The Condition of Postmodernity*. 2nd ed. Cambridge, Mass.: Blackwell, 1996.

Hassan, Ihab. *The Postmodern Turn: Essays in Postmodern Theory and Culture*. Columbus: Ohio State University Press, 1987.

Hays, Richard B. "Salvation by Trust? Reading the Bible Faithfully." *The Christian Century* 114 (1997): 218-23.

Hofius, Otfried. "ὁμολογέω." In *Exegetical Dictionary of the New Testament*, vol. 2, edited by Horst Balz and Gerhard Schneider, pp. 514-17. Grand Rapids: Eerdmans, 1991.

Hogan, Lucy Lind. "Rethinking Persuasion: Developing an Incarnational Theology of Preaching." *Homiletic* 24, no. 2 (Winter 1999): 1-12.

Hogan, Lucy Lind, and Robert Reid. *Connecting with the Congregation: Rhetoric and the Art of Preaching*. Nashville: Abingdon Press, 1999.

Hubbard, Dolan. *The Sermon and the African American Literary Imagination*. Columbia: University of Missouri Press, 1994.

Hunsinger, Deborah van Deusen. *Theology and Pastoral Counseling: A New Interdisciplinary Approach*. Grand Rapids: Eerdmans, 1995.

Jacks, G. Robert. *Just Say the Word! Writing for the Ear*. Grand Rapids: Eerdmans, 1996.

Jacobson, Rolf. Review of *Theology of the Old Testament: Testimony, Dispute, Advocacy*, by Walter Brueggemann. *Koinonia* 11 (1999): 124-26.

James, Henry. "The Art of Fiction." In *Partial Portraits*. London: Macmillan, 1888. Cited in Hans Frei, *The Identity of Jesus Christ: The Hermeneutical Bases of Dogmatic Theology*, p. 88. Philadelphia: Fortress Press, 1975.

James, William. *A Pluralistic Universe*. Cambridge, Mass.: Harvard University Press, 1977 (1908). Cited in Ihab Hassan, *The Postmodern Turn: Es-*

says in Postmodern Theory and Culture, p. 207. Columbus: Ohio State University Press, 1987.

———. *The Will to Believe and Human Immortality.* New York: Dover, 1956. Cited in Ihab Hassan, *The Postmodern Turn: Essays in Postmodern Theory and Culture,* p. 207. Columbus: Ohio State University Press, 1987.

Jameson, Fredric. "The Linguistic Model." In *Language and Politics,* edited by Michael J. Shapiro. New York: New York University Press, 1984.

Jodock, Darrell. *The Church's Bible: Its Contemporary Authority.* Minneapolis: Fortress Press, 1989.

Kaper-Dale, Stephanie. "Miriam's Song." Sermon preached at Princeton Theological Seminary, February 21, 2000.

Käsemann, Ernst. *Commentary on Romans.* Translated by Geoffrey W. Bromiley. Grand Rapids: Eerdmans, 1980.

———. *The Wandering People of God.* Translated by Roy A. Harrisville and Irving L. Sandberg. Minneapolis: Augsburg Press, 1984.

Kay, James F. *Christus Praesens: A Reconsideration of Rudolf Bultmann's Christology.* Grand Rapids: Eerdmans, 1994.

———. "The *Lex Orandi* in Recent Protestant Theology." In *Ecumenical Theology in Worship, Doctrine, and Life: Essays Presented to Geoffrey Wainwright on His Sixtieth Birthday,* edited by David S. Cunningham, Ralph Del Colle, and Lucas Lamadrid, pp. 11-23. New York: Oxford University Press, 1999.

———. Review of *Preaching Jesus,* by Charles Campbell. *Theology Today* 56 (1999): 403-5.

———. "Myth or Narrative: 'New Testament and Mythology' Turns Fifty." *Theology Today* 48 (1991): 326-32.

———. "The Word of the Cross at the Turn of the Ages." *Interpretation* 53 (1999): 44-56.

Keck, Leander. *The Church Confident.* Nashville: Abingdon Press, 1993.

Kennedy, George A. *Classical Rhetoric and Its Christian and Secular Tradition from Ancient to Modern Times.* Chapel Hill: University of North Carolina Press, 1984.

Kleinhaus, Kathryn A. "Why Now? The Relevance of Luther in a Postmodern Age." *Currents in Theology and Mission* 24, no. 6 (December 1997): 488-95.

Krieger, Murray. *A Window to Criticism.* Princeton: Princeton University Press, 1964. Cited in John H. P. Reumann, "After Historical Criticism,

What? Trends in Biblical Interpretation and Ecumenical, Interfaith Dialogues," *Journal of Ecumenical Studies* 29 (1992): 59 n. 15.

Kuhn, Thomas. "Reflections on My Critics." In *Criticism and the Growth of Knowledge*, 3rd ed., edited by Imre Lakatos and Alan Musgrave, pp. 231-78. Cambridge: Cambridge University Press, 1970.

————. *The Structure of Scientific Revolutions.* 2nd ed. Chicago: University of Chicago Press, 1970 (1962).

Kümmel, Werner Georg. *Introduction to the New Testament.* Translated by Howard Clark Kee. Nashville: Abingdon Press, 1989 (1975).

Küng, Hans. *Credo: The Apostles' Creed Explained for Today.* New York: Doubleday, 1992.

Landmesser, Christof, Hans Joachim Eckstein, and Hermann Lichtenberger, eds. *Jesus Christus als die Mitte der Schrift: Studien zur Hermeneutik des Evangeliums.* Berlin: Walter de Gruyter, 1997.

Lathrop, Gordon. *Holy Things: A Liturgical Theology.* Minneapolis: Fortress Press, 1993.

Levinas, Emmanuel. *Totality and Infinity: An Essay on Exteriority.* Translated by Alphonso Lengis. Pittsburgh: Duquesne University Press, 1961.

Lindbeck, George A. "The Gospel's Uniqueness: Election and Untranslatability." *Modern Theology* 13 (1997): 423-50.

————. *The Nature of Doctrine: Religion and Theology in a Postliberal Age.* Philadelphia: Westminster Press, 1984.

Lischer, Richard. "Why I Am Not Persuasive." *Homiletic* 24, no. 2 (Winter 1999): 13-16.

Long, Thomas G. "And How Shall They Hear? The Listener in Contemporary Preaching." In *Listening to the Word: Studies in Honor of Fred Craddock,* edited by Gail R. O'Day and Thomas G. Long, pp. 167-88. Nashville: Abingdon Press, 1993.

————. *Preaching and the Literary Forms of the Bible.* Philadelphia: Fortress Press, 1989.

————. "The Use of Scripture in Contemporary Preaching." *Interpretation* 44 (1990): 348.

————. *The Witness of Preaching.* Louisville: Westminster/John Knox Press, 1989.

Long, Thomas G., and Cornelius Plantinga, Jr. *A Chorus of Witnesses: Model Sermons for Today's Preacher.* Grand Rapids: Eerdmans, 1994.

Lowry, Eugene. *The Sermon: Dancing the Edge of Mystery.* Nashville: Abingdon Press, 1997.

Luther, Martin. *Luther's Works.* American edition, 55 vols. Edited by Jaroslav Pelikan and Helmut T. Lehman. St. Louis and Philadelphia: Concordia Publishing House and Fortress Press, 1955ff.

—————. "The Smalcald Articles." In *The Book of Concord: The Confessions of the Evangelical Lutheran Church,* translated and edited by Theodore G. Tappert, pp. 287-318. Philadelphia: Fortress Press, 1959.

Lutherans and Catholics in Dialogue VI: Teaching Authority and Infallibility in the Church. Edited by Paul C. Empie, T. Austin Murphy, and Joseph A. Burgess. Minneapolis: Augsburg Press, 1978.

Lyotard, Jean François. *The Differend: Phrases in Dispute.* Translated by George Van Den Abbeele. Minneapolis: University of Minnesota Press, 1988.

—————. *The Postmodern Condition.* Translated by Geoff Bennington and Brian Massumi. Theory and History of Literature, vol. 10. Minneapolis: University of Minnesota Press, 1984.

—————. *The Postmodern Explained.* Edited by Julian Pefanis and Morgan Thomas. Minneapolis: University of Minnesota Press, 1993.

Lyotard, Jean François, and Jean-Loup Thébaud. *Just Gaming.* Translated by Wlad Godzich. Minneapolis: University of Minnesota Press, 1985.

Mananzan, Mary-John. *The Language Game of Confessing One's Belief: A Wittgensteinian-Austinian Approach to the Linguistic Analysis of Creedal Statements.* Tübingen: Max Niemeyer Verlag, 1974.

Martyn, J. Louis. "Epistemology at the Turn of the Ages." In *Theological Issues in the Letters of Paul.* Nashville: Abingdon Press, 1997. Originally published as "Epistemology at the Turn of the Ages: 2 Corinthians 5:16," in *Christian History and Interpretation: Essays Presented to John Knox,* edited by W. R. Farmer, C. F. D. Moule, and R. R. Niebuhr, pp. 269-87. Cambridge: Cambridge University Press, 1967.

McClendon, James Wm., Jr., and James M. Smith. *Convictions: Defusing Religious Pluralism.* Rev. ed. Valley Forge, Pa.: Trinity Press International, 1994.

McClure, John. Review of Charles Campbell's *Preaching Jesus.* In *Journal for Preachers* 21, no. 2 (1998): 35-37.

—————. *The Roundtable Pulpit: Where Leadership and Preaching Meet.* Nashville: Abingdon Press, 1995.

McGowan, John. *Postmodernism and Its Critics.* Ithaca, N.Y.: Cornell University Press, 1991.

Mead, Loren B. *The Once and Future Church.* Washington, D.C.: Alban Institute, 1993.

Megill, Allan. *Prophets of Extremity: Nietzsche, Heidegger, Foucault, Derrida.* Berkeley: University of California Press, 1985.

————, ed. *Rethinking Objectivity.* Durham, N.C.: Duke University Press, 1994.

Meyers, Robin R. *With Ears to Hear: Preaching as Self-Persuasion.* Cleveland: Pilgrim Press, 1993.

Michel, Otto. "ὁμολογέω." In *Theological Dictionary of the New Testament,* vol. 5, edited by Gerhard Kittel and Gerhard Friedrich, translated by Geoffrey W. Bromiley, pp. 199-220. Grand Rapids: Eerdmans, 1967.

Mitchell, Henry. *Celebration and Experience in Preaching.* Nashville: Abingdon Press, 1990.

Moffatt, James. *A Critical and Exegetical Commentary on the Epistle to the Hebrews.* Edinburgh: T. & T. Clark, 1957 (1924).

Morse, Christopher. *The Logic of Promise in Moltmann's Theology.* Philadelphia: Fortress Press, 1979.

————. *Not Every Spirit: A Dogmatics of Christian Disbelief.* Valley Forge, Pa.: Trinity Press International, 1994.

Mueller-Vollmer, Kurt, ed. *The Hermeneutics Reader.* New York: Continuum, 1997.

Murphy, Nancey C. *Anglo-American Postmodernity: Philosophical Perspectives on Science, Religion, and Ethics.* Boulder, Colo.: Westview Press, 1997.

Neudorfer, Heinz Werner. "Ist Sachkritik nötig? Anmerkungen zu einem Thema der biblischen Hermeneutik am Beispiel des Jakobusbriefs." *Kerygma und Dogma* 43 (1997): 279-302.

Neufeld, Vernon H. *The Earliest Christian Confessions.* Grand Rapids: Eerdmans, 1963.

Nielson, Kai. "Searching for an Emancipatory Perspective: Wide Reflective Equilibrium and the Hermeneutical Circle." In *Anti-foundationalism and Practical Reasoning,* edited by Evan Simpson, p. 148. Edmonton, Alberta: Academic Press, 1987. Cited by Calvin Schrag, *Resources for Rationality: A Response to the Postmodern Challenge,* p. 177. Bloomington: Indiana University Press, 1992.

Nietzsche, Friedrich. *Beyond Good and Evil: Prelude to a Philosophy of the Fu-*

ture. Translated by Walter Kaufman. In *Nietzsche's Basic Writings,* edited by Walter Kaufman. New York: Modern Library, 1968.

————. *The Gay Science.* Translated by Walter Kaufmann. New York: Random House, 1975.

Norén, Carol M. *The Woman in the Pulpit.* Nashville: Abingdon Press, 1992.

Nygren, Anders. *Commentary on Romans.* Translated by Carl C. Rasmussen. Philadelphia: Muhlenberg Press, 1949.

Oberman, Heiko Augustinus. *The Harvest of Medieval Theology: Gabriel Biel and Late Medieval Nominalism.* Durham, N.C.: Labyrinth Press, 1983.

O'Day, Gail. *Revelation in the Fourth Gospel: Narrative Mode and Theological Claim.* Philadelphia: Fortress Press, 1986.

O'Donnell, James J. *Augustine.* Boston: Twayne Publishers, 1985.

Olson, Dennis. "Biblical Theology as Provisional Monologization: A Dialogue with Childs, Brueggemann, and Bakhtin." *Biblical Interpretation* 6 (1998): 171-80.

Osmer, Richard Robert. "Practical Theology as Argument, Rhetoric, and Conversation." *Princeton Seminary Bulletin* 18, no. 1 (1997): 61-67.

Patte, Daniel. *Paul's Faith and the Power of the Gospel: A Structural Introduction to the Pauline Letters.* Philadelphia: Fortress Press, 1983.

————. *Preaching Paul.* Philadelphia: Fortress Press, 1984.

Pelikan, Jaroslav. *Jesus Through the Centuries: His Place in the History of Culture.* New Haven: Yale University Press, 1985.

Petersen, Norman R. *Literary Criticism for New Testament Critics.* Philadelphia: Fortress Press, 1978. Cited in John H. P. Reumann, "After Historical Criticism, What? Trends in Biblical Interpretation and Ecumenical, Interfaith Dialogues." *Journal of Ecumenical Studies* 29 (1992): 59 n. 15.

Plantinga, Cornelius Jr. "Dancing the Edge of Mystery." *Books and Culture,* September/October 1999, pp. 16-19.

Polanyi, Michael. *Personal Knowledge: Towards a Post-Critical Philosophy.* Chicago: University of Chicago Press, 1962.

————. *The Tacit Dimension.* Gloucester, Mass.: Peter Smith, 1983 (1966).

Powell, Mark Allan. *What Is Narrative Criticism?* Minneapolis: Fortress Press, 1990.

Proctor, Samuel. *The Certain Sound of the Trumpet: Crafting a Sermon of Authority.* Valley Forge, Pa.: Judson Press, 1994.

Putnam, Hilary. *Reason, Truth, and History.* Cambridge: Cambridge University Press, 1997 (1981).

Reid, Robert Stephen. "Postmodernism and the Function of the New Homiletic in Post-Christendom Congregations." *Homiletic* 20, no. 2 (Winter 1995): 1-13.

Rengstorf, Karl Heinrich. "ἀπόστελλω." In *Theological Dictionary of the New Testament,* vol. 1, edited by Gerhard Kittel, translated by Geoffrey W. Bromiley, pp. 398-446. Grand Rapids: Eerdmans, 1964.

Rescher, Nicholas. *Pluralism: Against the Demand for Consensus.* Oxford: Clarendon Press, 1993.

Resner, André Jr. *Preacher and Cross: Person and Message in Theology and Rhetoric.* Grand Rapids: Eerdmans, 1999.

Reumann, John H. P. "After Historical Criticism, What? Trends in Biblical Interpretation and Ecumenical, Interfaith Dialogues." *Journal of Ecumenical Studies* 29 (1992): 55-86.

Ricoeur, Paul. "Appropriation." In *Hermeneutics and the Social Sciences: Essays on Language, Action and Interpretation,* edited, translated, and introduced by John B. Thompson. Cambridge: Cambridge University Press, 1981.

———. *Freud and Philosophy: An Essay on Interpretation.* Translated by Denis Savage. New Haven: Yale University Press, 1970.

———. "The Hermeneutical Function of Distanciation." In *Hermeneutics and the Social Sciences: Essays on Language, Action and Interpretation,* edited, translated, and introduced by John B. Thompson. Cambridge: Cambridge University Press, 1981.

———. "The Hermeneutics of Testimony." In *Essays on Biblical Interpretation,* edited by Lewis S. Mudge. Philadelphia: Fortress Press, 1981.

———. *Interpretation Theory: Discourse on the Surplus of Meaning.* Fort Worth: Texas Christian University Press, 1976.

———. "The Model of the Text: Meaningful Action Considered as a Text." In *Hermeneutics and the Social Sciences: Essays on Language, Action and Interpretation,* edited, translated, and introduced by John B. Thompson. Cambridge: Cambridge University Press, 1981.

Robinson, Anthony B. "Beyond Civic Faith." *The Christian Century* 115 (1998): 933-36.

Robinson, Wayne Bradley, ed. *Journeys in Narrative Preaching.* New York: Pilgrim Press, 1990.

Root, Michael. "Truth, Relativism, and Postliberal Theology." *Dialog* 25 (1986): 175-80.

Rorty, Richard. *The Consequences of Pragmatism*. Minneapolis: University of Minnesota Press, 1982.

———. "Habermas and Lyotard on Postmodernity." In *Habermas and Modernity*, edited and with an introduction by Richard J. Bernstein, pp. 161-75. Cambridge, Mass.: MIT Press, 1985.

———. *Philosophy and the Mirror of Nature*. Princeton: Princeton University Press, 1980 (1979).

———. "Solidarity or Objectivity?" In *Post-Analytic Philosophy*, edited by John Rajchman and Cornel West. New York: Columbia University Press, 1985.

Rose, Lucy. *Sharing the Word: Preaching in the Roundtable Church*. Louisville: Westminster/John Knox Press, 1997.

Rutledge, Fleming. *The Bible and the New York Times*. Grand Rapids: Eerdmans, 1998.

Schleiermacher, Friedrich. "Foundations: General Theory and the Art of Interpretation." In *The Hermeneutics Reader*, edited by Kurt Mueller-Vollmer, pp. 72-97. New York: Continuum, 1997.

Schmidt, Karl Ludwig. "ἀσφάλεια." In *Theological Dictionary of the New Testament*, vol. 1, edited by Gerhard Kittel, translated by Geoffrey W. Bromiley, p. 506. Grand Rapids: Eerdmans, 1964.

Schrag, Calvin O. *Resources for Rationality: A Response to the Postmodern Challenge*. Bloomington: Indiana University Press, 1992.

Schwartz, Regina M. "Introduction: On Biblical Criticism." In *The Book and the Text*, edited by Regina M. Schwartz, p. 11. Cambridge, Mass.: Blackwell, 1990.

Searle, John R. *Expression and Meaning: Studies in the Theory of Speech Acts*. London: Cambridge University Press, 1979.

Smith, Barbara Hernstein. *Contingencies of Value: Alternative Perspectives in Critical Theory*. Cambridge, Mass.: Harvard University Press, 1988.

Smith, Christine M. *Preaching as Weeping, Confession, and Resistance: Radical Responses to Radical Evil*. Louisville: Westminster/John Knox Press, 1992.

———. *Weaving the Sermon: Preaching in a Feminist Perspective*. Louisville: Westminster/John Knox Press, 1989.

Solberg, Mary. *Compelling Knowledge: A Feminist Proposal for an Epistemology of the Cross*. Albany: State University of New York Press, 1997.

Sternberg, Meier. *The Poetics of Biblical Narrative*. Bloomington: Indiana University Press, 1985.

Stout, Jeffrey. *The Flight from Authority: Religion, Morality, and the Quest for Autonomy*. Notre Dame: University of Notre Dame Press, 1981.

Strathmann, Hermann. "μάρτυς." In *Theological Dictionary of the New Testament*, vol. 4, edited by Gerhard Kittel, translated by Geoffrey W. Bromiley, pp. 474-514. Grand Rapids: Eerdmans, 1967.

Talbert, Charles H. *Reading Luke: A Literary and Theological Commentary on the Third Gospel*. New York: Crossroad, 1982.

Tanner, Kathryn. *Theories of Culture*. Minneapolis: Fortress Press, 1997.

Taylor, Barbara Brown. *The Preaching Life*. Cambridge, Mass.: Cowley Publications, 1993.

Thiel, John. *Nonfoundationalism*. Minneapolis: Fortress Press, 1994.

Thiemann, Ronald F. "Response to George Lindbeck." *Theology Today* 43 (1986): 378.

———. *Revelation and Theology: The Gospel as Narrated Promise*. Notre Dame: University of Notre Dame Press, 1985.

Thulin, Richard L. *The "I" of the Sermon: Autobiography in the Sermon*. Minneapolis: Fortress Press, 1989.

Tilley, Terrence W. "Incommensurability, Intratextuality, and Fideism." *Modern Theology* 5 (1989): 87-111.

Tillich, Paul. "You Are Accepted." In *The Shaking of the Foundations*. New York: Charles Scribner's Sons, 1953.

Tisdale, Leonora Tubbs. *Preaching as Local Theology and Folk Art*. Minneapolis: Fortress Press, 1997.

Toulmin, Stephen. *Cosmopolis: The Hidden Agenda of Modernity*. Chicago: University of Chicago Press, 1990.

Toynbee, Arnold. *An Historian's Approach to Religion*. Oxford: Oxford University Press, 1956. Cited in Terence E. Fretheim and Karlfried Froehlich, *The Bible as Word of God in a Postmodern Age*, p. 64 n. 5. Minneapolis: Fortress Press, 1998.

Tracy, David. *Plurality and Ambiguity: Hermeneutics, Religion, Hope*. San Francisco: Harper & Row, 1987.

———. "Theology and the Many Faces of Postmodernity." *Theology Today* 51 (1994): 104-14.

van Huyssteen, J. Wentzel. *Essays in Postfoundationalist Theology*. Grand Rapids: Eerdmans, 1997.

———. *The Shaping of Rationality: Toward Interdisciplinarity in Theology and Science*. Grand Rapids: Eerdmans, 1999.

Veling, Terry A. *Living in the Margins: Intentional Communities and the Art of Interpretation.* New York: Crossroad, 1996.

Volf, Miroslav. *After Our Likeness: The Church as the Image of the Trinity.* Grand Rapids: Eerdmans, 1998.

Wainwright, Geoffrey. *Doxology: The Praise of God in Worship, Doctrine, and Life.* New York: Oxford University Press, 1980.

Wilder, Amos. *Early Christian Rhetoric.* Cambridge, Mass.: Harvard University Press, 1971 (1964).

Willimon, William H. *Peculiar Speech: Preaching to the Baptized.* Grand Rapids: Eerdmans, 1992.

Wilson, Paul Scott. *Imagination of the Heart: New Understandings in Preaching.* Nashville: Abingdon Press, 1988.

————. "Postmodernism, Theology, and Preaching." In *Papers of the Annual Meeting of the Academy of Homiletics,* December 1-3, 1994, pp. 149-58.

Wingren, Gustaf. *Credo: The Christian View of Faith and Life.* Translated by Edgar M. Carlson. Minneapolis: Augsburg Press, 1981.

————. *The Living Word: A Theological Study of Preaching and the Church.* Philadelphia: Muhlenberg Press, 1960.

Wolterstorff, Nicholas. *Divine Discourse: Philosophical Reflections on the Claim That God Speaks.* London: Cambridge University Press, 1995.

Index of Names and Select Subjects

Index of Scripture References

Index of Scripture References

10:10	74	2:6-8	206	6:6	76
14:11	65	2:7	207	6:20	76
15:9	65n.6, 66	2:9-11	72	7:27	76
		2:11	65n.6, 66	8	76
1 Corinthians				9:11-28	76
1:18-25	80, 206	**Colossians**		10:23	75
1:18-31	215n.70	1:15	72	10:29	76
1:23	74	2:15	72	11:1	62
2:1	74n.40			11:13	66, 75n.47
2:1-5	206	**1 Timothy**		13:15	66, 75n.47
4:1	97	1:3-4	77		
9:1	68	1:3-20	79	**James**	
9:19-23	206	3:16	66n.10	2:19	74
12:3	74n.40, 79	4:1-2	77	5:16	65
13	99	4:7-16	79		
15:1-3	74n.40	6:1-11	79	**1 Peter**	
15:3-5	70, 74	6:12	67n.13, 76	3:22	72
15:3-8	74n.40	6:13	77n.56, 97		
15:8	68			**1 John**	
		Titus		1:1	68
2 Corinthians		1:16	66	1:1-4	80
4:13	68, 80			1:9	65
4:13-14	216	**Hebrews**		2:22	68n.20
6:3-10	206	1:1-4	76	2:23	67n.13, 77
6:11	209	2:17	76	4:2	77
7:2-13	209	3:1	75	4:3	67n.13, 77
9:13	75	4:2	156	4:15	67n.13, 77
11:4	85	4:12-13	157	4:20	77
		4:14	75, 76		
Philippians		4:14-16	76	**Revelation**	
2:1-11	74n.40	5:10	76	3:5	66-67, 68, 80
2:6	97	6:1-3	76		

264